Products Liability
and the Search for Justice

Products Liability
and the Search for Justice

Marshall S. Shapo

Carolina Academic Press
Durham, North Carolina

For
BEN
Budding Scientist
Himself Full of Wonders

Contents

Table of Cases

Acknowledgments

I have many people to thank for their help in my writing of this book.

Over a quarter century of studying and teaching about the fascinating development of the law of products liability, my ideas about the law have been shaped by many scholars across the country who have stimulated my thinking with their ideas about torts and products liability. I hesitate to name just a few, but I have expressed my debts to these fellow workers in many media.

I also acknowledge a more general obligation to colleagues at three great institutions: Texas, Virginia, and now Northwestern. Their probing from many points of view has enabled me to think about the law more deeply.

A particularly bright star in this firmament remains my first dean and my first academic collaborator, the remarkable Page Keeton. He gave me a sense of the complexity of the young law of products liability and a scholarly standard at which to aim. Roy Mersky, who came to Texas as law librarian when I began my law teaching career, provided suggestions that were important to my early scholarly development, as well as setting a high standard in his crucial craft. I also express my particular appreciation to two other eminent lawyers: Judge Robert Keeton, who as a professor at the Harvard Law School oversaw my dissertation in this area, and Charles Alan Wright, President-elect of the American Law Institute, for whose encouragement across the years I am grateful.

I owe many institutional and personal debts to the Northwestern University School of Law and its faculty and staff. Its deans, Bob Bennett and David Ruder before him, have provided me support for my ongoing research in this subject. Bill Elwin, associate dean and executive director of the Corporate Counsel Center at Northwestern, has been very helpful in arranging this support.

Another great librarian, George Grossman, has directed a wonderful staff at Northwestern, without whose aid I could not do this sort of work. Professor Grossman's departure from Northwestern will leave us poorer. Marcia Lehr has provided extraordinarily consistent and cheerful assistance as a research librarian. Others among her colleagues who have been especially helpful are Chris Simoni, Pegeen Bassett, and Irene Berkey.

I finished the manuscript for this volume at Wolfson College, Cambridge. I particularly appreciate the hospitality there of Sir David Williams, then President of the College as well as temporary vice chancellor of the University, and now permanent vice chancellor.

Some of my best teachers have been my students. There are now battalions of them from Texas, Virginia, and Northwestern. Their questions and comments in classes and seminars have made me think through many of the issues discussed in this book.

A long line of student assistants has aided me with the scholarly details of the research reflected in this volume. Over the past several years, among the most helpful of these have been Rob Drizin, Damon di Castri, Paige Harrison, Kevin Osborn, Chuck Regan, Paul Janaskie, James Phalen, and John Martin.

I am grateful for my association with Butterworth Legal Publishers, publisher of my treatise, *The Law of Products Liability*. The present book draws on the research and synthesis in that work.

Over the years, I have profited from conversation with many lawyers about various aspects of this subject. Notably, these have included Griffin Bell and the members of the A.B.A. Special Committee on the Tort Liability System, and Keith Davidson. Most recently, members of the firm of Sonnenschein, Nath and Rosenthal have provided object lessons in practical jurisprudence.

I appreciate the editorial assistance of Mayapriya Long of Carolina Academic Press. I express my special thanks to my secretary, Christy Bailey, who patiently helped with the completion of the manuscript, including several months at transatlantic distance.

My family is my greatest inspiration. Helene Shapo, who is as close to Superwoman as they come, edited some chapters of this volume. Quite as importantly, she provides an editing omnipresence, whatever her particular involvement with any manuscript. Her distrust of cant and jargon, and her insistence on analytical clarity, color all my thinking about the law. Our sons, Ben and Nat, provide many informal lessons in critical thinking, as well as family support, for a teacher who wants to understand the law as it relates to life.

Introduction: The Products Liability Puzzle

One morning in 1985 I was standing in Room 253 of the Senate Russell Office Building, waiting for the beginning of a committee hearing at which I was to testify on the subject of products liability. It was one of several occasions during the eighties when I, along with several other colleagues in the academic community, joined representatives of business and consumer groups to express to Senators our opinions on this subject.

It was about ten minutes to nine. The hearing was scheduled to begin at nine o'clock, although one could expect, from experience, that the lordly procession of Senators who were able to attend the hearing would arrive late. Yet the room already was full to overflowing, and bright with C-Span television lights.

Two middle-aged men, wearing typical Washington business uniform, stood nearby. I heard them chatting. One, blinking in the glare of the lights, looked around the crowded room. "This is a hearing on products liability," he said. "Why are all these people here?" His companion regarded him with pity for his ignorance. "Man," he said, "Half the people in this town make their livings from products liability."

The speaker was not referring primarily to lawyers who litigate cases concerning the rights of injured persons to recover damages from product sellers—the core of the legal problem that we call "products liability." He was talking about the lobbying efforts that had been proceeding, and that have continued to go on, over bills proposed in Congress to change the body of law that state courts and legislatures have developed to govern products suits.

The first speaker's bafflement was understandable. Why, in the halls of Congress, choked with deliberations over matters of national defense, tax policy, and welfare legislation, should the elected representatives of the entire nation concern themselves with matters that always had been resolved through private lawsuits?

The subject obviously is one that has engaged the emotions of many people in many different professional and consumer communities. Witnesses at a typical Congressional hearing on the subject might include such diverse persons as representatives of the National Association of Manufacturers, Consumers Union, the American Insurance Association, the Pharmaceutical Manufacturers Association, the White Lung Association, the National Conference of Chief Justices, and the National Stevedores Association.[1] The arguments that they have made, over the course of more than a decade, reflect such different views of the problem that we must ask, what is it that they really are arguing about?

At the simplest level, the answer is money. But although that is the occasion for the argument, it is not the reason. Some see the issue as focusing on the ability of people to choose product risk levels that are congenial to them, or on the effect of the law on technological innovation. However, what people basically are arguing about, when they express concern and even outrage about products liability decisions, is whether those decisions are fair. Both disappointed plaintiffs and losing defendants are saying, "It is not right to do this to me."

What are the various meanings of that sentiment? Frequently, especially when product sellers voice this idea, they mean that people should be given notice of what the rules are. As applied, this means that a seller should know in advance that there would be a significant possibility that it would be forced to pay compensation if its product caused an injury in a particular use. By comparison, what many consumers may mean is that sellers should be held more rigorously to the way they portray their products.

In the background of judgment on these questions there are all kinds of suppositions, intuitions, assumptions—and occasionally facts—about people's desires, and about how people actually behave. Beyond those considerations, however, when courts apply the rules of products liability to particular cases, they are making a series of judgments about what is fair.

Political efforts to change products liability law have attacked the problem from many angles. They have focused on matters ranging from theories of liability and the economic position of the seller to the amount of damages that a plaintiff can recover and the span of time in which one can sue. Many of the recent criticisms of products law have echoed broader attacks on our general law of injuries. One of these arguments asserts that Americans have come to rely too much on the law as a vehicle for "solving social problems."

Yet, in what has become a national debate, there has been insufficient discussion about the reasons for, and the fairness of, the rules of products liability and their specific applications. In an effort to enrich that discussion,

---

1. See, e.g., Product Liability Reform Act: Hearings Before the Consumer Subcommittee of the Senate Commerce Committee on S. 1400, 101st Cong., 2d Sess. iii–iv (1990).

I shall show that the law of products liability has emerged as an important illustration of our views about justice in private litigation. Emerging from moments of high tension over perceived grievances, it captures our working morality, a morality that arises in part from concerns about the uses and abuses of power. In particular, it responds to the images projected by our mass media, while incorporating common sense intuitions about the trade-offs inherent in most product purchases.

Products Liability
and the Search for Justice

1

Products Injuries in Context

Injury Law and Products Liability

Along with death and taxes, the injury problem is always with us.

One of the most fascinating missions of the law is to respond fairly to the personal and social problems caused by injuries.[1] There are many sorts of occasions on which a person may claim that he or she has been injured. Some of these "claims" are just gossipy grousing and do not give rise to litigation. In this class of cases are thousands and even millions of events that involve personal nastiness and pettiness. Affairs of the heart present countless situations in which people feel very deeply hurt but would not think of suing for damages.

Other situations, also very familiar, involve rather formal demands for compensation from the person who is supposed to have done the injury. One of the most obvious, and numerically important, of such cases, is the automobile accident. Ask any group of one hundred people how many of them have been involved in a motor vehicle accident in the last five years, and a substantial majority of hands will go up. Many of those incidents result in claims, at least against insurance companies. A few finally wind up in lawsuits, and fewer still actually come into the courtroom.

Other kinds of situations in which people historically have demanded that alleged injurers pay some form of compensation include events involving slips and falls on someone else's property, injuries caused by contact with high tension wires, harms associated with common carriers such as railroads or buses, and injuries caused by other people's animals.

---

1. This book is the first of a series of volumes that seeks to analyze the way that the law deals with this task.

The occasion of going to the doctor has now become a more frequent basis for damage claims. Suing one's physician is not a new idea, not even new to this century, but as any newspaper reader knows, it is now an event that occurs much more often than it did a generation ago.

This book focuses on one kind of injuries, those arising from the use of products, which also have become the center of legal attention in the last quarter century. Product injuries are a particularly interesting subject because they arise from situations that all of us frequently encounter, and thus we can relate to them easily.

Because of the central role that products play in all our lives, this body of law presents an unusual combination of patterns of conflict, legal rules, and social symbols. It has fueled some of the fiercest discourse about private law today—among judges, scholars, business persons, and politicians. The problems arising from this branch of the law include issues involving both the content of concepts and definitions of terms. They involve not only law as a study detached from other branches of social science, but law as it relates to economics, psychology, and politics.

Products Law and the Law Generally

In this book, I shall scrutinize the law that has developed in response to products injuries, analyzing that body of rules as symbols of justice in the area of private law. In the course of that analysis, I shall assess some of the controversies that now occupy people who think and write about these issues.

In describing the history of this branch of the law and the ferocious argument that has attended it, I shall show why the law has evolved as it has. I shall also try to formulate working principles that show the way to the most just solution to this set of legal problems. Because so many aspects of the problem of product injuries make it a representative case of how our law works today, I shall point out how this particular legal battleground illuminates strengths and weaknesses of the law in a more general sense.

Much of the focus of the book will be on case law—judicial decisions dealing with individual disputes. Since the cases deal mostly with personal injury, there is a constant sense of tragedy. From the case of the worker who loses an arm to an industrial machine, to that of the consumer who dies because of a reaction or disease caused by a pharmaceutical product, there often is an overhanging sense of tragic destiny. At the same time, in the high personal drama of the cases, the questions arise, "Did it have to be this way?" "Was someone sufficiently in control of the situation to have averted the harm?"

This book will also show more generally how what lawyers call "private law" is a remarkable mirror of society. In recent decades, Congress and state legislatures have enacted more law in the form of legislation, and more and more litigants have argued about issues that arise under the Constitution. The Constitution is undoubtedly our most important general guide to law, and statutes—enactments of Congress and state lawmaking bodies—represent significant resolutions of social disputes that have been fought out in the legislative arena. With increasing frequency, constitutional and statutory issues arise in the context of private litigation. But an enduring feature of the private law itself—the judge-made law that develops from particular disputes in court—is that it remains perhaps the most important grassroots reflection of where we stand as a society on dozens of issues that arise between ordinary citizens.

The Statistics of Injury

The statistics of products injuries are complicated. Such injuries tend to be tied with particular activities from which we derive much of the relevant data. Notably, these activities include motor vehicle accidents (46,300 deaths and 1,700,000 disabling injuries in 1990)[2], and workplace injuries (10,500 deaths and 1,800,000 disabling injuries in the same year).[3] Since consumers often attribute the severity of injuries in vehicle accidents to auto design, and since many workplace injuries occur when workers use machines with propensities to maim, these statistics include many "products" injuries.

Another fertile source of data deals with things generally classified as "consumer products." This is the estimates of the National Electronic Injury Surveillance System (NEISS) of the Consumer Product Safety Commission. NEISS makes projections of national injury data from emergency room statistics at selected hospitals. The NEISS estimates for 1986 include 106,607 injuries suffered by people working with workshop manual tools, more than 276,000 injuries apiece in two categories called "beds, mattresses, pillows," and "chairs, sofas, sofa beds," and, not surprisingly, more than 353,000 injuries associated with "cutlery, knives, unpowered." Sports and recreation equipment accounts for a substantial number of injuries—from 514,738 for bicycles and accessories to 106,792 for "all-terrain vehicles, mopeds, mini bikes" and 15,866 injuries associated with trampolines.[4]

---

2. Accident Facts, 1991 edition, at 51.
3. *Id.* at 34.
4. *Id.* at 96.

A sub-category of at least two of these classifications is one that increasingly has provoked claims for compensation under both tort law and workers compensation statutes. This is the category of "toxics," an umbrella label that principally refers to chemicals and fibers associated with many workplace processes and consumer products. The Bureau of Labor Statistics reported in 1986 that 41,900 workers suffered skin diseases and disorders as a result of their occupations, that 18,900 suffered "respiratory conditions due to toxic agents," and that there were 2,600 cases of "dust diseases of the lungs."[5] The latter figure would appear very low, given the amount of litigation that has been generated by lung diseases associated with the workplace. In its data on accidents in the home, NEISS estimated that over 99,000 injuries in 1986 were related to various chemical products used for "home maintenance," including cleaning agents, drain cleaners, solvents and lubricants.[6]

What we have said so far has not even touched the toll exacted by the traditional recreational substances: the involvement of alcohol in 22,000 fatal accidents;[7] the millions of illnesses associated with drinking; the more than 300,000 lives shortened each year by the use of tobacco products. And we do not deal here with illegal drugs, except to note that large questions of policy surround our political choices about where to draw the line of legality.

The data on litigation have themselves been controversial. In the 1970s seventies, two respectable sources gave astonishingly different estimates that varied by a factor of ten. In 1977, the federal Interagency Task Force on Products Liability produced an estimate of 60,000 to 70,000 suits annually,[8] but in the same year another source asserted that the figure was one million.[9] Perhaps the cynic would say that these widely differing numbers reflected the political agendas of those who offered them.

The Tradeoffs: Injury and Illness for Production

An important aspect of these statistics is that in one way or another, they reflect the gains that people derive from the activities in which the injuries

---

5. *Id.* at 50.

6. *Id.* at 96.

7. *Id.* at 56.

8. Task Force Study Cites Major Causes, Proposed Cures for Insurance Rate Rise, 7 O.S.H. Rep. (BNA) 824 (1977).

9. Product Liability Meeting Told of Crisis Facing Insurers, Businesses, Consumers, 5 Prod. Safety & Liab. Rep. (BNA) 226 (1977).

occur. Many of these injuries are directly related to the activities of businesses that, taken together, contribute many billions of dollars to the economy. Machines that mangle limbs and chemicals that cause a variety of serious illnesses are the heart of activities that provide wages for millions of workers, goods for a nation of consumers, and profits for millions of shareholders. Less easy to quantify, but still of obvious significance to ordinary people, are accidents attributable to the management and improvement of home life made possible by products like household chemicals. Some of the statistics mentioned above reflect the fact that leisure itself is profitable both to fun seekers and suppliers of goods. Thus, as we focus on the harmful consequences of productive enterprises—what economists call "negative externalities"—we must keep in mind the goods that they provide us.

Seeking Justice

Sorting Out Complaints

Thousands of injury incidents find their way to lawyers, and a certain percentage of those cases get to court, at least in the sense that a lawyer files a complaint on behalf of the injured person. One should note, however, that many more thousands of injury incidents never come to the attention of a lawyer. An important question that is beyond the scope of this book concerns the factors that impel people to pursue legal remedies of various kinds. Many of these factors may be cultural, related to American notions of what "rights" are and corresponding conclusions about the appropriate level of litigiousness.[10] Yet, faced with levels of litigation that are relatively high in the modern world, we should remember that the legal system provides screening mechanisms that keep many more cases of perceived injury out of court than those that get there.

Why People Complain

In considering the process of sorting out complaints, we should not neglect the fundamental issue of why people complain—why they protest so bitterly that they are willing to carry their case to the lawyer's door, and sometimes even through the door of the courtroom. If we can answer that

---

10. For critical commentary touching this point, see Sally Lloyd-Bostock, Common Sense Morality and Accident Compensation, in Psychology, Law and Legal Processes 93, *e.g.*, at 96-98 (D. Farrington, K. Hawkins and S. Lloyd-Bostock eds. 1979).

question, we also will shed light on the question of why some injured persons do *not* complain.

We might reasonably suppose that behind most injury claims is the feeling that somehow an accident, and an injury, were avoidable. A good part of this has to do with a concept of fault: the idea that the alleged injurer should have behaved differently. This "should" may encompass a variety of reasons. It is probable that for most people, the "should" has a high degree of moral content. An important normative aspect of the law of personal injuries arises from a belief that a person ought to have acted in a way different than he or she did act because it was "wrong" to do what he or she did. This belief may exist, for example, because the injurer took advantage of a situation or of a person. It may exist because the injurer exposed a large number of other people to a high degree of risk, although he or she was lucky enough only to injure the one person who has sued.

A related point has to do with our notions—often vague but frequently also very powerful—of what is "fair." One aspect of fairness has to do with the relationship of individual injury claimants to distributors of the product or service that caused the injury. Another concerns the relationship of the injured person to other users of the product or service. In the latter connection, the issue becomes whether it is unfair that the victim should bear the entire cost of the injury while all the other users benefit without injury. At the margins of this idea there are even some reactions connected to how the injured person's plight relates to the rest of society. Usually, we do not take this sort of thing into consideration in judging specific cases. As President Kennedy said in another connection, "Life is unfair." That intuition itself governs many of our reactions to legal claims.

Many people with a knowledge of economic theory will say that the "should" has only to do with the question of whether it would have been cheaper to take the precautions necessary to avoid the injury than the cost of the injury to the victim. But for most people, this factor is only one of several that enter our minds when we judge injury cases.

When we ask ourselves why it is that people make formal complaints about injuries, we need also to consider a variety of things that have to do with the effects of the harm. One such factor is that the injury has violated the expectations that people ordinarily would have in the situation that confronted the victim at the time of the injury. Another, more obvious point is that the injuries destroy or damage lives.

A collateral consideration—not one directly confronted by the private law—is the victim's need, usually defined in the law in financial terms. Need is not the same thing as being injured. If a very rich person is hurt in an accident, it may be that he or she will not suffer the kind of need that a laborer will suffer. For example, whereas the laborer's family may be deprived of earnings and also face serious medical bills, the rich person, or the well-insured middle-class person, will have access to funds that will pay for those losses.

Yet, there is a community of feeling and interest between rich and poor. Both feel pain in the same way. Thus, if pain can be translated into money, compensation for pain should not differ between people of different economic classes. Moreover, feelings of anger against the injurer are emotions likely to arise in much the same way in people of diverse social and economic status.

Some Basic Criticisms

I have said that one of my aims is to present the "most just" solution to the problems of liability law that I have been discussing. In this regard, I should emphasize the complexity of these problems, a point that much of the discussion of this area of the law tends to omit. The author of one well-publicized book, for example, speaks of how "[m]odern tort law" has "failed."[11] In a span of two or three pages, writing of the law of products warnings, he says that "[o]verstatement is worse still" and that "[t]he law's larger message to the consumer is falser still," and he describes the developing law of torts as "an octopus."[12] In somewhat more restrained fashion, a draft document prepared by a distinguished committee of the American Law Institute singled out tort law as "unduly costly and contentious" and as a system that "distributes compensation in erratic and inconsistent fashion." That draft referred to the "specter of costly and uncertain tort liabilities" as undercutting productivity and competitiveness.[13]

Other critical pronouncements have run in the same vein. Jeffrey O'Connell, a strong critic of tort law for a quarter century, declared it "small wonder that the tort system is often characterized as a form of roulette."[14] The writers of each of these statements have impressive credentials as students of the subject. But each tends to oversimplify a complex problem.

Indeed, these oversimplifications only underline the point that when people disagree to the point of filing lawsuits, the problem of justice is frequently a complicated one. Thus, although I have strong opinions of my

11. Peter Huber, Liability: The Legal Revolution and Its Consequences 15 (1988).
12. *Id.* at 15-17.
13. American Law Institute, Compensation and Liability for Product and Process Injuries: Progress Report 1 (April 13, 1987).
14. Jeffrey O'Connell, Offers That Can't be Refused: Foreclosure of Personal Injury Claims by Defendants' Prompt Tender of Claimants' Net Economic Losses, 77 Nw. L. Rev. 589, 591 (1982).

own on many of the issues discussed in this book, I am inclined to speak of the "most just" resolution of a problem rather than using words like "failure" and "false." Because injuries often arise from activities that confer benefits on workers, consumers, and business owners, the difficult problem is how to define the appropriate level of barriers to injury-causing activity and the proper level of compensation to those who are hurt. The task of achieving these goals presents subtle nuances, which should not be obscured by polemics.

Principal Threads of the Problem

What are the major threads of personal, social and economic life that bear on this problem?

A central feature of any analysis of products liability law, and of the broader field that encompasses it—tort law—is that of *risk*. The standard insurance definition of risk is uncertainty about loss. When a firm puts a new product on the market—for example, an industrial machine or a prescription drug—it may know in a general way that the product has certain dangerous propensities in the context of its probable use. Someone who purchases or uses the product may have some inkling of those propensities as well. Neither has a precise idea of when the product will cause injury. Both are dealing with risk.

An interlinked piece of the problem has to do with *knowledge*. A significant amount of products liability law deals with what sellers and consumers know about the risks associated with a product, and with their access to information about the product's risks, as well as its benefits.

The factors of risk and knowledge are in turn connected with still another important aspect of products law, which is *choice*. Both implicitly and explicitly, the law makes decisions based on assumptions about the relative ability of persons to choose courses of action. Choice in this sense implies not only the possession of information, but freedom, in some sense, to make a decision in favor of a particular course of action: for example, to purchase a product, to use it, or to encounter it in a place of work or recreation.

Among other relevant considerations are these:

• *The power relationship between the parties.* Did the parties bargain on relatively even terms? Was one party in a position to impose terms on the other, in a situation in which the other had no meaningful choice and it could be said that the imposition of terms was "unfair"?

• *Judgments concerning each party's relative ability to avoid the accident.* Was one party able to keep the injury from happening more cheaply than the other? Or, from a moral point of view, could one say that one party, more than the other, *ought* to have avoided the accident?

• *The representational background of the event.* How did the seller mean to represent the product, and what portrayal of the product could the consumer fairly be said to have received?

• *The role of insurance.* Which party is best able to purchase insurance against the consequences of the accident?

• *Loss spreading.* The factor of loss spreading, which is closely related to the existence and availability of insurance, arises from a point that we made earlier about the benefits that products confer. Since each risky product comprises a package of benefits and risks, each satisfied consumer is a beneficiary of the good fortune that comes from being one who derives the advantages of a product, rather than one who is injured by its hazardous characteristics. The technique of loss spreading seeks to assure that a portion of the benefit to the many will cover the costs of misfortune to the few.

Two Illustrative Cases

Julie Heldman was an outstanding American tennis player in the 1960s and 1970s. Not quite in the class of Martina Navratilova and Chris Evert, she was ranked in the top ten players in the world in four years between 1969 and 1975,[15] and was a strong enough competitor to represent the United States in three battles against British players for a historic prize, the Wightman Cup.

One of the injuries athletes fear most is the knee injury. That is what befell Heldman in her Wightman match against the British star Virginia Wade on August 21, 1971. The Wightman matches that year were played on a synthetic rubber surface made by Uniroyal, Inc., called the "Uniroyal Roll-A-Way Tennis Court." Heldman attributed her injury to uncertain footing caused by bubbles that formed under the surface of the Uniroyal court on a moist day. Although Heldman had complained about the condition of the court to her captain, Carole Graebner, she said that she did not refuse to play because she was a professional, and, as the court characterized her testimony, "the show must go on."

A jury thought the damage to Heldman's knee was worth $67,000, but an Ohio appellate court reversed the jury's award because the trial judge had refused to give an instruction to the jury on the doctrine of "assumption of the risk." The appellate court conceded that it could not say as a

---

15. Biographical information in Who's Who in Tennis (1983), provided by the United States Tennis Association.

matter of law that Heldman had "actual knowledge of the danger or that the condition was so patently obvious that she can be taken to have known it." However, the court thought the case presented a question for the jury on whether Heldman knew "that the bubbles created a dangerous condition" and assumed the risk by playing. It cited not only her testimony about the hazard, but also evidence from other players in the Wightman matches, including statements by both Graebner and Wade that the players were afraid of getting hurt.[16]

Heldman's case presents several of the controversial elements that have occupied courts when they deal with cases under the heading of "products liability." What was the relevant risk, and how much did either party know about it? How might the way that Uniroyal portrayed its product have influenced Heldman, or the parties who bought or leased the "Roll-A-Way Tennis Court"? How much choice did Heldman have about confronting the hazard posed by bubbles forming under wet conditions? Who, if anyone, was in the best position to avoid the accident? Would it be appropriate to charge the cost of Heldman's injury to the price of tickets to Wightman Cup matches?

An interesting comparison appears in another Ohio case, which involves a more tragic set of injuries. The product in question was a Jeep CJ-7, manufactured by American Motors Corporation. The accident occurred at the Hall of Fame Four-Wheel Club, near Dundee, Ohio, an "off-the-road" recreation facility that included a driving course of hills and trails around an abandoned strip mine. The CJ-7 came to market on the crest of a big TV advertising campaign, which included appeals to the macho instinct as well as strong claims that the vehicle could negotiate rough countryside. One film clip challenged a young man, in the company of his girlfriend: " . . . [Y]ou guys aren't yellow, are you? Is it a steep hill? Yeah, little lady, you could say it is a steep hill. Let's try it. The King of the Hill is about to discover the new Jeep CJ-7. . . . " The advertisement also featured such colorful statements as, "Ever discover the rough, exciting world of mountains, forest, rugged terrain? The original Jeep can get you there, and Jeep guts will bring you back."[17]

Unfortunately, this Jeep did not bring its riders back. It executed a "pitchover" on a hill, flipping through the air in a 180-degree arc. The owner of the vehicle and his wife died in the accident. One of their passengers, Jeanne Leichtamer, was rendered paraplegic, and her brother Carl Leichtamer suf-

---

16. Heldman v. Uniroyal, Inc., 53 Ohio App.2d 21, 36, 371 N.E.2d 557, 567 (1977).

17. Leichtamer v. American Motors Corp., 67 Ohio St.2d 456, 459-460, 424 N.E.2d 568, 572-573 (1971).

fered a depressed skull fracture. The Ohio Supreme Court affirmed jury verdicts for the Leichtamers—one million dollars in compensatory damages and another million in punitive damages for Jeanne and $100,000 under each measure of damages for Carl. The court specifically said that it was appropriate to give instructions to the jury that permitted it to find liability on the basis of the doctrine of strict liability in tort, based on the fact that the roll bar on the vehicle did not protect the plaintiffs from the effects of the Jeep landing on its top. "The only protection provided the user in the case of roll-overs or pitch-overs," said Justice William B. Brown for a majority of the court, "proved wholly inadequate." Commented Justice Brown, "A roll bar should be more than mere ornamentation."[18]

Many of the same questions that arose in Julie Heldman's case repeat themselves in the gruesome setting of the Leichtamer case: Who created the risk, and by what means? Who knew about it? What was the ambit of meaningful choice about the risk that the situation permitted? Was the loss feasibly insurable? On whom should the price of insuring it fall? The answers to these questions, in both the Heldman and Leichtamer cases and in thousands of other episodes involving products claims, come from a mixture of history, social and personal choices, and legal doctrine. This book will critically explore those answers—the law's response to product injuries.

---

18. *Id.* at 465, 424 N.E.2d at 576.

2

The Law and its Social Background

"The Law": A Group of Systems

When we approach the question of how the law should respond to product injuries, we first must ask a very abstract question: What do we mean by "the law"? It is also useful to ask what the social background is from which the law springs. This chapter deals with those questions.

Tort

From a purely descriptive point of view, "the law" itself has many facets. The part of the law that is described in the most detail in this book is judge-made law: the decisions of courts in disputes between or among named parties, at least one of whom complains of a particular grievance against another. The major corpus of the law of "products liability" is part of judge-made law, more specifically the general branch of personal injury law known as "tort law."

Compensation Statutes: Workers Compensation

There are other components of the legal system that deal with products injuries, and they may overlap with respect to the same injury. One of these components is the workers compensation system. Workers compensation, which is always statutory, aims to provide speedy compensation, without a lot of litigation, to workers who have been injured on the job. Under workers compensation laws, it is not necessary for an employee to show that his employer was at fault—only that the injury happened in the course of employment. There are numerous sub-systems of workers compensation. Each state has its own scheme, there is a special system for longshoremen and harbor workers, and another for federal employees.

We implied in the previous chapter how workers compensation arcs into the products liability arena: many injured workers are hurt in encounters with products, typically industrial machines. In an illustrative Washington case,[1] James Glass, a worker for the Morel Foundry Corporation, sued for severe injuries that occurred when a molding machine closed on his hand.

Because of his injury, Glass had received compensation benefits from his employer, Morel. But besides receiving those benefits—which as we have noted do not require a showing of employer culpability—Glass also sued Stahl Specialty Company, the maker of the molding machine. He apparently claimed that Stahl had been negligent in making the machine and had sold a defective product. This suit led to a further complication that often arises in cases of workplace injury involving products: Stahl asserted that if it were liable to Glass, then the employer, Morel, should have to pay some of the tort damages assessed against Stahl in addition to having paid the workers compensation benefits.

The Washington Supreme Court denied the manufacturer any relief from the employer. Lining up with most states that had ruled on the issue, it pointed out that workers compensation is an exclusive remedy for employees and does not permit them to bring tort actions against employers. Elaborating the logic of the workers compensation system, the court said it would not require an employer to contribute to a firm that had been sued in tort by an employee who could not bring a direct tort action against the employer.[2] This decision simply provides an illustration of the complications that can occur because two systems of law—the "products liability" branch of tort law and the no-fault system of workers compensation—may apply to the same accident.

Regulation: Safety Statutes

The other major system of law that comes into play in this setting is regulatory. To continue with the example of workplace accidents, regulations

---

1. Glass v. Stahl Specialty Co., 97 Wash.2d 880, 652 P.2d 948 (1982).
2. *See id.* at 883-888, 652 P.2d at 950-953.

of the Occupational Safety and Health Administration may become relevant in products liability cases.

Other kinds of regulation may similarly affect litigation about products injuries. The consumer who attributes harm to a prescription drug may confront the drug maker's argument that approval of the product by the Food and Drug Administration constituted an effective declaration that the drug was not defective and that its warnings were adequate. Motorists who assert that their vehicles lacked sufficient crash protection must contend with the argument that federal motor vehicle legislation has occupied the relevant legal territory, thus fencing out tort claims for design defects. And, under a recent Supreme Court decision, smokers attributing illness to a tobacco maker's failure to warn must deal with the contention that federal cigarette labeling and advertising regulation raises a bar to their litigation.

Systems of Law Compared

Each of the systems I have mentioned—the private law action in tort, the system of workers compensation, and regulation under safety statutes—has its own set of advantages and disadvantages.

Tort law, for example, gives us the costs as well as the benefits of individualization. An injured person who thinks that her injury is the fault of someone else can get a lawyer who believes in the case to argue the matter on her behalf, and hers alone. This may carry a substantial risk: the risk of losing—and getting no compensation at all. Moreover, a tort action may be very time consuming. But at the end, win or lose, the claimant will know that she has had her "day in court." If she wins a tort award, it is also possible that she will recover amounts well in excess of those available through a workers compensation claim, in part because tort law provides a niche for a kind of recovery not explicitly granted by compensation legislation—damages for pain and suffering.

Workers compensation type schemes exhibit a different set of advantages and drawbacks. Some of these features are mirror images of the tort system. Typically, workers compensation is quicker to respond than tort. This is in large part because it is less argumentative about certain kinds of questions on which tort law spends a long time. Where tort asks, "Was the defendant at fault?" workers compensation typically inquires only, "Was the claimant worker on the job when the injury occurred?"

This is not to say that workers compensation does not generate a lot of litigation; indeed, we have had considerable increases in the numbers of "comp" cases in which workers and employers carry their disputes to court. In this sense, workers compensation is beginning to move closer to tort. Still, in trading off relatively quick and certain, if comparatively small, recoveries against the sometimes larger but less certain awards of tort, and in foregoing tort requirements like those that demand that plaintiffs show "fault" or a "defect," workers compensation buys efficiency at the price of diminished opportunities for individualized litigation.

Some similar patterns, as well as some different ones, appear when we consider the pros and cons of safety regulation. Regulation seeks to do at least two things that are not part of the formal job description of tort law: to deal comprehensively with an area of activity, and to set definitive standards. Some people might add that another primary task of regulation that is not a principal part of the job of tort is to prevent accidents. But here we encounter controversy. A lot of other people think that one of the missions of tort law—some think virtually its only mission—is to communicate standards of conduct to people who engage in risky activity: for example, to fashion at least negative guidelines for those who design products or sell them.

However, even if one believes that tort is primarily a mechanism for behavior control, one must recognize that regulation is very different from tort because of the breadth of the regulatory net. Although judges' decisions in tort cases do have an effect on the conduct of others engaging in the same sort of activity, the regulations of safety agencies specifically govern everyone whose conduct falls within their scope. Moreover, regulation typically is highly prescriptive and specific, as well as forward looking. A judicial decision in a tort case may say, in effect, "It was unreasonably dangerous to design this workplace machine without a guard, and since this worker was injured because the machine did not have a guard, you as the maker of the machine will have to pay." By contrast, a safety agency's regulation would say, "You as an employer had better have a guard on your machine, and if the inspector sees a machine without a guard, he will fine you, even if no one has been hurt—yet." As a practical matter, a severely limited number of inspectors may not be looking for a particular sort of problem unless they have heard about accidents that already have occurred, but the difference in approach between tort and regulation is an important one in principle.

To summarize, we have at least three different major systems through which law regulates injuries, including product injuries. It is not unusual for at least two of these systems to apply to the same case of product injuries, or even for all three of them to have some application in a single case. These systems do overlap, and share features whose commonality is not always superficially apparent. But in significant ways, they are also distinct.

The Special Role of Tort Law

An underlying premise of this book, which focuses principally on the law of torts in the field of products injuries, is that because of its individualizing focus on particular cases, tort law is the bedrock of our law of injuries. In situations where a new injury pattern develops, tort gives us our initial insight into how we feel as a society about what constitutes justice in that kind of case. And even when legislatures have adopted compensation statutes on the model of workers compensation, and have enacted systems of safety regulation, tort law still creates an intellectual and practical foundation for society's response to injuries. It provides the primary refuge for the injured party who claims no more, and no less, than that the injurer should pay full compensation as a matter of simple justice.

Some Summary History

The history of products liability law is fascinating and complex.[3] This part of the chapter summarizes a few, especially representative, historical highlights.

Landmark Decisions

Mazetti v. Armour & Co.

It would be difficult to say that any one decision is the fountainhead of modern products liability law, but surely one of the leading nominees for that honor would be the 1913 decision of the Washington Supreme Court in *Mazetti v. Armour & Co.*[4] That case arose from the economic consequences of a potential public health problem. The plaintiffs owned a restaurant. They served a customer a plate of foul tongue that had been packed by the defendant Armour. The patron's loud public complaint, in the presence of other diners, produced expectably bad consequences for the plaintiffs' reputation and profits. They sought damages for those losses. The trial court dismissed the action, apparently on the basis of a rule, already

---

3. *See generally* Shapo, A Representational Theory of Consumer Protection: Doctrine, Function and Legal Liability for Product Disappointment, 60 Va. L. Rev. 1109, 1135-1152 (1974).
4. 75 Wash. 622, 135 P. 633 (1913).

time-honored in 1913, that a manufacturer could not be liable to anyone to whom it had not directly sold a product. Armour apparently was willing to concede that someone who ate unfit food could sue the manufacturer under an exception to the rule for food products, but it "strenuously" argued that this exception did not extend to include a retailer's suit for loss of reputation and profits.

The case thus presented the general issue of the responsibility of manufacturers for damage caused by dangerous products to parties with whom the manufacturers did not have a direct contract. The case was especially interesting because it involved only economic loss to the plaintiffs Mazetti. The Washington court grasped the nettle and reversed the lower court's dismissal of the claim. Among the interesting features of the case is the court's doctrinal flexibility. It based its precise holding on the theory of implied warranty for food products "dispensed in original packages."[5] However, the court spun out its decision on the basis of a mixture of warranty and negligence theory,[6] referring to allegations that the defendants had made representations of pureness, wholesomeness and fitness, and to claims that the plaintiffs had relied on those representations.[7]

What is important, beyond the technical legal doctrine, is the policy perspective from which the court viewed the case. Summarizing some precedents, it referred to "the general public policy as declared in the pure food laws" as well as to a rationale emphasizing danger to life derived from cases of patent or proprietary drugs.[8] Perhaps most interesting, as revelatory of the worldview of the court, is its quotation of a few sentences from a trichinosis case decided just the year before—the 1912 decision in *Ketterer v. Armour & Co.*[9] In the era of modern products liability law, it is fascinating to turn the yellowed pages of the volume that contains the *Ketterer* decision, which covers just a page and a half in the old Federal Reporter. Here is the language that the *Mazetti* court quoted:

> The remedies of injured consumers ought not to be made to depend upon the intricacies of the law of sales. The obligation of the manufacturer should not be based alone upon privity of contract. It should rest, as was once said, upon "the demands of social justice."[10]

---

5. *Id.* at 630, 135 P. at 636.

6. I have summarized the technical language in Shapo, A Representational Theory of Consumer Protection, 60 Va. L. Rev. 1109, 1135-1136 (1974).

7. 75 Wash. at 623, 135 P.2d at 633.

8. *Id.* at 626, 135 P. at 634.

9. 200 F. 322 (S.D.N.Y. 1922).

10. Ketterer v. Armour & Co., 200 F. 322, 323 (S.D.N.Y. 1912), quoted in Mazetti v. Armour & Co., 75 Wash. at 627, 135 P. at 635.

This language captures, rather powerfully, an historical frame of reference. It seems more than coincidence that these two decisions against a major packing company appeared just six and seven years after Upton Sinclair had joined the crew of journalists called "muckrakers" with a screed against conditions in the packing industry.[11] In view of the national fame Sinclair's *The Jungle* had achieved, it is reasonable to speculate that some of the members of the *Mazetti* court, as well as the *Ketterer* judge, had read the book. In any event, the same perspective influenced both tribunals. The *Mazetti* court makes four references to *Ketterer*, a trial court decision that did not cite a single source for its oratorical flourish.

Some may suggest that the decisions provide no more than a transcription of economic efficiency into the corpus of the law, with an implicit emphasis on information costs; after all, the *Mazetti* court stressed that there was no opportunity to check the contents of the tongue before it reached the consumer. But when judges turn so declamatory, with little reference to precedent, they manifest a commitment. The climate that yielded these early "consumer protection" decisions—the year of the Bull Moose and the first year of Wilson's New Freedom—was one of concern for underdogs. It was one of a commitment—to which even judges could unashamedly subscribe—to "social justice."

MacPherson v. Buick Motor Co.

The same decade brought one of the most famous decisions of a master of the craft, the majority opinion by Judge Benjamin Cardozo of the New York Court of Appeals in *MacPherson v. Buick Motor Co.*[12] The plaintiff in this case would not really rather have had a Buick; MacPherson sued the young auto company for injuries that occurred when a wheel of his vehicle crumbled. The legal obstacle for Cardozo in this case, as generations of law students have learned, was the same "privity of contract" doctrine that the *Mazetti* court had hurdled. The ancient wisdom was that plaintiffs claiming negligence could sue only their direct seller. Chief Judge Bartlett, dissenting, reflected the antique character of that point of view with his characterization of *MacPherson* as a case involving "the original vendor of an ordinary carriage."[13]

Cardozo, by contrast, pulled the law of New York—and eventually that of every other American jurisdiction—into the twentieth century. He refused to accept the "verbal niceties" that prior judges had used to distin-

---

11. U. Sinclair, The Jungle (1906).
12. 217 N.Y. 382, 111 N.E. 1050 (1916).
13. *Id.* at 400, 111 N.E. at 1056 (Bartlett, C.J., dissenting).

guish products that were "inherently" and "imminently" dangerous[14]—jurists of the past having conceded that manufacturers could be held liable without privity for the "inherently" dangerous product. Cardozo's eloquence carried him past the barrier of direct sale, past the idea that the duty of sellers "grows out of contract and nothing else":

> We have put the source of the obligation where it ought to be. We have put its source in the law.[15]

Thus, the greatest judge of that rough and ready day was not inclined to be ruled—or to have consumers be ruled—by the formal boundaries—and bonds—of contract. Rather than the law of bargains, the most closely applicable law was the law of injuries.

Henningsen v. Bloomfield Motors, Inc.

The story now leaps almost a half century, to the 1960 decision of the New Jersey Supreme Court in *Henningsen v. Bloomfield Motors, Inc.*[16] During the time since Cardozo's pathbreaking synthesis in the *MacPherson* case, practically every American jurisdiction had fallen in line on the proposition that no wall of "privity" barred suits for negligence by consumers against sellers high up in the distributional chain, including manufacturers. The battlefield now shifted to the question of whether a remote seller could be held liable to a consumer without a showing of negligence.

The *Henningsen* case arose from a one-car collision involving a ten-day-old vehicle. The driver, the purchaser's wife, testified that she heard a sudden, loud noise "from the bottom, by the hood" of the car, and felt the steering wheel spin in her hands. She suffered personal injuries in the resulting crash.

Justice John Francis's opinion for the court synthesized a group of arguments in favor of eliminating the privity requirement under the doctrine of implied warranty. At that point in the nascent history of what became "products liability" law, the implied warranty theory, of contractual origin, appeared to present the principal hope for a plaintiff like Ms. Henningsen, suing without being able to prove negligence.

Justice Francis carried forward, by quotation from the *Mazetti* and *Ketterer* cases, the theme of " 'the demands of social justice.' "[17] But he ex-

---

14. *Id.* at 394, 111 N.E. at 1054-1055.

15. *Id.* at 390, 111 N.E. at 1053.

16. 32 N.J. 358, 161 A.2d 69 (1960).

17. *Id.* at 384, 161 A.2d at 83, quoting Mazetti v. Armour & Co., 75 Wash. at 627, 135 P. at 635, which had quoted Ketterer v. Armour & Co., 322 F. at 323, *see* text accompanying note 10 *supra*.

panded that idea both within the representational framework drawn by the *Mazetti* court for early twentieth century law, and in the broader perspective of an era of "large scale advertising by manufacturers."[18] On this base of product portrayal, he fashioned an argument that emphasized the power of a few automobile manufacturers, selling cars on the basis of standardized contracts and disclaimer clauses from which the consumer had no practical escape. He described a setting of "gross inequality" and "gross disproportion" in bargaining power, one in which the "ordinary buyer" lacked "freedom of choice." In this context, he said, "[a]n instinctively felt sense of justice cries out against such a sharp bargain."[19]

Henningsen, therefore, adds to notions of "social justice" and a general concern with reliance on representations a more particularized concern with the effects of modern media and a focus on the uses of power.

Greenman v. Yuba Power Products, Inc.

Henningsen dramatically carried forward the banner of recovery for products claimants who could show neither negligence nor privity of contract. But Henningsen's theory of recovery, still bound to the past, was that of warranty—as we have noted, a doctrine with contractual origins. It remained for Justice Roger Traynor of the California Supreme Court to stake out a place for consumers, suing without proof of negligence, in the territory of injury law—specifically, the field of tort. Traynor's vehicle was *Greenman v. Yuba Power Products, Inc.*,[20] a 1963 case in which the plaintiff was hurt when he was using a combination power tool to make a chalice. He attributed his injuries, caused when a piece of wood flew out of the tool, to defects in the device.

Traynor could have rested his decision for the plaintiff on the rather straightforward theory of express warranty, based on representations that the defendant had made in a brochure that the plaintiff claimed to have studied. But this was an opportunity for which the great California judge had been waiting for the better part of two decades. In a separate opinion in a 1944 case involving an exploding Coke bottle, Traynor had suggested that it was time to stop playing semantic games in order to force such cases into a negligence framework. He wrote in that case, *Escola v. Coca-Cola Bottling Co.*, that the more candid, and appropriate, theory for such situations was one of what he then called "absolute liability."[21]

---

18. *Id.* at 373, 161 A.2d at 77.
19. *Id.* at 384, 388, 161 A.2d at 83, 85.
20. 59 Cal.2d 57, 377 P.2d 897, 27 Cal. Rptr. 697 (1963).
21. Escola v. Coca-Cola Bottling Co., 24 Cal.2d 453, 150 P.2d 436, 440 (1944) (Traynor, J., separate opinion concurring in the judgment).

Now, in *Greenman,* Judge Traynor seized the tactical opportunity. For the first time, an American judge articulated a theory of strict products liability:

> A manufacturer is strictly liable in tort when an article he places on the market, knowing that it is to be used without inspection for defects, proves to have a defect that causes injury for human being.[22]

Traynor rested this blunt holding on at least two major pillars. One of these appeared rooted in the marketing process, foreshadowed by Traynor's declaration that "[i]mplicit in the machine's presence on the market ... was a representation that it would safely do the jobs for which it was built":

> [I]t should not be controlling whether plaintiff selected the machine because of the statements in the brochure, or because of the machine's own appearance of excellence that belied the defect lurking beneath the surface, or because he merely assumed that it would safely do the jobs it was built to do.[23]

Traynor founded his other rationale upon notions of power and economic obligation. He submitted as a principal policy basis for his holding the need "to insure that the costs of injuries resulting from defective products are borne by the manufacturers who put such products on the market rather than by the injured persons who are powerless to protect themselves."[24]

The moment of the *Greenman* decision, in January 1963, fixed in place the basic doctrinal foundation of modern products liability. The theoretical basis of Traynor's opinion reflected an evolving society: although the governing law had arisen from direct portrayals of products from sellers to buyers, it had now become recognized as part of the law of injuries and not of contract. The judges who had fashioned these theories, surveying a period of immense growth in the variety and sophistication of products, had developed a body of law with a normative emphasis: one that concerned itself with "ought" and "should," with power, and even with "social justice."

Junctures of Scholarship

In the nineteen fifties, a few scholars began to venture into an area that some already began to define as "products liability."[25] In 1957 the Tennes-

---

22. *Greenman,* 59 Cal.2d at 62, 377 P.2d at 900, 27 Cal. Rptr. at 700.

23. *Id.* at 64, 377 P.2d at 901, 27 Cal. Rptr. at 701.

24. *Id.* at 63, 377 P.2d at 901, 27 Cal. Rptr. at 701.

25. George Priest presents a short bibliographical essay on this literature in The Invention of Enterprise Liability: A Critical History of the Intellectual Foundations of Modern Tort Law, 14 L. Legal Studies 461, 500-505 (1985).

see Law Review published a symposium on the subject that incorporated papers delivered at the annual meeting of the Association of American Law Schools.[26]

It was in 1960 that the most influential scholarly essay appeared on the subject. This was William L. Prosser's heavily footnoted synthesis of a body of law that had developed under theories like implied warranty, an essay that concluded that it was time for courts to call this development by a more conceptually descriptive name: "strict liability in tort."[27]

When he wrote this article, Prosser carried two portfolios that generated still more publication in favor of his thesis. In one role, he was the author of a much cited treatise on general tort law, a book that reflected the development in his thought as he brought out successive editions.[28]

More important from the point of view of the politics of legal scholarship, Prosser was the Reporter for the Second Restatement of Torts, a massive project under the auspices of the American Law Institute. It was in this capacity that he developed, through a relatively swift succession of drafts over a three year period,[29] a conception of strict liability that found its ultimate expression in section 402A of the Second Restatement. That provision sketched a form of strict liability against sellers for products that were "in a defective condition unreasonably dangerous to the user or consumer or to his property." This form of liability—applicable although "the seller has exercised all possible care in the preparation and sale of his product"—governed even cases in which there was no direct sale to the plaintiff or "any contractual relation" between the plaintiff and the seller.[30]

Although a comment to section 402A asserted a disinclination to base this version of strict liability on representations,[31] it spoke of a rationale of forced reliance—that the public "has the right to and does expect, in the case of products which it needs and for which it is forced to rely upon the seller, that reputable sellers will stand behind their goods."[32] Whatever ten-

---

26. Strict Liability of Manufacturers: A Symposium, 24 Tenn. L. Rev. 923 (1957). The events of the meeting are briefly recounted in Priest, supra note 25, at 501-502.

27. Prosser, The Assault Upon the Citadel (Strict Liability to the Consumer), 69 Yale L.J. 1099 (1960).

28. W. Prosser, Torts 672-85 (3d ed. 1964); *id.* 650-58 (4th ed. 1971).

29. A summary of this history appears in Putman v. Erie City Mfg. Co., 338 F.2d 911, 918-919 (5th Cir. 1964).

30. Restatement (Second) Torts § 402A (1965).

31. Comment n to section 402A says that the rule "does not require any reliance on the part of the consumer upon the reputation, skill, or judgment of the seller ... nor any representation or undertaking on the part of that seller."

32. *Id.,* comment c.

sions might inhere in the comment's ideas about the representational background of products liability, however, it was forthright about its social views concerning the underpinnings of the law. The seller, said the comment, had "undertaken and assumed a special responsibility toward any member of the consuming public who may be injured by" the product.[33] Moreover, the comment declared, "public policy demands" that the cost of product-caused injuries "be placed upon those who market them, and be treated as a cost of production against which liability insurance can be obtained."[34]

Thus it was that by the date of publication of the final version of section 402A, in the first set of volumes of the Second Restatement in 1965, the adherents of strict liability for products had made a powerful case for their position. They explicitly rooted that position in social policy, although arguably it also drew nourishment from the process of product marketing.

The Social Background and Related Assumptions

Having sketched some of the main lines of judicial and scholarly authority on products liability, and their stated rationales, we can now begin to probe the relationship of the social background of the subject and the assumptions of decision makers.

Consumer Desires and Preferences

The vulnerable consumer

An important set of issues in the law of product injuries concerns the nature of the consumer. What kind of person are we dealing with? Possessing what level of intelligence? What degree of vulnerability to glittering generalities? How much does this person seek risk, or how willing is he or she to accept a risk in order to use a product that will do a specific job? What generates this person's preferences for particular kinds of goods? The law has begun to make educated guesses about the answers to some of these questions and related issues. It has proved fairly supple, and generally sensible, in responding to the question of what kind of animal the consumer is.

---

33. *Id.*
34. *Id.*

Consumer intelligence and sophistication; subjective and objective standards. Consider, first of all, the question of what assumptions the law makes, either by factual determination or as a matter of convenience, about consumer intelligence and sophistication. One straightforward way to solve this problem is to announce, and stick to, an objective standard. An injured person may claim that for some reason or another—age, disability, lack of experience—he or she was unable to measure up to the standard of most people who use the product that caused the injury. Advocates of an objective standard will reject this plea. In essence, they tell such claimants, if you're going to play in this product league, you have to have the physical, intellectual, and emotional equipment that will allow you to be as alert as at least the average person.

Tort law certainly has taken that position in many cases in which it is the *defendant* who seeks to be judged by a standard special to himself. A legal classic is the nineteenth century decision in *Vaughan v. Menlove.*[35] In that case, the defendant kept on his property a hay rick that gave grave promise of combustibility. The plaintiff, who owned neighboring cottages, remonstrated with the defendant for five weeks that the hay was a fire hazard. But the defendant continued his apparently doltish insistence that "he would chance it." When a fire in fact occurred, the defendant argued that the court should take account of his "misfortune of not possessing the highest order of intelligence." But Chief Judge Tindal of the Court of Common Pleas rejected that defense. In a much quoted formulation of the objective standard, he said that to make fault "co-extensive with the judgment of each individual ... would be as variable as the length of the foot of each individual." Thus, he concluded that in "all cases" each person must observe the degree of "caution such as a man of ordinary prudence would observe."[36]

Courts have followed this lead in many tort cases, adhering to the idea that people who engage in grown-up activities must behave like at least average grownups, and insisting that various mental and emotional limitations will not lower the general standard of care. Thus, a child who operates a snowmobile cannot plead his tender years to lower his duty of care to others.[37] And, on the other side of the liability coin, a drunk who climbs a power pole and is electrocuted cannot use his intoxication to lower his duty to take care of himself.[38]

---

35. 3 Bing., N.C., 468, 132 Eng. Rep. 490 (1837).

36. *Id.* at 476, 132 Eng. Rep. at 493.

37. Robinson v. Lindsay, 92 Wash.2d 410, 598 P.2d 392 (1979).

38. Martin v. Louisiana Power & Light Co., 546 F. Supp. 780 (E.D. La. 1982), aff'd, 719 F.2d 403 (5th Cir. 1983) (table).

Yet, in the broad legal area denominated "consumer protection," of which products liability law is a part, the courts have sometimes reacted more forgivingly to lack of talent and sophistication. One of the most famous statements of this point of view appeared in a trademark decision issued by a federal court of appeals in 1910. The law, that court said, must respond to "the ignorant, the unthinking and the credulous, who, in making purchases, do not stop to analyze, but are governed by appearances and general impressions."[39]

Courts have employed an analogous approach in situations in which inexpert consumers have to deal with complex mechanical products. One such decision dealt with a terrible accident that killed a couple and orphaned two children. The accident involved a big diesel Freightliner truck owned by Billy Maxey and Mary Delia Maxey, which tilted on its right side and then slid a distance of almost a hundred yards.

The truck had its fuel in aluminum "saddle tanks," located near the frame rails of the vehicle. There was a tank only on the left side of the vehicle when the couple purchased it, but the manufacturer's design allowed users to add a right tank, and Billy Maxey added one. The tanks did not have certain safety features that were supposed to reduce fire hazards in crashes: a flexible, impact-absorbing bladder and "fuel line fittings which would separate in a crash." After the truck slid to a stop, a fire occurred and the couple was burned alive, leaving daughters aged twelve and nine.

The jury found that Billy Maxey had "voluntarily assumed the risk of his injuries," a finding that both a federal trial judge and the appellate court could not tolerate. Setting aside the jury's finding on this point, the trial judge conceded that it was reasonable for the jury to think "that in the event of a turnover the tanks would probably contact the ground." However, he noted that the manufacturer had not tried to prove that Maxey "was aware of the extent of the fire hazard," for that presumably would have shown that the maker itself had been culpable in putting the product on the market. Moreover, the court noted that Freightliner had not shown "that Maxey was aware that the right tank lacked a safety bladder and cutoff valves, much less any proof that Maxey knew and appreciated the scope and risk of the danger created by this defect."[40]

Two sittings of the Fifth Circuit agreed on this point. As Judge Daniel Thomas put it in a panel decision of that court, it was "untenable" to argue that a "national manufacturer of truck/tractors" did not know of the hazards of the tanks, "but that Billy Maxey, a truck driver and mechanic with

---

39. Florence Mfg. Co. v. J.C. Dowd & Co., 178 Fed. 73, 75 (2d Cir. 1910).
40. Maxey v. Freightliner Corp., 540 F. Supp. 955, 961 (N.D. Tex. 1978).

a high school education should be charged with knowledge and appreciation of the nature and extent of this risk."[41]

The decisions of both the trial and appellate courts focused on the technical meaning of the doctrine called "assumption of risk," which to be successfully argued by a defendant requires that the plaintiff must have voluntarily and unreasonably encountered a known risk. A central lesson of the decisions, focusing on the knowledge element, is that one cannot require a nonspecialist user of complicated machinery, even a business person, to possess expertise about it.

The "sophisticated user" doctrine

There is, to be sure, another face to expertise. It presents itself in the "sophisticated user doctrine," under which courts bar suits by injured persons who by personal training and experience are well acquainted with particular product hazards. An illustrative federal case involved the death of Joseph Martinez, a member of a crew working to strip a barge that had carried a chemical laden with benzene. At the time the barge was loaded with the chemical, DuPont—its manufacturer—had put a Benzene Warning and Cargo Information Card on the craft. It also had placed in a special compartment on the barge a product identification card that described the toxicity of the chemical.

As the crew labored to strip the barge, the foreman smelled fumes and ordered an evacuation of the tank in which they were working, but Martinez collapsed before he could get out. An autopsy attributed his death to acute benzene intoxication. In a complicated lawsuit, one of the issues was whether DuPont was liable under either strict liability or negligence doctrines for failing to warn Martinez of the dangers of the product. The Fifth Circuit held it improper to impose liability on DuPont under those theories. The court emphasized that DuPont sold the product principally through a petrochemical broker and intended it for a limited market of "professionals" who would know how to handle such chemicals. Since Martinez' crew was "in fact composed of such professionals," the court said that the warning and identification cards "should have been adequate to apprise crew members of the hazards of entering the barge's tanks."[42]

Another Fifth Circuit panel even applied the "sophisticated user" defense against a tire serviceman with a second grade education. In this case,

---

41. Maxey v. Freightliner Corp., 623 F.2d 395, 399 (5th Cir. 1980), aff'd on this point, 665 F.2d 1367, 1377 (5th Cir. 1982) (quoting the panel decision).

42. Martinez v. Dixie Carriers, Inc., 529 F.2d 457, 465 (5th Cir. 1976) (negligence); see similar language, id. at 467 (strict liability).

57-year-old Milton Davis had been mounting agricultural tires—hundreds or even thousands of them—for two years. The court relied on evidence that "he could read and understand the meaning of the word 'warning,' " which appeared on a label the manufacturer had placed on the tire.[43]

However, there are limits to the protection that this doctrine confers on manufacturers, limits related to the plaintiff's particularity of knowledge. Yet another Fifth Circuit decision makes this clear. This case arose from extensive property damage, in addition to several deaths, that resulted when a blowout occurred on a drilling barge off the Texas Gulf Coast. The issue relevant to this discussion arose from the corporate plaintiffs' claims that the manufacturer of a blowout preventer had failed to give adequate warnings of its limitations. The device had a rated capacity of 5,000 psi, but only had been tested to 3,500 psi. As the crew struggled with the blowout during its early stages, the blowout preventer failed at 3,700 psi. In rejecting the "sophisticated user" defense, the court emphasized that the "defense applies only when the user knew of the particular danger"— namely, the unreliability of the product between its rated capacity and its tested capacity. The trial court had decided that there had been negligent use of the product, but the appellate court thought that this holding did "not necessarily imply . . . a finding of knowledge" by the plaintiffs "or that the manufacturer's warnings were adequate."[44]

The traditional concept of assumption of risk, as we have noted, includes the idea that a plaintiff should not recover when he or she has voluntarily and unreasonably confronted a known risk. When a court weds this concept to the "sophisticated user" doctrine, as occurred in the case of the blowout preventer, it appears that the judicial sympathy for the "ignorant" manifested in the 1910 trademark decision discussed above[45] carries forward to modern cases involving products injuries. The law has to walk a fine line in this area, one that meanders among several important legal theories, including "duty to warn" doctrine and the concepts of "contributory negligence" and "assumption of risk." The courts appear to be aligning their decisions with the idea that in a meaningful free market, consumers must process enough information to make sensible choices about packages of risks and benefits.

---

43. American Mut. Liab. Ins. Co. v. Firestone Tire & Rubber Co., 799 F.2d 993, 995 (5th Cir. 1986)(quoting Ducote v. Liberty Mut. Ins. Co., 451 So.2d 1211, 1213 (La. App.), cert. denied, 457 So.2d 15 (La. 1984) on the "sophisticated user" doctrine).

44. In re Incident Aboard the D/B Ocean King on August 30, 1980, 813 F.2d 679, 687 (5th Cir. 1987).

45. *See supra*, text accompanying note 39.

Ethical Premises

A set of ethical issues overlays the questions we have been discussing. These issues have to do with willingness to accept risk, and they have psychological and behavioral aspects. We speak of some people being "risk averse" and others as "risk preferrers." Some people have a zest for danger. They enjoy living on the edge, at least part of the time. They may view such conduct as sharpening perceptions; they may find that it stimulates alertness.

The known hazard and overlapping systems of justice. If we accept that there is a smooth curve of risk preference among members of the population, we next face a challenging "should" question. Let us consider the case—there are many—in which a worker uses a product with a serious built-in hazard. For a lawyer, some of the most interesting cases of this kind are those where two conditions exist: (1) the worker knows of the hazard and (2) the maker of the product could have made it safer but did not because it did not think that doing so would aid its market position.

Two overlapping sets of problems come into play here. One involves systems of justice and the other has to do with the number of actors in the drama. A regulatory scheme may make the parties' choice for them. In workplace cases in particular, tort law focuses on two of the three parties that make choices: the manufacturer who designs the product and the employee who works with it. By comparison, a workers' compensation plan will not overtly take individual choice into account. Workers' compensation legislation primarily controls the legal relation between the worker and the employer, who has purchased the product and ordered the worker to use it, but we cannot ignore the fact that the relationship is triangular.

A set of relevant technical rules deals with the relationship between tort law and workers' compensation. Workers compensation is basically an exclusive remedy, limiting employees only to its benefits and barring them from tort suits. As we noted in our discussion above of James Glass's suit against the Stahl Specialty Company, this limitation effectively cabins the liability of employers for workplace injuries, including those that occur in the use of industrial machines.[46]

The aim of an integrated system of justice would be to divide up the burdens of injuries appropriately among all three of these parties to a work-

---

46. *See supra*, this chapter, text accompanying notes 1-2. For discussion of the general rule that bars manufacturers of workplace machines from suing workers' compensation employers, *see* 1 M. Shapo, The Law of Products Liability ¶ 15.03 (1990).

place injury. A touchstone of such a system, in our society, would be the concept of free choice.

What freedom means. We now must confront the issue of what we mean by freedom when we speak of "free choice." In a sharply defining decision in a case involving a household product, a lawn mower, the Maryland Court of Appeals rejected the plaintiff's claim. The owner of the machine, Harold Myers, was mowing on a slope. He suffered severe injuries when he slipped and fell and his foot went under the mower and into the whirling blade. He argued that there were various ways that the maker of the machine, Montgomery Ward, could have made it safer. For example, it could have put a "dead-man" control on the mower, or it could have designed the housing of the mower so that it would stay close to the ground no matter what the level of the cutting blade.

The court was unsympathetic to these contentions. In words that would appeal to many philosophers and economists, building on its observation that it "was apparent at the time of purchase" that there were no safety devices, the court declared that "in a free market, Myers had the choice of buying a mower equipped with them, of buying the mower which he did, or of buying no mower at all."[47]

This point of view—a straight you-pays-your-money-and-you-takes-your-choice approach—has been influential. It is not surprising that, apart from such household settings as the Myers case, it also has captured courts dealing with workplace cases. An illustrative decision involved Gary Prince, a coal miner who was hurt while he was using a roofbolter machine to implant metal bolts in a mine ceiling to keep it from collapsing. The injury occurred when a wrench used to tighten a bolt flew out of a chuck on the machine and hit Prince in the face. The roofbolter he was using did not have a wrench retainer, even though another type of bolter did have such a device.

Prince, who had more than three years of mining experience and had worked with the roofbolter for about three months, was aware there was a danger from wrenches flying out of the chuck; he answered "yes" to a question about whether he thought the operation of the bolter without the wrench retainer "present[ed] hazards to you." On these facts, an Illinois appellate court thought it must decide that Prince "assumed the risk of his injuries as a matter of law." The court specifically rejected Prince's argument "that there can be no duty imposed upon a plaintiff to refuse to operate machines because he knows that a machine could be designed in a safer fashion."[48]

---

47. Myers v. Montgomery Ward & Co., 253 Md. 282, 297, 252 A.2d 855, 864 (1969).
48. Prince v. Galis Mfg. Co., 58 Ill. App.3d 1056, 374 N.E.2d 1318, 1321 (1978).

A similar philosophy has governed other decisions on workers' claims. An example is a case in which Perry Orfield, a bulldozer operator, was using the machine to arrange uprooted brush and trees in long piles—an operation called "windrowing"—on a Tennessee construction site. Orfield, who knew his bulldozer did not have a steel canopy guard, was hit in the chest by a fifty-foot-long oak tree. Orfield had used dozers with and without guards in his many years of operating such equipment. He said that he liked the safety that the guards provided and that he and his fellow workers had mentioned that to their foreman. However, he testified that he worked without the canopy because he was afraid that if he did not, he would lose his job.

It was the fact of Orfield's actual knowledge and contemplation of the danger that most influenced the Sixth Circuit to hold against him. Technically, the decision drew on a notion that many courts associate with the defect requirement under strict liability doctrine. This idea is that for a product to be defective, it must be dangerous beyond the contemplation of the ordinary consumer. In Orfield's case, the court viewed his admitted awareness of the danger as meaning that the dozer "was not dangerous beyond his own contemplation as a user possessing ordinary knowledge" of the product's characteristics.[49]

We can now discern several possible bases for this kind of decision. One lies in the broad notion of free choice in free markets. Another is more of a lawyer's idea, yet one relatively accessible to non-lawyers: the concept of "assumption of risk." A third is the somewhat more technical idea that a product is not "defective" if its dangers lie within the contemplation of the user. In a fourth variation, courts frequently use the coverall term "obviousness" to link the obtrusive nature of a danger to a decision to deny recovery to product users.

The constraints on choice.   This set of ideas does not go unchallenged as a description of human behavior. The Fifth Circuit provided an antidote in another case in which a wrench figured in the dispute, although it was not the wrench that ultimately caused the injury. A worker, William Green, was working on the gearbox of a machine that twisted several electrical fibers together to make a single cable of fiber. Kneeling near a low-slung gearbox, Green had used an Allen wrench to loosen an oil-soaked gear, which itself weighed 52 pounds, from the lubrication system of the machine. As he put his hands around the gear and pulled it down along its shaft, the gear slipped off the shaft and crushed his left ring finger. The injury required a

---

49. Orfield v. International Harvester Co., 535 F.2d 959, 964 (6th Cir. 1976).

series of operations and resulted in a "severe depression" over a two-year period.

A witness for the manufacturer testified if the firm had provided a different kind of wrench—a T-wrench—Green would not have had to grip the oily gear with his hands. The jury found that the machine was "defective" and "unreasonably dangerous" and "was a producing cause of the accident," but also said that Green had "assumed the risk." On the basis of the "assumption of risk" finding, the trial court held that the jury's verdict for Green could not stand. The Fifth Circuit reversed, with reasoning diametrically opposed to that of the roofbolter and bulldozer cases discussed above. Emphasizing that "voluntariness is a mandatory prerequisite to a finding of assumption of risk," the court said that Green could not "be found to have assumed the risk" when he had followed the manufacturer's procedures for gear changes in a context where the manufacturer "offered no alternative course of conduct to accomplish the task."[50]

This emphasis on voluntariness collides head-on with the idea that one who continues to work with a dangerous machine—as, for example, Orfield did—cannot recover for injuries attributable to its hazards. Of course, one need not call that kind of conduct assumption of risk to deny recovery; the court in *Orfield*, for example, chalked up its decision under the "no defect" heading.

It is easy enough for skilled lawyers to wrap the question in various kinds of terminology. Some formulations of the issue entangle notions of factual causation and metaphysics: did the design of the machine Green was using really "cause" the injury? Or was it Green's "choice" to try to wrestle a slippery 52-pound gear off its shaft?

Overarching such competing characterizations is a choice that defines the law, and arbitrates the question of how free the employee's behavior is. This is a judicial choice among philosophies. Judge Garrity of the federal district court in Boston made such a choice in the case of Elizabeth Downs, injured when her hand was caught in the stroking mechanism of a punch press. In one aspect of the case—Ms. Downs's awareness of the hazard of putting a hand near the mechanism when one could inadvertently start the press with a foot pedal—Judge Garrity indicated that he was dubious that she had the requisite particular knowledge.

But he also directly confronted the problem inherent in the sale of a machine that will put a worker in the position of either having to work in a dangerous way or quit her job. In this case, a co-worker of Downs had suggested to her a safer way to do the job, but her foreman had ordered her to work in the way that led to the accident. Ms. Downs testified, as Judge

---

50. Green v. Edmands Co., 639 F.2d 286, 290 (5th Cir. 1981).

Garrity noted, "without refutation or rebuttal, that she saw no realistic choice but to follow the foreman's orders." It is worth quoting his comment rather fully:

> The option of quitting her job was no doubt available, but it was effectively foreclosed, or at least quite circumscribed. The plaintiff lacked a trade or college degree and had to help support a family. For a woman in her constrained position, commanded to follow a questionable practice but needing her job, the facts strongly rebut voluntariness in the ordinary sense of the word.[51]

What should we say about this decision as a matter of judicial performance? That this is an "activist" judge, who is performing a "legislative" function? What should we say about decisions with the opposite holding? That it is equally "activist" to base judgments on a thoroughgoing "free market" approach? That in the twentieth century, we do not view this market as "free"? That it is as free as can be, because in Singapore, or even in Boston, there are many people who would take their turn at the same punch press, perhaps for even less wages?

These are hard questions to answer. Observers' responses will vary according to many factors: experience of life and work, personal philosophy, professional training. What we can say is that sometimes knowledge is not power; that sometimes awareness is helplessness. We can add that in situations where a product manufacturer sets up a situation in which an employer benefits from an employee's vulnerability, it seems just that the manufacturer should contribute to the alleviation of injuries that are likely to occur. A judicial decision in a single case of this kind may seem an imperfect way to deal with this problem; we have noted the legal complexities inherent in the overlapping systems of law that bear on workplace injuries. But sometimes the law must deal episodically with a poor, and imperfect world.

The Role of Product Portrayal

A crucial factor in the background of products liability law is the way that products are portrayed in the marketplace. The principal way that happens is through what we conventionally call advertising. But by product portrayal, I refer to a broader concept that embraces more than the use of television, radio, newspapers, and magazines to market particular products. I mean all of the subtle ways in which sellers both create demand for their products, and establish images in the minds of consumers about the

---

51. Downs v. Gulf & Western Mfg. Co., Prod. Liab. Rep. (CCH) ¶ 11,459, at 32,217 (D. Mass. 1987).

nature of those products—their utility for particular functions, their safety, and even their hazards.[52]

These methods of image creation, within a broader concept of product promotion, include not only media communication but the appearance of the product itself. The images themselves include general conceptions in the public mind, built up over time, about the functions and risks of certain types of products. Every product sale draws on these reservoirs of meaning in the minds of consumers, and the main current of products liability law represents a response to the way in which sellers tap those impressions.

Some doctrines of products liability law deal rather explicitly with the process of image creation. The most direct applications appear in theories like fraud and express warranty. Among others, this catalog includes failure to warn theories under both strict liability and negligence classifications, and the doctrine of assumption of risk in many manifestations. Beyond that, more general judicial uses of negligence doctrine, strict liability, and theories of defect have roots in the way that products are portrayed.

Insurance

All of the sociological, and legal, action described in this chapter plays out against a background occupied by one of the biggest businesses in the country, the insurance industry. Insurance pervades the planning sectors of our personal and commercial lives. It is an important consideration, although one not always explicitly identified, at every turn in the law of products liability.

What are the principal threads of the insurance fabric that surrounds this area of the law? For our present purposes, insurance represents a way for people to deal with the financial risk arising from the chance that a product will cause injury. Insurance depends on a relatively large number of potential exposures to injury and relative certainty, over time, about the rate of injuries for which protection is sought.

There are two kinds of insurance that are theoretically relevant to the subject of products liability, but only one usually figures in practical discussions of the subject. The more theoretical of the possibilities is that of first-party accident insurance: in theory, a person who feared injury from products could buy insurance that protected her against the financial consequences of such an accident, for example, lost wages or medical bills.

---

52. I have showed how hundreds of products liability decisions reflect this concern, implicitly as well as explicitly, in Shapo, A Representational Theory of Consumer Protection: Doctrine, Function and Legal Liability for Product Disappointment, 60 Va. L. Rev. 1109 (1974).

Many people hold this kind of insurance against the general fortuities of life, of which product accidents are only a small subset, often carrying that coverage through their employers. Most people do not think in those terms vis-a-vis particular products, or even products in general, nor are they likely to, nor are insurers likely to provide so specific a type of first-party insurance. This hypothetical possibility is useful, however, in helping us to frame the subject. It points up the fact that, at least in theory, potential accident *victims* have an opportunity to cushion their own losses, putting aside such factors as the defendant's fault and the moral implications of the act of selling an unreasonably dangerous product.

The more practically relevant form of insurance in this context is liability insurance, which typically is funded by premiums paid by firms that wish to avoid paying a court-ordered judgment for injuries caused by their products. We can identify at least two principal issues raised by liability rules in this connection. One concerns calculability of the risk, and the other relates to the effect of high liability premiums on production costs.

As we have indicated, it is a fundamental requirement of insurance that it involve risks that are calculable. If legal rules change very quickly, or if they are uncertain in their application, insurers will find it difficult to set premiums for the risk of liability, because they will not have sufficient information to calculate an average for their future exposures. In the early years of the expansion of tort doctrine to include strict products liability, one might have speculated that the shock of doctrinal change affected the calculability of insurance rates. Certainly at the present time, the question is whether the law as it has evolved gives insurers reasonable assurance that they can calculate rates for classes of products injuries that will enable them both to absorb the losses that will in fact occur and to gain a reasonable rate of return.

We should observe, in this connection, that there is no more uncertainty in the basic verbal formulas of strict liability, which basically require a plaintiff to prove that a product was defective and unreasonably dangerous, than there has been in the general law of negligence. That negligence body of rules, which relies on the equally abstract standard of reasonable prudent conduct, has reigned for more than a century without serious complaint about its abstractness or allegations about its vagueness. To this, I would add an observation based on my reading of tort and insurance literature over the last quarter century. There surely have been complaints about the uncertainty generated by products liability rules. But market conditions for investment by insurance companies appear to have been as much at the root of uncertainty that troubles these firms.

To be sure, there is evidence that some features of the legal climate have contributed to substantial increases in liability insurance premiums, and therefore seller costs. And critics have asserted that liability rules have had at least two destructive effects: they have created disincentives to research and development,[53] and they have caused manufacturers to stop producing products that consumers, on balance, would desire.[54]

The "uncertainty" and costs factors join together to create a problem in estimating the costs of future production. Wrapped up in that problem are questions about what kinds of products the law keeps off the market, and about the amount of deterrence to the sale of "good" products that is created by legal condemnation of "bad" products. That, in turn, leads to the question of whether the law is reasonably distinguishing "good" from "bad" products.

Later chapters will assess the law with that issue in mind, but presently I present this hypothesis: there is very little proof that products liability rules have deprived consumers of products that, on balance, they would really "want." Here and there one finds a special case, of which the case of vaccines is a primary example. But that unusual situation demanded and received a special solution, one now proceeding through a combination of federal legislation and judge-made law.

I understand that it is very difficult to prove that a general rule has kept one of many possible things from happening. I do suggest, however, that there is a heavy burden on those who argue that we should feel panicked about a trend in the law in which a large majority of courts have participated. In general economic reporting, products liability is notable by its absence in the identification of causes for economic stagnation. Against that background, advocates of the panic hypothesis must produce a lot of evidence to justify a dolefulness that verges on prophecies of disaster.

Some Systemic Features of the Law

Relevant to this discussion are certain features of our legal system that most people tend to take for granted. These features have evolved as part of our society's general response to disputes that cannot be resolved in the ordinary course of negotiation. They include the employment of adversary trials as the last line of dispute resolution, the use of juries to resolve dis-

---

53. *See, e.g.,* Who Should Be Liable? 95, Table 5.5 (Research and Policy Committee of Committee for Econ. Development 1989) (21 percent of large firms and 18 percent of small firms surveyed "[d]iscontinued product research" as a result of "actual liability experience").

54. *See, e.g., id.* (36 percent of large firms and 27 percent of small firms "[d]iscontinued product lines"; 30 percent of large firms and 31 percent of small firms "[d]ecided against introducing new products").

puted issues in those trials, and the method of financing litigation. Each of these matters has generated volumes of analysis and commentary. In this analysis, we can advert only briefly to these aspects of the system.

First, our system of justice is adversary. It relies on the parties to marshal the facts and the applicable legal arguments. The judge in this system, unlike judges in so-called inquisitorial systems, takes a rather passive role. He does not seek evidence on his own. Nor does he, except in the most extraordinary situations of mismatch between counsel, seek affirmatively to develop arguments in favor of one party or the other. This system, which has many meritorious features, including a tendency to turn up evidence in favor of parties initially disadvantaged,[55] also has some negative consequences. It creates incentives to twist facts, to push arguments unduly, to generate mountains of paper and in general to invent tactical problems for one's opponent. In such litigation as products cases involving complex goods, these features of an adversary system may be very costly for both the litigants and the system. We should note, however, that one purpose of the doctrine of strict liability is to overcome some of the problems of proof inherent in the labyrinthine nature of corporate files related to design procedures and manufacturing processes.

An important question is whether products liability law has so enhanced the opportunity for successful litigation that it encourages plaintiffs to sue on what is essentially an extortionate basis, utilizing small chances of large verdicts to demand settlements unjustified by the law. So far as I know, there are no hard data on that issue, although a frequent complaint of defense lawyers is that the availability of punitive damages in products cases creates opportunities for plaintiffs to demand settlements far beyond the true value of a case. I should add that I have heard of no feature of the adversary system that makes it more of a vehicle for injustice in products liability cases than in the law generally.

Another built-in feature of our present system is the use of trial juries, a right effectively granted to litigants by the Seventh Amendment to the Constitution. I shall not rehearse at any length the arguments for and against the use of juries. I do note the frequent complaints that juries are unduly sympathetic to victims of personal injury—a category that includes products liability plaintiffs—but I also observe that there is a substantial literature indicating that juries are not unreasonably swayed by emotion. I know of no evidence that the ability of juries to understand judicial instructions in products liability cases suffers by comparison with that of juries in

---

55. *See, e.g.*, J. Thibault & L. Walker, Procedural Justice: A Psychological Analysis 40 (1975).

other tort cases, or indeed in any other class of cases typically tried to juries.

One other common factor in tort litigation, including products litigation, is that claimants principally rely on lawyers who employ the "contingency fee." This method of conducting legal business also arouses controversy. Advocates of the contingency fee defend it, in part, on the basis that it permits people to seek vindication of their legal rights when they literally could not afford to do so otherwise. Opponents claim that these fee arrangements are the root of frivolous and even extortionate litigation.

Conclusion

In this chapter we have set products liability law against its background in other areas of injury law, as well as framing it by some systemic features that are common to litigation generally, especially tort litigation. Our summary review of judicial history in the last three decades has revealed the roots of modern products liability law both in the representational background of product sales and in courts' desire to do justice between consumers and sellers in the context of the relevant power relationships. Focusing in part on product injuries in the workplace, we have seen how differing results may be explained not only on the basis of the knowledge of the parties, but also on the basis of competing moral principles on which judges draw in discerning relative degrees of freedom of choice. We are now ready to extend our exploration of products liability cases with an eye to the symbolic content of this branch of the law.

3

Stakes and Symbols

Our survey of the history and the social background of products liability law provides a foundation for an examination of some representative case profiles, with a view to analyzing the social symbolism of those decisions. I shall be using concrete cases as gateways to insights on human activity that the litigation process has translated into law.

Some Representative Activities and Decisions

Industrial Machines

One of the most important areas of products liability law, from both a quantitative and a social point of view, involves industrial machines. The volume of cases in this area makes it numerically significant. Beyond that, we noted in the last chapter the problems of practical legal philosophy that arise when employees lose limbs, or even their lives, to the dangerous features of machines used in the workplace. The kinds of choices that the law makes about these cases therefore carry important messages about how Americans view their society.

Michigan: Living by the machine. A recurrent issue in the industrial context concerns allegations of a lack of adequate safety devices. An illustrative Michigan decision involved a worker at a Chrysler plant, Karl Tulkuu, who suffered a severe hand injury while he was operating a press with another worker. When the press was working normally, each operator had to depress and hold down two palm buttons to activate the machine. When the accident happened, Tulkuu's co-worker had pushed down both of his palm buttons and Tulkuu had depressed one button while he tried to use his other hand to blank a piece of metal that was caught in the machine. Although the two workers had thus depressed only three of the four palm buttons, the machine cycled, causing the injury. The immediate cause of the event was the broken condition of a plastic case on a microswitch on the button that the plaintiff had not pressed. This caused the switch to fail and allowed the machine to go through its cycle even though the plaintiff was not pushing that button. Tulkuu sued the makers of the palm button assembly and of the switch.

At the trial, the judge gave an instruction to the effect that Tulkuu's claim would be barred if he was contributorily negligent. So instructed, the jury held for the defendants and the intermediate appellate court affirmed. The Michigan Supreme Court reversed, in a 1979 decision that is noteworthy because of its origins in a state where the competing interests of both employers and workers are particularly well developed. The supreme court's decision drew on the impression of safety that safety devices develop in employees, on the assumption that tort judgments would influence conduct, and on a general rationale of consumer protection.

First, the court emphasized the image that the machine communicated: "The employee has become 'conditioned' to believe that the equipment being used is what is says it is, namely, safety equipment." An employee who has "come to rely on the effectiveness" of such equipment, said the court, "cannot and should not be required to temper his or her behavior because of a defect about which the employee has no awareness."[1]

In this context, the court thought that to permit the defense of contributory negligence "would be tantamount to subverting ... safety concerns" that it had mentioned in prior decisions. The court now fired a double-barreled sentence that evinced both a concern for justice and a view that its holding should and would affect conduct. Emphasizing the need to "foster the protection of the worker and to encourage manufacturers to take all reasonable precautions in designing and manufacturing safety devices," Justice Blair Moody, Jr. wrote that the court could not "allow the discredited doctrine of contributory negligence to undermine these goals." Justice Moody then announced the broad rule "that contributory negligence is no bar where evidence has been presented of defendant's causal negligence in the design or manufacture of a safety device."[2]

In a state that has lived by the industrial machine, this decision exhibits a significant empathy for the conduct of a party who is on the disadvantaged side of a power relationship. In its insistence that it should "foster the

---

1. Tulkuu v. Mackworth Rees, 406 Mich. 615, 622, 281 N.W.2d 291, 294 (1979).
2. *Id.* at 622-623, 281 N.W.2d at 294.

protection of the worker," the court also hints at a broad conception of the judicial role in fostering social justice. This combination of empathy and justice-oriented ideas fixes state policy in an environment that affects millions of people—the dangerous workplace.

New Jersey: No defense in strict liability. The liability doctrine in the *Tulkuu* case was negligence. The New Jersey Supreme Court contemporaneously applied analogous principles in a case involving a strict liability theory, and later expanded the protection of its liability rules with respect to workers who pleaded negligence.

On the first of these occasions, the plaintiff was Frank Suter, who was part owner of a firm that fabricated sheet metal products and worked in the plant himself. In a situation similar to Tulkuu's, Suter sustained a serious injury to his hand on a machine used to flatten metal sheets and form them into cylindrical shapes. He had operated this machine "on innumerable occasions" over an eight-year period preceding his injury.

Suter was hurt as he tried to pull a piece of slag out of the machine. When he reached over, his body brushed a gear lever. The result was to activate the rollers, pulling Suter's fingers into them. There was evidence that he knew that pushing the lever would activate the rollers. He also was aware that there were two ways to deactivate the machine so that the rollers would not operate: he could have touched a foot treadle or pushed a red stop button. Although Suter did have this knowledge, an expert testified on his behalf that either of two design features would have prevented the accident—the use of a rotary guard or the placement of the lever mechanism higher on the machine.

These facts, exhibiting as they do Suter's ability to have avoided the accident, give special sharpness to the court's affirmance of a judgment in his favor. Emphasizing the breadth of protection for product users provided by the doctrine of strict liability, the court viewed that theory as "in a sense but an attempt to minimize the costs of accidents and to consider who should bear those costs." Speaking of the case of factory employees, presumably even those who could avoid accidents themselves, the court drew on a law review article to buttress its factual generalization that it was manufacturers of workplace machines, rather than workers, who were " 'in the better position both to judge whether avoidance costs would exceed foreseeable accident costs and to act on that judgment.' "[3]

Given this economic premise, the court advanced a broad legal principle for strict liability cases involving design defects in the workplace setting. In

---

3. Suter v. San Angelo Foundry & Machine Co., 81 N.J. 150, 173-174, 406 A.2d 140, 152 (1979), quoting Calabresi & Hirschoff, Toward A Test for Strict Liability in Torts, 81 Yale L.J. 1055, 1060 (1972).

such cases, the court declared, the defense of contributory negligence would not apply when an employee was "using the machine in an intended or reasonably foreseeable manner" and was "injured because of [the] defect."[4]

New Jersey: No defense in negligence.   Five years later, in a 1984 case, the New Jersey court issued a decision that was even more powerful because it extended to negligence cases its bar to invoking plaintiffs' conduct as a defense. In its basic fact pattern, the case was sadly repetitive of many other litigations. The plaintiff, John Green, was working on a plastic blow molding machine to make plastic toy baseballs and bats. As he tried to remove a piece of plastic that got stuck in the machine, the presses "slammed shut," crushing the fingers on his right hand. Green's supervisor asserted that company procedures required workers who wanted to remove pieces of plastic from the machine to use a "stop" button on the side of the press.

Green admitted that he "certainly" knew that he would be hurt if the die presses slammed shut while his hand was inside, but he also insisted that he had not been warned of the dangers of reaching inside the machine and said he "did not think that the die presses could actually close on his hand."[5]

Drawing on precedents including Suter's case, the court held that there was no defense based on "a factory worker's fault . . . in an action grounded solely in negligence."[6] Among the ingredients in the factual mixture that yielded this decision were the manufacturer's knowledge of the probable use of its product, and the relative lack of choice available to factory workers. The manufacturer's negligence, the court said, consisted of selling a machine whose dangers it "should have foreseen might cause injury to one in the position of the plaintiff." Moreover, the court asserted, the employees who operate such machines have "no real choice." The "practicalities" of their "workday world" mean that "the employee works 'as is' or he is without a job." The court could see no reason why it should deny the defense of contributory negligence to manufacturers on strict liability claims involving workplace machines but permit it against claimants alleging that manufacturers were negligent.

A certain empathy.   Products liability rationales now begin to thicken around workplace realities. The employer may make the economic decision closest to the employee, but the court discerns an important center of power

---

4. *Id.* at 177, 406 A.2d at 153.

5. Green v. Sterling Extruder Corp., 95 N.J. 263, 267, 471 A.2d 15, 17 (1984).

6. This language comes from the court's statement of the issue, 95 N.J. at 264, 471 A.2d at 16.

in the manufacturer and its knowledge of the conditions of employment. This fact of power links up with a posited lack of choice on the part of the claimant. Along with these elements of the case go an empathy for semi-informed conduct that does not truly represent a decision, and for the natural inclination of people to take shortcuts. That empathy appears to have a morality of its own. In a variety of settings, legal and non-legal, many people may tend to the view that the wages of carelessness must be uncompensated injury. Why, in the face of that view, have these courts inclined in the way they have in cases involving industrial machines? It would appear that the empathy we have described is a creature of judicial reading of the power relationship, of relative abilities to deliberate concerning the relevant decisions, and of the image projected by the product itself.

Machines in the public sphere. One may apply an analogous analysis in cases in which large machines used in the public sphere injure people who are not workers. One of the most important Florida products liability cases is exemplary. It involved the death of a pedestrian, Gwendolyn West. As her brief fatal chapter began, West was standing on a street curb talking with a friend who was waiting for a bus, while a road grader lumbered by from left to right. As the bus approached, West began to walk across the street. At the same time, unfortunately, the grader—now to West's right—began to back up, having reached one terminus of its designated path. As she walked across the street, West looked to her left and then looked in her purse. While she was walking and looking in her purse, the grader, backing along its path from her right, ran her over. After six days in the hospital, she died from massive internal injuries.

An expert for the plaintiff asserted that the grader was defective in several ways: configurations that obstructed rear visibility and produced a "blind spot" for the operator, a lack of mirrors, and a lack of backup signals.

The Florida Supreme Court's decision focused on whether it should adopt the strict liability doctrine and how broad the ambit of the doctrine should be. For our present purposes, the most interesting part of the decision appears in the court's declaration that not only should strict liability apply, but it should embrace a "bystander" who is not a direct user or consumer of a product. The court defined a duty "to those who suffer personal injury or property damage as the result of using or being within the vicinity of use of the dangerous instrumentality furnished by a manufacturer which fails to give notice of the danger."[7] Implicit in the decision are the many of the same considerations we have been discussing in cases involving industrial machines, including the product designer's ability to deliberate and to

---

7. West v. Caterpillar Tractor Co., 336 So.2d 80, 89 (Fla. 1976).

choose. But perhaps the most salient lesson of the Florida court's language is that appearances count, even in a negative sort of way. Ms. West apparently was aware of the grader when it passed by her. The court is saying, in effect, that the maker of the grader had an obligation to be sure that the machine signalled its return.

Crashworthiness

Second collisions and "intended purpose."   One of the most interesting functional categories of products liability law deals with the "crashworthiness" of vehicles. More than a quarter century ago, an Indiana state policeman named Elmer Paul analyzed the problem of automobile injuries in terms that Ralph Nader later made famous in his book *Unsafe at Any Speed*. Paul's most memorable phrase was that of the "second collision"—the moment when occupants of a motor vehicle slam against the inside of the vehicle after the "first collision—the impact of the vehicle with whatever it hit."[8] It did not occur to the generations before 1960 that injuries occurring in that way would, or should, give rise to a lawsuit against a vehicle manufacturer. After all, the primary accident was not in any way caused by the car maker: it may have been due to the fault of a third party, the carelessness of the driver of the car whose occupants were injured in the "second collision," or an "unavoidable accident." In its 1966 decision in *Evans v. General Motors Corp.*, the Seventh Circuit epitomized the reason that there was no law supporting consumer complaints in this kind of situation. The court said in *Evans*, "the intended purpose of an automobile does not include its participation in collisions with other objects, despite the manufacturer's ability to foresee the possibility that such collisions may occur."[9]

The realities of vehicle use.   But General Motors' luck—and that of its cousins in the auto making industry—did not hold beyond *Evans*. In the 1968 decision in *Larsen v. General Motors Corp.*, the Eighth Circuit focused precisely on the feature of foreseeability of accidents about which the Seventh Circuit had been dismissive. It was true, Judge Floyd Gibson conceded in *Larsen*, that "automobiles are not made for the purpose of colliding with each other." Yet, Judge Gibson observed, "a frequent and inevitable contingency of normal automobile use will result in collisions and injury producing impacts." In that accident-filled environment, he wrote,

---

8. See R. Nader, Unsafe at Any Speed 86 (1965) (characterizing Elmer Paul's analysis).
9. Evans v. General Motors Corp., 359 F.2d 822, 825 (7th Cir. 1966).

there was "[n]o rational basis" to distinguish injuries occurring in "second collisions" from those caused by a "defect in design or manufacture."[10]

Where there had been no cases prior to the mid-sixties, *Larsen* supplied a foundation for a small industry of litigation. Hundreds of complaints followed, presenting variations on the basic theme that vehicles were inadequate to protect their occupants against injuries resulting from crashes. Rigid steering wheels that impaled drivers, door locks that did not hold, fuel tanks that exploded when vehicles were hit from the rear—all these became fair game for litigation. The Mississippi Supreme Court even placed a powerboat in the "crashworthiness" category.[11]

To be sure, some courts imposed stringent proof requirements on plaintiffs who sued under this theory. The Third Circuit, for example, required claimants to show how an alternative design would have prevented the type of injuries that occurred, and to "offer some method of establishing the extent of enhanced injuries attributable to the defective design."[12]

Yet the "crashworthiness" cases clearly had created a new body of law where none had existed before, and we should ask why. We already have implied some potential answers. Perhaps the steel-hulled makeup of the modern motor vehicle conveys an aura of safety to its occupant, especially in the context of auto advertising. Perhaps, by analogy to what we suggested has been the case in the arena of workplace machines, the courts empathize with the sort of inadvertence that afflicts even the best drivers in fast-moving traffic.

Officiousness challenged and applied. But other concerns seem to lie close to the surface. They center on judicial vexation with accident statistics. Some critics will view the concern as officious. It is true that in a certain sense, the statistics are two-edged. The accident data available to the manufacturer is also, at least in a general way, the province of every driver and passenger who has seen and heard ambulances screaming away from the wreckage of an accident. But there is more. The manufacturer makes the initial design decision; the motorist's choice is secondary. Too, the manufacturer has a precision of knowledge about weak points that most motorists lack, as well as information about the comparative costs of strengthening the product and of injuries.

None of this is to deny that motorists participate in a dangerous game. The economist Sam Peltzman has presented data indicating that as cars are

---

10. Larsen v. General Motors Corp., 391 F.2d 495, 502 (8th Cir. 1968).
11. Rose v. Mercury Marine, Div. of Brunswick, 483 So.2d 1351, 1352 (Miss. 1986).
12. Huddell v. Levin, 537 F.2d 726, 737-738 (3d Cir. 1976).

made safer in response to regulation, the accident rate goes up.[13] Some may scoff at the suggestion of causality, but there is a common sense core to it: if people felt more secure against second collisions, might there not be an increase in accidents as they took more chances with their primary driving activity? Is it not plausible that if you could get from here to there in a few fewer minutes, without getting yourself hurt in the process, you might subconsciously behave in a way that was riskier to others?

By analogy, it might be argued that there would be a marginal fall-off in driving care if people knew that vehicle manufacturers would have to compensate them for their own driving injuries. Even if that insight were correct, however, we must explain why the tradition of judicial officiousness about crashworthiness took root almost instantly after *Larsen*. As we have suggested, some of its foundations lay in the specificity of knowledge of vehicle manufacturers, and the deliberate character of their design choices. Undoubtedly, and perhaps less appealingly to purists, officiousness arose from judicial concern with the massive social problem of automobile-caused injuries. Perhaps the contribution of auto manufacturers to those injuries was relatively small as compared with other inputs. Perhaps a national injury Tsar could develop and enforce a comprehensive panacea.[14]

But courts are not inclined to wait for overall solutions. When they perceive a way to save a life, or a few thousand lives, they will take it. The tension between the judicial method of doing business and the heralded virtues of the comprehensive solution is high here. But the judicial way of doing things has virtues of its own. Among other things, it provides a social spearhead. To exaggerate the metaphor: let the judicial Pattons take the first objectives; the more timorous can legislate at leisure.

Medical Products

A different set of considerations appears in decisions involving medical products for which there is a widespread perception of critical need, such as prescription drugs. In the drug area, much of the law centers on the question of whether the manufacturer has been negligent, either because it has been insufficiently diligent in searching out side effects or because it has not warned adequately of inherent hazards. These questions themselves often present difficult factual problems. But one of the most contentious issues is whether there should be a separate category of strict liability for drugs— either with respect to inherent dangers or, with subtle logic, for failures to warn.

---

13. *See, e.g.*, Peltzman, Regulation of Automobile Safety (Am. Enterprise Inst. 1975).

14. I have explained the problem inherent in assuming a Tsar who does not exist in M. Shapo, Tort Reform: The Problem of the Missing Tsar, 19 Hofstra L. Rev. 185 (1990).

The strict liability salient.   A few decisions provide a challenging standard, imposing straight strict liability because of the dangerous nature of a product. A leading case of this sort in the general area of medical products is *Cunningham v. MacNeal Memorial Hospital*, decided by the Illinois Supreme Court in 1970. That case involved a plaintiff's contraction of serum hepatitis from a blood transfusion at a time when, the defendant argued, there was no way it could have detected the virus in whole blood. In the particular case at issue, it was unclear whether that was so. But the Illinois court opined that the detectability of the virus was "of absolutely no moment." In effect, it said that if one is going to impose strict liability, it should be strict. The court pointed to language in section 402A of the Second Restatement declaring that the section's strict liability rule applies "although . . . the seller has exercised all possible care in the preparation and sale of his product." As applied, this meant that a unit of blood that carried a disease-causing virus provided grounds for liability "whether or not defendant can, even theoretically, ascertain the existence" of the virus. If one allowed defendants to avoid liability in this situation, the court said, the result would be to "emasculate the [strict liability] doctrine and in a very real sense would signal a return to a negligence theory."[15]

The *Cunningham* decision—which was overruled by the Illinois legislature[16]—exemplifies the pure theory of strict liability, under which the court must focus not on the conduct of the seller but on the condition of the product. Under that doctrine, it does not matter how the situation looked to the seller when it put the goods on the market; what counts is the risk apparent at the time of trial, and whether a reasonable seller, forewarned with that knowledge, would have elected to take that risk at the time of *sale*. To the rejoinder that this is an imposition of liability without a showing that the defendant should or even could have known of the risk, the response is: Yes, that is the meaning of strict liability.

A social premium.   *Cunningham*, however, is unusual. Not only have most legislatures—including Illinois'—limited the liability of blood suppliers to negligence. Most courts have been relatively lenient to suppliers of certain medical products. Prescription drugs and their medical cousins, biological products such as blood and vaccines, have presented to courts an especially sympathetic defense case. They inspire a judicial attitude that opposes the theoretical argument that courts should not take into account the special utility of particular products. Whether it is automobiles or blood, workplace machines or drugs, let the market set the price; that is

15. Cunningham v. MacNeal Mem'l Hosp., 47 Ill.2d 443, 453, 266 N.E.2d 897, 902 (1970).
16. *See* Ill. Ann. Stat. ¶ 5102 (Smith-Hurd 1988).

how the argument runs. Yet, however one may demonstrate theoretically that the market will sort out risks and benefits through the price system, many courts insist on building an extra social premium into the equation where the liability issue focuses on drugs and biologicals.

The California Supreme Court emphasized the special niche of these products in a 1988 decision. It specifically rejected the application of strict liability to claims for failure to warn of the dangers of prescription drugs, in cases where the defendant "neither knew nor could have known by the application of scientific knowledge available at the time of distribution that the drug could produce the undesirable side effects suffered by the plaintiff."[17] The court expressed concern that if it were to impose strict liability, "[t]he likelihood of the producer's liability would increase with significant advances in scientific knowledge, discouraging the development of new and improved drugs to combat disease."[18]

Running parallel to this opposition to strict liability in drug cases is judicial hostility to putting adequacy of warning questions to juries when a pharmaceutical manufacturer has given warnings to physicians. At least in a case where a manufacturer "repeatedly warned" doctors against prescribing its product to people with aspirin sensitivity, the Fifth Circuit "reject[ed] [the] suggestion that a mere allegation of inadequacy of warning of side effects on a prescription drug makes a jury issue."[19]

The Case of the Exploding Soda Bottle

Among the leading heroines in the trench-level history of products liability was a California waitress named Gladys Escola. The 1944 case that made Escola's name a household word—at least in the households of torts analysts—began when she took a Coca Cola bottle from a case under a restaurant counter to put it in a refrigerator. The bottle exploded in her hand, with frightful consequences. Another employee said that the contents of the bottle "flew all over herself and myself and the walls and one thing and another." Escola sustained a five-inch cut that severed blood vessels, nerves, and muscles in her thumb and palm.

The res ipsa approach.   Do Coke bottles explode just by accident? Asking itself that question, the California Supreme Court said that a jury could

---

17. Brown v. Superior Court, 44 Cal. 3d 1049, 751 P.2d 470, 480, 245 Cal. Rptr. 412 (1988).

18. *Id.* at 1066, 751 P.2d at 481, 245 Cal. Rptr. at 422.

19. Anderson v. McNeilab, Inc., 831 F.2d 92, 93 (5th Cir. 1987). This result lines up with the theory of the so-called "learned intermediary" doctrine. *See generally* 1 M. Shapo, The Law of Products Liability ¶ 19.07 [9] [a] [ii] (1990) and Supps. 1991, 1992.

answer in the negative. Affirming a jury verdict for Escola, it drew on the doctrine of "res ipsa loquitur." That theory permits plaintiffs to use circumstantial evidence—in this case centering on the occurrence of the explosion itself—when a jury reasonably could infer that an event would not have happened unless the defendant was negligent. Drawing on testimony that the available methods for testing bottles were "almost infallible," a majority of the court concluded that "a defect which would make the bottle unsound could be discovered by reasonable and practicable tests."[20] Even in the early 1940s, the question was not a novel one. The California court cited seven cases that had applied the res ipsa doctrine to cases of exploding bottles, as well as a dozen decisions that for various reasons refused to do so.[21]

Judge Roger Traynor, already building a reputation as a preeminent state court judge, was inclined to agree on the result, but he took issue with the majority's reasoning. For him, the issue was not really one of negligence. Rather, it focused on the liability of manufacturers for any product that turned out to be defective. That liability, as he viewed it, should be "absolute" when a firm places an article "on the market, knowing that it is to be used without inspection," and that product "proves to have a defect that causes injury to human beings." Traynor advanced several reasons for this conclusion: the ability of product makers to anticipate and guard against some hazards; the fact that "[t]hose who suffer injury from defective products"—which "may be an overwhelming misfortune" to the injured person—"are unprepared to meet its consequences"; the ability of manufacturers to insure injury risks and distribute them among the consuming public; the inability of consumers to investigate the soundness of modern products; the tendency of advertising to "lull[ ]" previously "vigilan[t] consumers."[22]

Operative elements in judicial thought. In this decision in an everyday product setting, involving a consumer good that in the era of glass soda bottles was used millions of times a day, we discern a combination of several concepts: a consumer, (1) relatively powerless and (2) unaware of relevant knowledge, (3) who comes into contact with an advertised product (4) in a setting in which the manufacturer is better able to bear the risk.

We may focus the case in 1990's terms by asking about the present validity of these propositions. Here are the current realities:

---

20. Escola v. Coca Cola Bottling Co., 24 Cal.2d 453, 461, 150 P.2d 436, 440 (1944).
21. *Id.* at 457, 150 P.2d at 438.
22. *Id.* at 462, 467, 150 P.2d at 440-441, 443 (Traynor, J., separate opinion, concurring in the judgment).

(1) Many consumers still are relatively unprepared to "meet [the] consequences" of a serious product injury, although there have been significant improvements in both public and private insurance against the medical and employment consequences of injuries.

(2) Consumers typically still have very little knowledge about the production processes that send even simple products to market, for example, the tests used to detect defects in shatterable bottles. Moreover, most product sellers would not be inclined to provide relevant statistics ("Caution: Under the testing system used in this plant, one bottle in 50,000 will explode in normal use").

(3) The sophistication of advertising has risen considerably over the last few decades. Although there has been a parallel increase in the worldliness of consumers and their ability to discount the blandishments of advertisers, new persuasive techniques have contributed mightily to a powerful background aura of quality, including safety, in advertised products.

(4) The ability of firms to insure and to distribute the risk of products injuries presents factual issues, in a world whose corporate population ranges from enormous conglomerates to small family factories. At one end of that spectrum, we must ask whether loss bearing ability is a sufficient basis on which to impose tort liability; at the other, we should ask whether inability to absorb or distribute losses from advertised products that injure relatively ignorant consumers should inspire judicial concern about the effects of liability on small enterprises.

The exploding soda bottle may be passing from the scene, but the cases endure as examples of how a ubiquitous consumer product of a disappearing age symbolizes a cluster of legal issues that are very much present in the law of the nineties.

The Collapsing Stepladder

There are plenty of comic moments in the movies that involve the fall of stepladders. But that sort of occurrence is not usually funny for the person who was on the ladder, and it is not unusual for such events to lead to lawsuits. What do decisions in suits against sellers of ladders teach us about the relationship of law to our ordinary lives, particularly the relation of law to the things we buy? Many of the lessons cluster around issues of what we mean by proof, how proof relates to our idea of what a defect is, and how we think people should behave in the presence of everyday dangers.

Res ipsa rehearsed. A central question when a stepladder fails is whether we may deduce from the failure itself that there was something defectively wrong with the product. We may first approach this question from the standpoint of the doctrine of res ipsa loquitur, which we explained briefly above in relation to the case of Ms. Escola's exploding Coke bottle.

One way to deal with this problem is to hold that there is enough evidence for a jury to find a defect when a ladder cracks under the weight of a person of normal poundage. That was the holding of a Massachusetts appellate court in a case in which Joseph Calvanese sued the W.W. Babcock Company, a ladder maker. In a decision reversing a defendant's judgment, the court's analysis implied the connection between the proof issue and consumer expectations. The court viewed a wooden stepladder as "a relatively uncomplicated and sturdy product the parts of which are not likely to fail under normal use or to deteriorate from natural causes." Rejecting the trial judge's refusal to give a circumstantial evidence instruction, the court concluded that it was "within common experience" that a ladder, properly cared for, "would not mysteriously fail if put to the use for which it was intended."[23]

In another case, this one in New York, the plaintiff said that he "heard the sound of breaking wood" when he was on the third rung of a ladder and felt it go out from under him. Although the court did not think the plaintiff had a case either for design defect or for inadequate warning, it held that he had presented "a question of fact as to the defective manufacture of the ladder," premising that "a defect in a product may be inferred from circumstantial evidence that the product did not perform as intended."[24]

Proof and substantive judgment. An interesting aspect of such decisions is the way they meld a substantive point about consumer expectations with a rather technical theory of proof. When we speak of issues of proof in the products context, we often are asking both whether there was a problem at all—a defect in a product, for example—and whether such a problem caused an accident to happen. Simple cases like the ladder cases make clear that an apparently technical inquiry may depend on a normative conclusion: a conclusion about how things should be, specifically, how a ladder ought to work. The ruling on proof thus embodies a judgmental statement about the strength of ladders, one might almost say a metaphysical declaration about an ordinary class of objects.

This theme further develops itself in other fact situations in the milieu of ladders. It becomes an easier case for the plaintiff when he is able to show that he was working on a level surface, that he had inspected the ladder and

23. Calvanese v. W.W. Babcock Co., 10 Mass. App. Ct. 726, 732- 733, 412 N.E.2d 895, 900 (1980).

24. Putnick v. H.M.C. Assocs., 137 A.D.2d 179, 183-184, 529 N.Y.S.2d 205, 208 (1988).

that his weight was evenly distributed; easier still if an onlooker testifies that the ladder "shot out" from under the claimant. The Illinois Supreme Court found on a packet of those facts that a jury reasonably could have concluded that "there was an absence of abnormal use and that the ladder failed 'to perform in the manner reasonably to be expected in light of' its 'intended function.' "[25] A similar factual profile—user inspection, placement on solid ground, normal use—supported a plaintiff's verdict in another Illinois case in which the ladder "crunch[ed]" beneath the plaintiff and carried him to the ground.[26]

Liability constrained. Another principal legal battleground in the stepladder cases, as in much products litigation, concerns the plaintiff's conduct. An Oregon case involving the collapse of an aluminum ladder exhibits some of the doctrinal refinements the law has developed. The trial court instructed the jury that it could find the plaintiff, Burrell Findlay, contributorily negligent if he did any of four things: if he placed the ladder on uneven ground, if he did not test it for stability and balance, if he used it in a way that overbalanced it, or if he did not maintain a proper lookout.

The Oregon Supreme Court drew on the idea that in products liability cases, one cannot be held contributory negligent unless one voluntarily and unreasonably encounters a known danger. It therefore held that the defenses of failure to test for stability and to maintain a proper lookout could not succeed in a strict liability action. As to defenses based on the way that the plaintiff actually used the product, offered under the label of "misuse," the court emphasized that " 'abnormal' use does not mean every instance of negligence, however, slight, in connection with the use of the product.' " A defendant seeking to bar a claim on the grounds of "misuse," the court said, must show "a use or handling so unusual that the average consumer could not reasonably expect the product to be designed and manufactured to withstand it—a use which the seller, therefore, need not anticipate and provide for."[27]

The legal focus in this case is somewhat unlike that of the ladder cases earlier discussed, for it is on the plaintiff's conduct, rather than the condition of the product. But the same issues appear at the heart of the case: how did the ladder appear to the consumer, and, therefore, how would the con-

---

25. Gillespie v. R.D. Werner Co., 71 Ill.2d 318, 322-323, 375 N.E.2d 1294, 1296 (1978) (quoting Dunham v. Vaughan & Bushnell Mfg. Co., 42 Ill.2d 339, 342, 247 N.E.2d 401, 403 (1969)).
   26. Tulgetske v. R.D. Werner Co., 86 Ill. App.3d 1033, 1038, 408 N.E.2d 492, 496 (1980) (employing the same language).
   27. Findlay v. Copeland Lumber Co., 265 Or. 300, 305, 509 P.2d 28, 31 (1973).

sumer think he could use the product? One might say that these issues resolve themselves into the question: how strong should a ladder be?[28] But that question is always contextual: how strong should it be in the situation in which the consumer used it, a situation that necessarily includes the image it communicated to him?

Not every claimant wins when a ladder breaks. In a Louisiana case, Kenneth Ducote fell from the second or third step of a ladder that he was climbing as he carried a bundle of shingles. His only recollection was that after he fell, he was "laying on the ground with the shingles still on my shoulder and the ladder was broke then." In denying recovery, an appellate court noted that there were "no apparently observable defects on the day that plaintiff fell," but one must read the decision in the light of what a consumer reasonably might expect from a ladder clearly labeled as being for "Occasional Light Household Use and Lightweight Climbers." An assumption about the image such a product would have created in consumer minds is implicit in the court's emphasis on the benefits conferred by stepladders, compared with the relatively "nominal" magnitude of risk they pose.[29] In this case, the court appears to tie together the lack of an identifiable defect with an intuitive estimate of the strength one might expect from a ladder so labeled.

Another boundary to liability is evident in the Fifth Circuit's holding that an expert has not proved a defect when he testifies that a particular part of a ladder is its weakest point. As that court commented, "[e]very design must by definition have a weakest point." It was also clear that the court did not view the happening of an accident as sufficient to prove a defect: the plaintiff testified that he fell after hearing a cracking noise and that he later saw a hairline crack, but the court thought this was not enough to sustain a verdict for him.

This survey of a few ladder litigations makes it evident that even in cases involving so homely a product, and with quite similar fact situations, we never will be able to make perfect sense of the decisions. There are too many variables that may influence courts. Nevertheless, we may draw a fairly consistent thread from the run of the cases. It is, indeed, a thread that appears throughout the world of products decisions.

The gist of the matter seems to be this: to prove a defect, apart from adducing direct evidence about an unacceptable weakness in a product, one

---

28. Compare Justice Goodwin's declaration, in an earlier Oregon decision, that judges, as contrasted with juries, "have . . . decided how strong products *should* be: they should be strong enough to perform as the ordinary consumer expects." Heaton v. Ford Motor Co., 248 Or. 467, 474, 435 P.2d 806, 809 (1967).

29. Ducote v. State Farm & Casualty Co., 488 So.2d 385, 392 (La. Ct. App. 1986).

must relate his or her case to the total image that the product presented, in light of the general expectations of the public, conditioned by experience and advertising, about the capabilities of that category of product. One way for a seller to tailor those expectations, and thus to cabin liability, is to signal to consumers the built-in limitations on a product's performance. To summarize this aspect of the stepladder's role as a symbol of products liability law, we may say that the "proof" issue, "What happened?" depends in large measure on the inquiry, "What did the user expect?" which itself turns on the question, "How did the product present itself?"

The Law and the Social Stakes

Analyzing judicial decisions from a diverse group of products contexts, we have identified several ways in which the law provides social benchmarks. Here we seek to integrate some of these insights into a discussion of the law as an agent for dealing with competing stakeholders.

Competing interests. What stakes are at issue? Sometimes in harmony and sometimes opposed, they are complex. They inhere, in part, in our demand for the development of new products, which by definition tends to include a certain amount of risk—always commercial risk and sometimes risk to consumers themselves. Running parallel to this stake in innovation, consumers have a stake in protection from injury. Alongside both these interests, and from time to time overlapping each, is our desire for a steady supply of reliable consumer goods.

Procedural concerns. Now the stakes become more abstract. They have to do with widely shared ideas about what justice means. One meaning of justice that is relevant here has a procedural character. It lies in a belief that people should not be unfairly surprised, either by the actions of others or by the legal system. With reference to consumers, this idea implies that people are entitled to compensation when a product surprises them by collapsing, blowing up in their faces, or causing illness in a way they could not have guessed from the way the product presented itself to them.

A parallel application of this principle is that sellers have a right not to have to pay for injuries that they would not have predicted would have been the subject of a successful lawsuit, given what they knew about their product and the way they portrayed it in the marketplace. This point has significant human dimensions. All consumers can empathize readily with Ms.

Escola, the waitress whose hand was torn apart by an exploding bottle, or Mr. Suter, the worker whose fingers were pulled into the rollers of a metal fabricating machine. But we also can empathize with the owners of a family company who face the prospect of going out of business because the machines they have made for many years have suddenly generated judicial decisions condemning them as unreasonably dangerous. In my experience as a witness and observer at Senate committee hearings on products liability, one of the most striking recurrent motifs was the complaint that uncertainty in the law was frustrating and sometimes ruining the owners of small businesses. One of the leading advocates of federal products liability legislation, Senator Robert Kasten of Wisconsin, emphasized in colloquies with me the volume and intensity of his mail on this subject.

This is not only a matter of fairness for producers of goods; it has implications for one of the most sophisticated businesses in our society, the insurance industry. Indeed, in significant measure, insurers rely on the law to present the profile of risk on which they must base premiums.

Substantive concerns. Existing alongside what I have labeled procedural interests, centering on the avoidance of uncertainty and surprise, we find a set of substantive stakes. These are wrapped up in notions of power and individual responsibility, ideas that thread through this analysis. One set of stakes concerns the use of power: in particular, the ability of sellers to make choices that dramatically affect the risk level of consumers. Since the beginning of the Republic, Americans have sought to check the exercise of governmental power in ways that impose on private individuals. In this century, we have become more sensitive to the way that individuals and firms can set the terms of other people's lives. Products decisions by the dozens provide incremental benchmarks concerning such uses of power.

Judicial decisions in products cases also reflect our commitment to individual responsibility as a prime value in social life and in law. This value ties in closely with sellers' exercise of the power to make various kinds of choices—about design, about the nature of warnings, about the character of advertising campaigns. Negligence law focuses on these matters explicitly. Strict liability law, even though technically it does not deal with conduct, often embodies implicit judgments about the responsibility of sellers.

But it is on the side of consumer conduct that this commitment becomes most apparent. Through various applications of doctrine—the refusal to call something a defect, the determination that a product carried adequate warnings, the use of defenses like assumption of risk and "misuse"—the law tells consumers that it adheres to the idea of individual responsibility. In an increasingly impersonal world, this message underlines our sense that something very important is at stake in cases where consumers themselves make choices, even choices somewhat constrained by circumstance. That vital idea is that product users are responsible for choosing their own level of risk, at least when another party has not unfairly used its power to impose that risk, and has not encouraged an unduly risky course of conduct.

This is a primer on some principal factors that lie behind the technical discussions that are part of every judicial decision in a products case: our personal and social stakes in reliable products, in innovative entrepreneurial conduct, in protection from injury, in fairness-based process, in a commitment to individual responsibility, and in freedom from imposition by our fellows. The law of products liability provides graphic reflections of how our culture evaluates and compares these interests.

4

Methods of Analysis: Economic, Behavioral, and Legal

The stakes in products litigation are lofty ones, but to resolve the disputes that result in that litigation, society requires the labors of professional craft workers. Our discussion now turns to some details of relevant crafts.

Consider a literary parlor game, recently staged by a newspaper in a book review: an artist draws a fanciful picture, and a dozen novelists each tell a story about what the picture describes. One can only imagine—since what is called for is an act of imagination—how diverse will be the yarns that professional storytellers will spin.[1]

In our simple aspirations for the law, most of us probably desire less room for imagination and correspondingly more certainty. Yet the law always has been fertile territory for interpretation, and therefore for at least lawyers' creativity. Surely, that has been the case since the first judge who wrote a dissenting opinion put quill to parchment.

It is even more the case today, when delegates from many other areas of academic life have begun to apply their specialized kinds of knowledge to the law. In this chapter I will sketch how some non-lawyer specialists, as well as attorneys, employ their professional tools to analyze legal problems, examining some of the premises their methods of analysis involve concerning the law. I will relate this discussion to an idea that represents a major thread of this book: that decision making in products liability cases should begin with an examination of the representational background a product carries with it into the worlds of commerce and personal life.

---

1. *See* A Gorey Christmas, N. Y. Times Book Review, Dec. 2, 1990, at 1 & 16-18.

Economic Theory

Early in this century, Louis Brandeis stressed that lawyers and judges must study "economics and sociology and politics" to prepare themselves to deal with rapid "economic and social transformation."[2] Over the last three decades, economic theorists have sought increasingly to vindicate their portion of Brandeis' prophecy. Or at least they have found one of the happiest of theoretical hunting grounds in the law.

It is interesting to examine some of the language that economists employ—their stock tools of the trade—to deal with problems involving personal injuries. For example, they speak in terms of actors competing for scarce resources even in situations where most people's intuitions would view this phraseology as at best a stretched metaphor. When two automobiles collide, for example, ordinary people would speak only whimsically of both motorists "trying to occupy the same space." Yet the economist sees this literal truth as a useful analytical description.

Information and the "bribe."   In an analogous fashion, economists begin their analysis of cases involving allegedly defective products by positing that if everyone were well informed about product hazards, it would make no difference with respect to efficiency whether the burden of injury costs was imposed on the seller or on the consumer. This was a basic insight developed by the Nobel Prize-winning economist Ronald Coase in a 1960 essay dealing with social cost and liability rules,[3] and then specifically applied to products liability in an article by Roland McKean in 1970.[4]

There is a good deal of theoretical attractiveness, and even some practical sense, in these ideas. The theory, as McKean explained it, depends on the notion that sellers and consumers could "bribe" their way to efficient results. Thus, for example, consumers might "hire producers to reduce product hazards . . ."; " 'bribe themselves' to exercise care so long as these actions [pay]"; and provide incentives to family and friends who used their products to take more care.[5] Conversely, of course, producers might "bribe" consumers to take more care in the use of products.[6]

This is not quite as precious as it sounds. If one can step around the perverse stretching of the terminology of the "bribe," one can see the practical

2. Louis D. Brandeis, The Living Law, address to Chicago Bar Ass'n., Jan. 3, 1916, in Brandeis, Business—A Profession 344, 361-362 (1933 ed.).

3. Ronald H. Coase, The Problem of Social Cost, 3 J. L. & Econ. 1 (1960).

4. Roland N. McKean, Products Liability: Trends and Implications, 38 U. Chi. L. Rev. 3 (1970).

5. Id. at 43, 46.

6. See id. at 46, adverting to the inefficiencies of that strategy.

import of the idea, as it translates into an ongoing bargaining process in which consumers and sellers haggle over price and quality. We all know that to a certain extent, we get what we pay for in safety as in other economic goods. A frequently given pairing links the motorcycle, which affords very little collision protection, with the large automobile, which provides a lot. One could say that in buying the weight, belting, and interior padding of a Lincoln Continental, a former motorcycle owner is "bribing" the Ford Motor Company to produce more collision protection. The label is not as important as the economic reality.

The reality, however, also includes the relative ability of the parties to acquire and use relevant information about product hazards. Economists have a word for this, too. They sum up this factor under the heading of "transaction costs," which include such things as finding out who you are going to bargain with, the costs of negotiating, and the expense of "undertak[ing] the inspection needed to make sure that the terms of the contract are being observed."[7]

Let us put aside, for the moment, any problems arising from the fact that many products liability cases do not involve a direct "contract" or anything approaching a "negotiation." If we do that, we can see that there is a common sense core to the theory. If I sell a product that has a variety of uses— to take a commonly used example, a hammer—it probably will be inefficient, not to mention unfair, to make me responsible for injuries that flow from every conceivable use of the product. It often may be much more efficient to impose burdens of accident avoidance on people who might want to use a hammer on very hard nails or other objects that may flake or chip. Thus, users can best decide whether to use face shields, to buy stronger hammers for particularly tough jobs, or to postpone non-emergency home repairs, perhaps hiring a carpenter who daily makes a prudent assessment of the risks of using one sort of hammer or another.[8] A lot of transaction costs analysis comes down to these simple kinds of questions: who is the best assessor of risks, and who is the cheapest cost avoider?

Modern microeconomic analysis of injury law tends to focus on the question of efficiency. This approach entails the notion that we can have too few, as well as too many, accidents. When do we have too few accidents? When the market—the collective body of consumers operating through individual purchasing decisions—would prefer to take a chance on a higher risk of injury in order to have a certain set of benefits from a class of products at a

---

7. *See* Coase, *supra* note 3, at 15.

8. Compare McKean, *supra* note 4, at 30, discussing the possibilities for manufacturers and consumers to promote incentives for each other to acquire crucial information about hammers.

particular price. On occasion, legislatures that pass safety statutes counter-act such preferences. Although some safety legislation aims to correct in-formation imbalances about risks, those who enact such laws are some-times saying that they are going to save us from ourselves, or at least from the risk levels that the market would choose.

Wealth distribution. Economists themselves are sensitive to the fact that an efficiency-based analysis does not always capture the essence of our social goals. They also concern themselves with questions of "wealth dis-tribution." At their simplest, in the area we are analyzing, these are issues about who winds up with the stakes in a particular litigation. Most people would agree that the fact that a seller is richer than an injured product buyer is not a reason to make the seller pay the cost of the buyer's injuries. Much criticism of products liability law has as its premise, implicit or explicit, that such redistribution is a primary motivation for judicial decisions—an assertion that is unproved.

There is, however, another area of concern about the wealth distribution effects of liability rules. It is one with an ironic twist. Intuitively, we see those injured by defective products as "victims." But some economic ana-lysts view the problem differently; they see what ordinarily are viewed as "pro-consumer" liability rules as being not only anti-consumer but anti-poor consumer. The theory runs this way: when we impose liability for cer-tain kinds of risks, we effectively will raise product prices. Who does this help? Yuppies who not only, perhaps excessively, are concerned for their own safety but who also have the income to pay the higher prices. And who does this hurt? Low-income consumers who would prefer to pay a few dol-lars, or a few pennies, less for a product and take their chances on a rela-tively small increased risk of injury.

This sort of discussion may seem at odds with common conceptions of justice. But it provides an interesting filter for the lens through which we look at one of the most fundamental questions in the law of the products liability: what is the meaning of the term "unreasonably dangerous"?

How the law communicates. An important issue in injury jurisprud-ence is how effective the law is in communicating standards to sellers and others who may be vulnerable to liability judgments. By necessity as well as by tradition, the law of torts is peppered with abstract standards, often turning on the concept of reasonableness: negligence is conduct that falls below the standard of care of a reasonably prudent person. Defective prod-ucts provide the occasion for liability if they are "unreasonably danger-ous." Consumers may be barred from recovery, or have liability awards re-duced, if they have behaved unreasonably for their own safety, especially if they have voluntarily and *unreasonably* encountered a known risk.

It is facile to complain that such language is insufficiently precise. However, as Judge Learned Hand said in a case involving a violation of a revenue statute, "[s]tandards of conduct, fixed no more definitely [than in the statute] are common in the law; the whole of torts is pervaded by them; much of its commands are that a man must act as the occasion demands, the standard being available to all."[9]

Even at the next level of generality, negligence standards can be very abstract. An important judicial tool in the determination of whether an actor has been negligent is that of foreseeability. One example among thousands appears in a case that arose from the electrocution of a worker who was helping to operate a crane that touched an uninsulated power line. In holding that the defendant utility could be found negligent for not posting conspicuous warnings of the hazard, the New Jersey Supreme Court said that the care required in "the handling of a highly dangerous and destructive agency" included "circumspection and foresight with respect to contingencies reasonably to be anticipated in the light of the current social, industrial and commercial ambience."[10]

Of course, judicial impositions of liability in negligence cases often imply a fairly precise quantitative standard. If there is testimony that a particular level of strength in a product component would have averted an injury, then a decision that it was negligent to use a part that was below that strength would send a signal that the higher level would be adequate.[11]

We should observe that the utility of the economic theory we have been discussing must turn ultimately on the answer to questions about how people behave: who knows most about a product? who can find out about its hazards most cheaply? Who will have the strongest incentive to make the other person change behavior in a way that reduces accidents? What kinds of trades will particular groups of consumers make between price and heightened risks of injury? How communicative are legal standards that depend on concepts like "reasonable" and "foreseeable"? The answers to questions of this sort do not come from theory; they come from social facts.

Behavioral Facts

Social researchers have deployed themselves along many fronts of investigation about consumer product markets. One field of inquiry that is es-

---

9. United Business Corp. of Am. v. Comm'r of Int. Rev., 62 F.2d 754, 756 (2d Cir. 1933).

10. Black v. Public Serv. Elec. & Gas Co., 56 N.J. 63, 77, 265 A.2d 129, 136 (1970).

11. *Cf.* John J. Kennelly, Trial of a General Aviation Aircraft Case Against Manufacturer, Component-Part Maker, and Overhaul Company—Defective 5¢ Screws Result in $660,000 Aggregate Awards for Two Deaths, 15 Trial Lawyer's Guide 281, 367 (1971)(discussing expert testimony that screw could be made out of higher strength steel).

pecially important to the law of products liability concerns the experience that consumers have with products. Consumer experience will influence the application of products liability doctrine at every stage of factual analysis, from the purchase decision to choices of how to use products, including choices made under pressure of time and events.

A tragic example.   A heart-rending Minnesota case involving a Hankscraft steam vaporizer illustrates the point in several ways. The plaintiff in this case was Andrea McCormack, three years and nine months old at the time of an accident in which she was horribly burned. The injury occurred when Andrea got up in the middle of the night to go to the bathroom and somehow tipped over the vaporizer, causing scalding water to spill on her.

A focal point of the litigation was the literature that accompanied the vaporizer, which was the second Hankscraft model of that kind that Andrea's parents had bought. Mr. McCormack had purchased the first vaporizer and the parents testified that they had read the instruction booklet "from 'cover to cover.' " Ms. McCormack obtained the second device from the same self-service drugstore where her husband had bought the first one. She said she selected the second vaporizer without help from a salesperson because it was a Hankscraft and because of that firm's representations in the booklet with the first vaporizer that its vaporizers were "safe" and "practically fool-proof." The defendant also had claimed, in advertisements for its vaporizers, that they were "tip-proof." Ms. McCormack said she completely read the instruction booklet with the second vaporizer, which was "substantially identical" to the first booklet.

As it turned out, the vaporizer was made in such a way that only two pounds of force could tip it over, with water as hot as 211 degrees gushing out of the jar that surrounded the heating unit of the device. There was evidence that officers of the defendant knew that as many as a dozen children had been burned in this way and that they knew that "a user could conclude from the booklet that steam was generated in the plastic core and be led to believe that the reserve water in the jar did not itself become scalding hot."

A jury awarded the plaintiffs $150,000 for the child's injuries, and although the trial judge granted a judgment overturning that verdict, the Minnesota Supreme Court reinstated it. It did so on the basis of several theories, including the relatively straightforward doctrine of express warranty, which it applied to language like the word "safe" in the defendant's instruction booklet.[12] No doubt it would be scant comfort to the McCormack

---

12. McCormack v. Hankscraft Co., 278 Minn. 322, 154 N.W.2d 488 (1967). The court also employed theories of negligence for failure to warn and design negligence, as well as strict liability.

family, but the manuals for later models of Hankscraft vaporizers included warnings about "accidental upset" that included statements that "the water can be scalding hot and could cause serious injury or damage if spilled."[13] These manuals also indicated that the newer models had a device that would lock the cap of the vaporizer to its water reservoir.[14] One might note, in addition, that cool mist vaporizers came to capture a substantial part of the market previously occupied by steam devices.

The underlying behavioral reality of this case, whatever the doctrinal basis for decision, is entwined with the way the product appeared to the plaintiffs when they bought it and set it up in their child's bedroom. In that regard, it is important to consider the prior contact that the McCormacks had with a Hankscraft vaporizer.

Various researchers have investigated the effects of product familiarity. An example of this line of inquiry is a report by Eric J. Johnson and J. Edward Russo, who tested a group of 54 graduate business school students on their recall of, and response to, an edited advertisement for a sub-compact car.

Johnson and Russo drew several lessons from their data, as well as the findings of earlier investigations. These included the conclusions that "familiarity with product classes has an effect on decision and search behavior," first leading "to an increase in external search and subsequent recall" but, "with high levels of familiarity," a decline in "both information search and memory."

The authors sought an explanation "for why experienced consumers search less information." They hypothesized that this phenomenon did not occur because "of relevant information stored in memory," but rather because of consumers' "higher-level knowledge of the product class and its important attributes." At this level, consumers "search less information and use more selective, phased decision rules that delete the preliminary exploration of external information."[15]

Particular behavioral research projects will not usually have a perfect fit with specific litigation, but often they will shed light on key factual hypotheses. The conclusions of Johnson and Russo seem consistent with the idea that the McCormacks reasonably would have gone to a Hankscraft vaporizer the second time, employing impressions of that product line formed from their prior reading of the first booklet. We now turn from this poten-

---

13. Manual for Model Nos. 5592B, 5593D, 5594B, and 5595B of Hankscraft vaporizer, at 1 (photocopy in possession of author).

14. *Id.* at 3.

15. Eric J. Johnson & J. Edward Russo, Product Familiarity and Learning New Information, 8 Advances in Consumer Research 151, 155 (1980).

tial specific application of behavioral research to a thesis about how courts should approach products liability cases, relating that thesis to judicial assumptions about behavior.

A Representational Approach and Judicial Assumptions

The roots of the thesis lie in what courts appear to be doing, but the thesis also suggests what courts should do. The basic proposition is that the judgment of controversies about product disappointment should focus principally on the seller's portrayal of the product. The thesis not only takes into account media advertising and product appearance, but defines "portrayal" to include all the ways in which the product "projects an image on the mind of the consumer."[16] That image would include widespread agreement about what the product is and does, an idea I shall elaborate in the next chapter under the concept of the "metaphysical product."[17] Most generally, it embraces "the integrated image of the product against the background of the public communications that relate to it."[18]

The thesis provides a frame for a notable remark of Justice Traynor in his landmark opinion for the California Supreme Court in *Greenman v. Yuba Power Products, Inc.*,[19] the first judicial articulation of the doctrine of strict products liability in a majority opinion:

> [I]t should not be controlling whether plaintiff selected the machine because of the statements in the brochure, or because of the machine's own appearance of excellence that belied the defect lurking beneath the surface, or because he merely assumed that it would safely do the jobs it was built to do.[20]

The representational thesis forces us to examine both our assumptions about how consumers come to encounter products and the evidence that exists about those encounters. Let us examine both assumptions and evidence in light of decided cases and legal doctrine.

We first should be clear about causes and effects. Many judges and commentators refer to a "consumer expectations" standard. Comment i to section 402A of the Second Restatement of Torts captures this idea with its

---

16. I originally spelled out this thesis in Marshall S. Shapo, A Representational Theory of Consumer Protection: Doctrine, Function and Legal Liability for Product Disappointment, 60 Va. L. Rev. 1109, 1370 (1974).

17. *See infra*, chapter 5, pp. 79–81.

18. *See* Shapo, *supra* note 16, at 1370.

19. 59 Cal. 2d 57, 377 P.2d 897, 27 Cal. Rptr. 697 (1963).

20. *Id.* at 64, 377 P.2d at 901, 27 Cal. Rptr. at 701.

declaration that in order to be defective, a product "must be dangerous to an extent beyond that which would be contemplated by the ordinary consumer who purchases it, with the ordinary knowledge common to the community as to its characteristics."[21] Because language of this sort has become quite common in discussion of the subject, I shall frequently refer to the "consumer expectations" test.

But I shall also emphasize that the key to much of products liability law lies in the way that image creation by product sellers generates those expectations. The distinction is a very important one, because an emphasis on image creation focuses analysis on the way that sellers generate product portrayals, which is usually quite deliberate, often subtle and usually in tune with sophisticated market research. I note that this approach seems fair to all parties to disputes over alleged product defects. As to consumers, it centers legal decisionmaking on the reason that they chose to use or encounter a product. As to producers and sellers, it fixes on methods of product promotion through various kinds of media, a judgmental strategy that seems especially reasonable in competitive markets.

For everyone whose interests are involved in products liability litigation, perhaps the most important contribution of a representational analysis is its recognition of the reality we see all around us—the effects of sophisticated image creation through a battery of media.

Many American courts have favored a focus on consumer expectations. We may illustrate the potential diversity of this approach by reference to the Pacific Coast jurisdictions. The Washington Supreme Court, for example, stressed that juries should not be asked to "evaluate the seller's actions," but rather only to judge "whether the product is dangerous to an extent beyond that which would be contemplated by the ordinary consumer."[22] The California Supreme Court, by comparison, employed a consumer expectations test as part of a two-pronged defect standard that included, as an alternative, a risk-benefit analysis. The first prong of this test allowed a consumer to show that a product failed to perform "as safely as an ordinary consumer would expect when used in an intended or reasonably foreseeable manner."[23]

The Oregon Supreme Court, whose defect test underwent a substantial evolution, arrived at the formulation that the question of whether a product was "dangerously defective" depended on whether a reasonable person would have marketed it *"if he had knowledge of its harmful character."*[24]

---

21. Restatement (Second) of Torts § 402A comment i (1965).

22. Ryder v. Kelly-Springfield Tire Co., 91 Wash. 2d 111, 118, 587 P.2d 160, 164 (1978).

23. Barker v. Lull Eng'g Co., 20 Cal.3d 413, 429, 573 P.2d 443, 454, 143 Cal. Rptr. 225, 236 (1978).

24. Phillips v. Kimwood Mach. Co., 269 Or. 485, 492, 525 P.2d 1033, 1036 (1974).

Yet the court elaborated this classic strict liability standard with an emphasis that this deemed perspective of the seller achieved the same result as a consumer expectations test "because a seller acting reasonably would be selling the same product which a reasonable consumer believes he is purchasing."[25]

These jurisdictions, all prominent in the development of products liability law, have thus developed different verbal formulas for deciding what a defect is. But all have insisted, in one way or another, on the importance of deciphering the expectations of ordinary consumers.

Let us now examine how courts have treated attributes that might affect the consumer's role as a receptor for the images that sellers, and their advertising agencies, create. In the background of this discussion is the effort of economic theorists to move beyond a simple bargaining model to an examination of "transaction costs." From an economic point of view, this part of the analysis deals with the sector of the products liability problem related to information costs.

The image.   We may begin with a North Carolina case featuring one of the simplest of products and one of the best known of sellers. Plaintiff Wanda Jean Morrison bought a pair of high-heeled shoes, which she claimed "looked to be of excellent quality," from a Sears store. Ms. Morrison alleged that the heel of the left shoe gave way the second time she wore it. When the heel buckled, she fell and suffered a back injury that required surgery. Ms. Morrison offered an affidavit by an engineer who opined that the left heel lacked sufficient rigidity, because its cast plastic compound was improperly formulated, to support a wearer in ordinary walking and working conditions. Sears, which was not the maker of the shoes, responded with a traditional retailer's defense: as the seller of a boxed pair of shoes, it did not have a reasonable opportunity to inspect in order to uncover the alleged defect.

The North Carolina Supreme Court issued a decision that favored Morrison under the theory of implied warranty of merchantability. The decision was not elaborate on this point. The court simply said that the plaintiff had alleged that the shoes "were not fit for the ordinary purposes for which they are used," summarized the affidavit of the plaintiff's expert, and concluded that the evidence presented a prima facie case that the shoe was defective when Sears sold it. Although the court was willing to entertain a defense based on a state statute that barred actions against sellers of products who had "no reasonable opportunity to inspect" them, it found that the plain-

---

25. *Id.* at 492-93, 525 P.2d at 1037.

tiffs had presented a question of fact about whether Sears had equipment that could have detected the alleged defect.[26]

The case is interesting from a doctrinal point of view. The North Carolina courts have been wary of the theory of strict products liability. Yet this decision, using the terminology of "defect" under the historic merchantability theory, vindicates a complaint that rests on the appearance of a product. It is a fair question whether a retail seller should be held for products it cannot reasonably inspect for defects; the North Carolina legislature had made that policy determination in favor of sellers. But despite that legislative choice, this decision effectively upholds a consumer's right to rely on the general image that a product presents. We should stress, from a doctrinal perspective, that this was not a case for an "express warranty," which requires a specific affirmation about a product's qualities. However, under the much more general standard of fitness for ordinary purpose, a state court that takes a relatively conservative stance on products liability doctrine found that the plaintiff had a case.

Ordinary and well-understood dangers.   An interesting comparison appears in judicial assumptions about the familiarity of consumers with ordinary, everyday dangers. Consider a piece of folk wisdom from a Massachusetts appellate court in a case against the Ford Motor Company. The plaintiff was Orlando Tibbetts, a car owner who was injured as he tried to remove a wheel cover in order to put snow chains on a tire. Attempting to pull the wheel cover off with his bare hand, he put his fingers into a decorative slot. As he unsuccessfully tugged at the cover in below freezing temperatures, he lacerated two fingers. Although a jury thought that the injury was worth $20,000 and that Ford should pay for it, the court was unwilling to find that Ford had a duty to remove burrs from the slots of the wheel cover. First using traditional judicial language, the court said that "[s]uch a common or straightforward product . . . is not defective simply because it is foreseeable that it may cause injury to someone using it improperly." The court's folk translation was perhaps quite as meaningful legally: "the world is full of rough edges."[27]

The idea that consumers must be held to recognize common dangers repeats itself in many product contexts and under several doctrinal headings. Indeed, the notion of "obviousness" has become an all-purpose description of undeservingness for many classes of plaintiffs. Thus, an auto passenger who sat in the middle of a front seat without a seat belt cannot claim there

---

26. Morrison v. Sears, Roebuck & Co., 319 N.C. 298, 301-04, 354 S.E.2d 495, 498-499 (1987).

27. Tibbetts v. Ford Motor Co., 4 Mass. App. 738, 741, 358 N.E.2d 460, 462 (1976).

was a duty to warn of the risk that she would be impaled on a front-mounted gearshift lever.[28] And a motorcycle rider must recognize that his cycle "is a light-weight, non-enclosed vehicle offering no protection in the event of collision."[29]

The notion that anything sharp can hurt people finds a particularly rending manifestation in a case that arose from an accident that brought a gruesome end to a picnic. The couple who gave the picnic owned some sharp lawn darts that had been bought by the mother of the hostess, who had reimbursed her mother for the purchase. Some children at the event got hold of the darts and started playing with them. An eight-year-old girl threw one of the darts in the air and it pierced the skull of a two-year-old boy, Jeramie Aimone. The maker had put a warning on the dart itself in raised letters. It read, in part:

WARNING
NOT A TOY FOR USE BY CHILDREN
MAY CAUSE SERIOUS OR
FATAL INJURY

The manufacturer repeated these warnings on its shipping cartons, on its game box, and in its instruction booklet. Moreover, it had made a point of trying to avoid sales of its product to children, for example, refusing to sell it to toy stores and telling retailers not to sell the darts in toy departments.

Citing these warnings, the Seventh Circuit rejected common law tort claims against the manufacturer, brought on behalf of Jeramie under strict liability and negligence theories. In its holding on the strict liability count, the court expressed its agreement with the district judge that the hazards of the product should have been "obvious even to children of the tender age of eight."[30] That was not to say that there could be no successful litigation on behalf of Jeramie; among the other defendants were the hosts of the picnic. But in the legal relation between the child and the dart maker, the court could find no compensable injury.

One cannot fix this holding to one factor; besides the "obvious" character of the danger, the facts included the warning and the manufacturer's efforts to keep the product from being characterized as a toy. We should note, moreover, that in an example of the pluralistic way that decisions emerge from complex bodies of relevant law, the court of appeals refused to dismiss a count based on the Federal Hazardous Substances Act. This part of the

---

28. Simpson v. Hurst Performance Inc., 437 F. Supp. 445, 447 (M.D.N.C. 1977).
29. Shaffer v. AMF, Inc., 842 F.2d 893, 898 (6th Cir. 1988).
30. First Nat'l Bank of Dwight v. Regent Sports Corp., 803 F.2d 1431, 1437 (7th Cir. 1986).

decision adduced evidence that the defendant had violated federal regulations intended to keep lawn darts from being used by children.[31]

Through our present lens, the salient aspect of the lawn darts case lies in the court's conviction that everyone knows the dangers of a metal dart. The court is saying that, although we may scrutinize the manufacturer's intent concerning the market, we may not doubt that anyone, including a third-grader, understands the hazards of such a product.

The captivating power of this idea is evident even in many decisions exonerating handgun manufacturers. As the Fifth Circuit put it in rejecting such a suit, "the dangers of handguns are obvious and well-known to all members of the consuming public."[32] To be sure, there are many reasons why one might choose not to impose liability on gun makers for shooting injuries. However, this seems a macabre premise on which to build the argument, given the irrelevance of the "obviousness" of the dangers of a firearm to most shooting victims.

Yet what such decisions show is the endurance of the idea in the judicial mind that dangers known to all are grounds for suit by none. We have suggested that while product image often presents a basis for seller responsibility, it is literally a two-edged concept in liability terms. Part of the image of many products, often deemed a facet of the knowledge of all who may encounter them, is the dangers intimately associated with the qualities that give them their useful character: the sharpness of knives, the openness of motorcycles, the piercing ability of darts. We should add that the idea of the obvious danger closely overlaps the concept of the metaphysical product.[33] It is part of the core concept of a knife that it is sharp and of a dart that it will pierce.

---

31. *See id.* at 1434-35.
32. Perkins v. F.I.E. Corp., 762 F.2d 1250, 1275 (5th Cir. 1985).
33. *See infra*, chapter 5, pp. 79-81.

5

Cognition and Choice in a Mass Culture

Choice in Context: The Creation of Demand

Advertising

Having established some basic features of consumer assumptions about the use of products in everyday life, or at least what many courts assume about consumer assumptions, we turn now to inquire about the effects of modern sales techniques on consumer outlooks. We thus ask what advertising builds into the "ordinary" expectations of which courts speak.

Judicial decisions in products cases have reflected the cultural heritage of many decades of mass media and, in particular, more than a generation of mass television. In 1961, at the dawn of the modern evolution of products liability law, the Connecticut Supreme Court referred to the consumer in the supermarket as "bewitched, bewildered and bedeviled by the glittering packaging in riotous color and the alluring enticement of the products' qualities as depicted on labels." The court noted, moreover, that the consumer would be likely to choose a product "which was so glowingly described by a glamorous television artist on the housewife's favorite program, just preceding the shopping trip." The court discerned "radio, magazine, billboard [and] newspaper" advertising as adding to the background of "the appeal directed to the ultimate consumer."[1] The next year,

---

1. Hamon v. Digliani, 148 Conn. 710, 717-18, 174 A.2d 294, 297 (1961).

the municipal appeals court for the District of Columbia referred to an environment in which "[l]avishly-presented publicity programs by TV, radio and the press cultivate public favor and are major inducements in the consumer's final decision to buy."[2]

Both the Connecticut and District of Columbia decisions approved suits based on theories of *implied* warranty. Thus, they seemed to find no more than nostalgic memories in the world of express representations in which, as the Connecticut court pictured it, "[t]he neighborhood storekeeper . . . called all of his customers by their first names and measured or weighed out the desired amount of the commodity ordered before packaging it."[3] As the person-to-person product claim faded into history, the media background came to the fore.

The lulling of the consumer. A compelling figure of speech appeared in a concurring opinion in an Arizona appellate case in 1970. In that case, arising from an injury attributed to a defect in a rental truck, Judge Jacobson undertook to summarize the "public policy considerations" buttressing strict liability for products.[4] In this catalog, later quoted in an important Montana case on vehicle crashworthiness,[5] he referred to the proposition that the "consumer's vigilance has been lulled by advertising, marketing devices and trademarks."[6]

Interestingly, this formulation of the "lulling" idea cited only another concurring opinion, this one in an Arizona Supreme Court case decided in 1965. The earlier litigation did not feature a most typical kind of consumer good, but rather a submersible pump motor used on a ranch. In his concurrence in that case, Chief Justice Lockwood stressed that the proper theory of liability should be strict liability rather than the implied warranty doctrine that seemed dominant in the majority opinion.[7] His principal references to the role of product portrayal appeared to reside in quotations from Justice Traynor's opinion for the California Supreme Court in the *Greenman* case, in particular to a passage that we have quoted above.[8] This rather

---

2. Picker X-Ray Corp. v. General Motors Corp., 185 A.2d 919, 920-21 (D.C. Mun. Ct. App. 1962).

3. Hamon, *supra* note 3, 148 Conn. at 717, 174 A.2d at 297.

4. Lechuga, Inc. v. Montgomery, 12 Ariz. App. 32, 37-38, 467 P.2d 256, 261-262 (1970) (Jacobson, J., concurring).

5. Brandenburger v. Toyota Motor Sales, U.S.A., 162 Mont. 506, 514-515, 513 P.2d 268, 273 (1973).

6. 12 Ariz. App. at 38, 467 P.2d at 262 (Jacobson, J., concurring).

7. Nalbandian v. Byron Jackson Pumps, Inc., 97 Ariz. 280, 287-89, 399 P.2d 681, 686-87 (1965)(Lockwood, C.J., concurring).

8. *See id.* at 287-88, 399 P.2d at 686-87, quoting Greenman v. Yuba Power Prod., Inc., 59 Cal.2d 57, 64, 377 P.2d 897, 901, 27 Cal. Rptr. 697, 701 (1963), quoted *supra*, chapter 4, text accompanying note 20.

intricate history leads to the point that even a quarter century ago, in what now appears as a medieval period of advertising techniques and at the very outset of the development of strict liability law, judges were reciting the idea that those techniques "lull" consumers.

Consumer Preferences

A wealth of social science literature testifies to the variety of influences on consumers. An evocative illustration of the techniques that work on the consumer mind appears in the field of life insurance sales. Investigators have shown a correlation between the number of sales and attempts by agents to establish themselves in the relationship with the buyer by citing their expertise, for example, by reference to their length of time in selling insurance or their winning of awards in that enterprise. Another positive correlation, but one less strong, tied successful sales efforts with attempts to show kinship based on work or activity ("I used to be somewhat of a bowler myself").[9]

The success of such diverse appeals in insurance sales leads to the question of how consumers form preferences about more tangible products. Some of the research on that subject has focused on the relationship of such factors as perceived quality of goods and distance from the consumer in the process of selecting grocery stores. One technical study, though self-critical of its own flaws, concluded that shoppers were "primarily concerned with the quality and price of merchandise" and less with such factors as "traveling distance, speed of service, and nearness of parking."[10] These findings seem consistent enough with a model premised on consumer rationality, but other questions arise when problems of consumer disappointment present themselves to the law. How do consumers make judgments on quality? How many consumers are relatively immobile with respect to sources of supply, for example, being constrained by the lack of an automobile to a point where "nearness of parking" is not even a factor?

A taste for risk. In the products field, where criticism of liability rules often focuses on their effects on innovation, some important behavioral issues concern consumer choices to try new goods. It seems reasonable to believe that a significant number of product accidents occur because people are in the experimental period of using a product they have not used before,

9. James L. Taylor & Arch G. Woodside, Effects on Buying Behavior of References to Expert and Referent Power, 117 J. Soc. Psych. 25, 28-31 (1982).

10. Harry J. Schuler, Grocery Shopping Choices: Individual Preferences Based on Store Attractiveness and Distance, 13 Environment & Behavior No. 3, at 331, 339 (1981).

and thus lack information on hazards and how to avoid injury. Why do people switch brands, or purchase new types of products? Some research indicates that at least a segment of the population seeks out stimulation in its product purchases, and that indeed, "[s]timulation needs are satisfied most by risk taking, followed by variety seeking, and the least by curiosity." Summarizing this research, P.S. Raju and M. Verkatesan saw it as holding "considerable significance for the promotion of new products": "For example, it may not always be to the marketer's advantage to place the promotional emphasis on reducing perceived risk," for that strategy "could turn away those who prefer to take risks."[11]

If consumer buying preferences relate significantly to individual inclination to risk taking, that fact arguably should influence judicial decisions on such questions as whether a particular plaintiff has fallen below a proper standard of care. It might even influence the question of whether to label a product feature as a defect, if it can be shown that significant numbers of purchasers have a preference for risk. At the same time, we would want to know what role the seller's scheme of product portrayal may have played in influencing those preferences.

In pursuing those inquiries, we might begin with the finding by Raju and Verkatesan that "those with higher optimum stimulation levels were . . . younger, more educated, and more likely to be employed."[12] We might, for example, determine that those characteristics correlate closely with decisions to purchase off-the-road vehicles. That would be not only because of the obvious point that employed consumers can afford such products but because of a certain carefreeness that goes along with affluence. At the same time, we would want to investigate the techniques sellers use to play upon such characteristics, and particularly to learn if those techniques may, by glorifying risk in general, mask specific catastrophic hazards.

We also might usefully examine the potential application of these findings to a case like *McCormack v. Hankscraft*, which we discussed earlier.[13] People buying a vaporizer for young children are not likely to have a high demand for risk. What they basically want is information—and Raju had found that information seeking was one of the activities that has the least correlation with "optimum stimulation."[14] When we combine the McCormacks' familiarity with the product and the company name, we reason-

11. P.S. Raju & M. Verkatesan, Exploratory Behavior in the Consumer Context: A State of the Art Review, 7 Advances in Consumer Research 258, 262 [photocopy typescript in possession of author], citing Raju, Exploratory Behavior in the Consumer Context, unpublished doctoral dissertation.

12. *Id.*

13. *See supra*, Chapter 4, text accompanying note 12.

14. *See* Raju and Verkatesan, *supra* note 11, at 262, citing Raju, *supra* note 11.

ably can hypothesize that they wished to minimize both the expense of search and the level of risk. Indeed, the image of the product that confronted them was one that was virtually riskless. It is factors like these, somewhat susceptible to quantification, that underlie the necessary judicial cloaking of the facts of such tragedies in legal doctrine.

By comparison, consumers who buy products of firms perceived to be relatively inexperienced in a product line—or newly developed products—must confront the argument that they are "risk preferrers." Entangled in this part of the subject are the issues of whether and how relative degrees of risk preference relate to lower price, and at what point the law should set minimums of quality and safety for particular products.

Other social research that might be relevant in products litigation has to do with the sequencing of information. One example appears in a survey of people who tried a new soft drink that carried a coupon incentive. Carol Scott and Alice Tybout found that subjects "evaluated the drink less favorably than those who did not receive an incentive for trial . . . *only* when . . . negative evaluations of others were received *prior* to tasting the product." By comparison, "when the negative information was received *after* the taste experience, . . . the incentive group . . . evaluated the drink more favorably than the no incentive group."[15] The order of receipt of information produced similar results when external information was positive, and the researchers decided that it must be "the ambiguity of the external information, and not its valence" that "caused the differential processing of cues."[16] Such findings provide at least some support for the idea that various kinds of information conveyed before purchase, presumably including information conveyed by advertising, weigh significantly not only in buying choices but decisions for product encounter and use.

In examining sellers' efforts to induce and change consumer behavior, we also should note the body of theories that may be employed to describe, and to take advantage of, market segmentation. One group of researchers, analyzing purchasing strategies, identified no fewer than sixteen "brand choice segments" in consumer markets, ranging from people who were "National Brand Loyal" to those who were "Private Label Loyal" and "Private Label Switcher[s]."[17] After surveying several hundred households with respect to a few homely product categories,[18] these authors concluded that "buying behavior may be more closely related to *general* characteristics of the house-

---

15. Carol A. Scott and Alice M. Tybout, Theroetical Perspectives on the Impact of Negative Information: Does Valence Matter?, 8 Advances in Csmr. Res. 408, 409 (1981).

16. *Id.*

17. Robert C. Blattberg, Peter Peacock and Subrata K. Sen, Purchasing Strategies Across Product Categories, 3 J. Csmr. Res. 143, 144 (1976).

18. Aluminum foil, waxed paper, liquid detergent, and facial tissue.

holds ... than might have been expected from past research."[19] This led to the practical conclusion that by "find[ing] certain general customer characteristics which distinguish members of one segment from another," marketers could more effectively "target segments because of the possibility of better media selection and a more selective distribution of free samples and coupons."[20] Thus, it would appear that even the most hardheaded consumer has characteristics which render him or her receptive to messages with particular textures.

The Framing of Choice

An important aspect of research on consumer decisionmaking involves the "framing" of consumer choices. A landmark contribution to this literature has come from the work of Daniel Kahneman and Amos Tversky. Literally playing games with experimental subjects, these authors have shown that if one poses alternative courses of conduct that involve the same degree of financial risk, employing different ways of describing the risk, subjects will make very different choices under the influence of the varying descriptions. They found, for example, that casting "objectively identical" alternatives in terms of how much one wins or how much one loses, or indeed whether one wins or loses at all, will significantly influence choice.[21]

Kahneman and Tversky have also observed that consumers keep mental books on product and service categories in terms of "topical accounts." That is, they make judgments about how to spend their money in terms of such categories. In that connection, these researchers discovered, subjects refuse to make exact substitutions of money for goods. Again these results depend on the framing of the problem, for example, relating to the sequence in which events occur.[22]

James Bettman and Mita Sujan have extended "framing" analysis to the question of how consumers formulate the criteria that govern product purchase. Bettman and Sujan "primed" certain research subjects with such criteria—either emphasizing "creativity" or "reliability"—and then presented them with choices involving "noncomparable" products, specifically, 35 mm. cameras and home computers, as well as comparable products. They found that "[w]hen no decision criterion was available ...

---

19. 3 J. Csmr. Res. at 154.
20. *Id.*
21. *See, e.g.*, Daniel Kahneman and Amos Tversky, Choices, Values and Frames, 39 American Psychologist No. 4, at 341, 346 (1984).
22. *See id.* at 347-348.

subjects appeared to construct one," involving such abstract ideas as " 'need,' 'function,' and 'fun.' "

By contrast, when a decision criterion was readily available, "subjects directly focus[ed] on concrete or specific attributes" of products, "such as 'several modes of operation' for cameras and 'constructed to operate under all climate conditions' for computers for both decisions involving comparable and noncomparable alternatives." These authors inferred "that rather than any inherent differences between noncomparable and comparable categories, the one fundamental distinction between them may be the ready availability of decision criteria for comparable sets—at least for experts—versus the need to construct them for noncomparable sets."[23]

Any lessons of this kind of research for liability judgments are likely to be indirect. Generally, however, such investigations indicate that up to the moment the consumer formulates an intention to buy a product, he or she confronts a powerful set of sequential conditioning agents. Those agents— "priming" vehicles and descriptions of product attributes—set the mental terms and conditions of product choice. In stages, they color our entire matrix of decision. We need not speak in terms of loaded concepts like "manipulation" and theoretically controversial ones like "creation of demand" to make the point: the choices of the assertedly sovereign consumer arise from a background prepared and infused with images created by professionals whose business it is to frame the question and then to answer it. Ever more subtly constructed, these images shape preferences, condition demand and should influence judgments of liability.

Consumers, Cognition, and Product Concept

The Metaphysics of Products

We turn now to a discussion of the metaphysics of products. We have seen that many important issues in products liability, including the question of what a defect is and how the law should treat the plaintiff's conduct, grow out of the relationship of the consumer's concept of a particular product to his or her level of information, to the framing of that information by both the seller and the consumer, and to the resultant choice of purchase or en-

---

23. J. Bettman & M. Sujan, Effects of Framing on Evaluation of Comparable and Noncomparable Alternatives by Expert and Novice Consumers, 14 J. Csmr. Res. 141, 151 (Sept. 1987).

counter. Tied in with all these factors is the way that product categories acquire a meaning of their own.

Cars.   We do not have to invoke the idea of Platonic forms to understand that classes of products present themselves to consumers as core ideas. For example, an object that had certain physical characteristics and was advertised as an "automobile" would convey to a prospective purchaser certain basic messages: that it included an engine that would start when one turned the key in the ignition, that it had a transmission that would translate the power of the engine into movement, and even that it possessed a set of devices with hard rubber surfaces that would clean the windshield.

Putting aside the question of the buyer's duty to inspect, an object described as an automobile that lacked any of those features would present a clear case for legal relief, at least for rescission and perhaps even for damages. In legal terms, courts would hold the vehicle to breach an implied warranty or to be defective. That is because the performance of millions of such objects over many years, in the context of many communications by sellers, has generated a consensus on the minimum meaning of objects with that appearance and that label.

Food.   A subtler set of problems appears in cases involving food products. For example, should someone who buys a can of oysters at a commissary expect that she will bite into a pearl when she begins to consume the delicacy? Sylvia O'Dell, an Oklahoma graduate student, thought not. After fracturing three teeth on "a little raw pearl" in an oyster in a soup she had made, she sued the canning company. The state appellate court reversed a jury verdict for the canner, rendered under a generalized instruction using the test of what a consumer could "reasonably expect." The court conceded that a purchaser of oysters in the shell "could 'reasonably expect' to find a pearl in one of the oysters." But it thought it "unrealistic to say" that a buyer of canned processed oysters would have that expectation, at least without further explanation. In its reversal, the court said that the jury instruction should have given "consideration . . . to the fact that the term 'reasonably expected' involves more of a probability than just a possibility."[24]

As the Oklahoma appellate court noted, we can draw several distinctions about the question of natural objects in food. Almost two decades before the Oklahoma decision, for example, the Ohio Supreme Court had said that the possibility that a 3 x 2 centimeter piece of oyster shell might appear in an oyster "is so well known to anyone who eats oysters that . . . as a matter

---

24. O'Dell v. DeJean's Packing Co., 585 P.2d 399, 402-03 (Okl. Ct. App. 1978).

of law . . . one who eats oysters can reasonably anticipate and guard against eating such a piece of shell."[25]

By contrast, in several other decisions involving other kinds of products, courts have been sympathetic to the consumer:

• In one case the plaintiff bit into a fried chicken wing and encountered something that "she perceived to be a worm," although expert testimony indicated that it was probably the aorta or trachea of the fowl. A federal trial judge was at pains to stress that he had been "born and raised south of the Mason-Dixon line (where fried chicken has been around longer than in any part of America)." Even with that background, though, he said he knew "of no special heightened awareness chargeable to fried chicken eaters" that should put them "on the alert for trachea or aorta in the middle of their wings."[26]

• In another case a Florida court invoked a reasonable expectations test in refusing to apply the defense of comparative negligence—for failing to chew sufficiently before swallowing—in a case in which a piece of metal wire in a doughnut lodged in the plaintiff's throat.[27]

• Recently other courts have held for consumers who found a piece of beef bone in a hamburger[28] and a bone in a cube of turkey meat.[29]

The homeliness of the cases should not obscure their philosophical aspect. Through the development of product images that create a certain security about safety—in fact the fashioning of images in which safety is not even imaginably an issue—consumers come to assume that they need not search for pearls, bones, or unaesthetic chicken parts. The exploitation of images gives practical meaning to the concept of a particular food. Part of products liability law depends, then, on a metaphysics of processed oysters, hamburgers, and chicken wings.

Consumer Intelligence and Sophistication

Another dimension of the problem relates to the sort of animal the consumer is. We have to ask what the law should assume about the level of consumer intelligence and sophistication, and how should it respond to varying levels of those attributes.

Cognitive Complexity. In academic terms, the problem may partly be cast as one of "cognitive complexity," which has been defined as "the num-

---

25. Allen v. Grafton, 170 Ohio St. 249, 259, 164 N.E.2d 167, 175 (1960).

26. Yong Cha Hong v. Marriott Corp., 656 F. Supp. 445 (D. Md. 1987).

27. Coulter v. American Bakeries Co., 530 So.2d 1009 (Fla. Dist. Ct. App. 1988).

28. Evart v. Suli, 211 Cal. App. 3d 605, 613-14, 259 Cal. Rptr. 535, 541 (1989).

29. Phillips v. Town of West Springfield, 405 Mass. 411, 540 N.E.2d 1331 (1989).

ber of dimensions used in a differentiated manner to evaluate objects."[30] Relevantly to products liability, this appears to translate as the number of ways in which a consumer slices up the qualities of a product. Looking into that question, two researchers combined a diverse group of product categories including automobiles, apartments, and toilet soap. They concluded that at least with respect to these categories, a person whose evaluations of one product were cognitively complex "tends to be relatively complex in his evaluation of the other product classes as well."[31] The researchers were careful to say that there was no indication of whether or not this complexity of classification would hold for other parts of life, for example, social encounters.[32] But if such findings extend across consumer goods generally, then those who make and interpret laws presumably should have that evidence in mind. Thus, those who fashion liability rules to govern product categories might tailor those rules to their best estimates about the complexity of analysis that typical classes of consumers are likely to bring to purchase decisions in those categories. In practice, this would sometimes produce a standard that protects the consumers with the least capacity for complex analysis.

As diverse as it is, the consumer population presents some interesting twists and turns with respect to the classification of people by their inclination to study and actively process product information. According to one pair of researchers, people who have a "moderate" amount of prior knowledge and experience about a product—microwave ovens in their study— will "do more processing of the currently available information" and will rely less on prior knowledge than people who score either "high" or "low" on prior knowledge and experience.[33]

One might have thought that the tendency to process information would correlate directly with prior knowledge. However, the investigators speculate that although "[t]he Low group may not possess the ability to process the information in the current choice task," members of the "High group" may have "enough ability" but may not "necessarily [be] motivated to process much current information, as they do not need to." Where members of the High group "can rely on information in memory and their prior experiences," "[t]he Moderate Group . . . may possess enough ability and have

---

30. Chin Tiong Tan & Ira J. Dolich, Cognitive Structure in Personality: An Investigation of its Generality in Buying Behavior, 7 Advances in Consumer Research 547, 548 (1979).

31. *Id.* at 549.

32. *See id.* at 550.

33. James R. Bettman & C. Whan Park, Effects of Prior Knowledge and Experience and Phase of the Choice Process on Consumer Decision Processes: A Protocol Analysis, 7 J. Csmr. Res. 234, 244 (December 1980).

enough motivation to devote substantial processing effort to the task."[34] Such conclusions add complexity to the issue of when and how the law should try to correlate seller liability with the knowledge and experience of classes of product users.

Personality traits. Another potential basis for legal differentiation among groups appears in findings about the correlation of consumer behavior with such factors as age, social class, and "cognitive personality traits." One study involved 120 housewives in a "midsized midwestern city." Researchers asked these women to perform shopping tasks related to three convenience foods—instant coffees, nondairy coffee creamers, instant lemonades—and one appliance, electric clothes dryers. The investigators found that "[w]ives who were younger, earlier in the life cycle, highly educated, and nonhomeowners drew more cues and examined more alternatives for all four decisions."[35]

Perhaps one might explain these findings by suggesting that yuppies, being relatively well educated and self-confident ("[t]he higher-status working wives . . . tended to be higher in self-esteem and lower in trait anxiety"),[36] are more incisive shoppers. The question for the law is, if the elder and less sophisticated cousins of the yuppies are "simplifiers, intolerant of ambiguity, and lower in self-esteem,"[37] how should we tailor the legal rules pertaining to consumer disappointment? This study appears to identify a population that is relatively vulnerable to messages that oversimplify, and relatively less inclined to analyze the features, presumably including safety features, of products. One might then argue that, in litigation involving members of targeted groups of relatively vulnerable buyers, such evidence should influence the application of legal rules.

As we analyze the role of product image and consumer reception, we should note that in the case of televised messages, one study has concluded that "non-advertising communications were associated with higher levels of miscomprehension than were advertising communications." The authors of this report noted that "though statistically significant, these differences are practically trivial."[38] Even so, this data suggests that despite our concern with the image-making power of mass media, we should not accuse television advertising as being inherently deceptive.

---

34. *Id.*
35. Charles M. Schaninger & Donald Sciglimpaglia, The Influence of Cognitive Personality Traits and Demographics on Consumer Information Acquisition, 8 J. Csmr. Res. 208, 213 (1981).
36. *Id.* at 215.
37. *Id.*
38. Jacob Jacoby, et al., Viewer Miscomprehension of Televised Communication: A Brief Report of Findings, 8 Adv. Consumer Res. 410, 412 (1981).

The Obviousness Issue

The metaphysics of products and the level of consumer sophistication link up in the concept of "obviousness." This concept increasingly surfaces in products liability cases in which courts must concern themselves with the mental set of consumers. The basic idea, which appears under various doctrinal guises, is that a seller should not be liable to someone injured by a product hazard that was obvious. An established collateral ancestor is the rule that visitors to land should not recover from landowners for injuries caused by "open and obvious" conditions.[39]

Swimming pool injuries. A symbolic group of cases, tragically typical of an affluent society, involves people who suffer crippling injuries from diving into the shallow end of residential swimming pools. The legal problem tends to arise when someone injured in that way claims that a pool manufacturer had a duty to warn of the hazard. Notions of causation and consumer responsibility whirl with the concept of obviousness in a legal centrifuge, with sometimes one and sometimes another being spun out to rationalize judgments. In a decision involving two such cases, the New York Court of Appeals crisply answered the plaintiffs' arguments in an opinion that captures the approach of most courts to such situations. "[E]ach plaintiff's conduct," said the New York court, "rather than any negligence by the defendants in failing to issue warnings, was the sole proximate cause of his injuries."[40]

A parallel doctrinal approach appears in a decision by an Illinois appellate court in another swimming pool case. That court applied a "subjective test," based on "what plaintiff actually knew," in affirming a jury finding that the claimant "assumed 96% of the risk." The court incorporated some of the salient facts of the case in its observation that the six-foot-five-inch plaintiff, who "had been taking swimming lessons when he was six or seven years old," had admitted that "he wouldn't want to dive virtually straight down into 4½ feet of water and agreed . . . that he might break his neck if he did so."[41]

It is true that the decisions have not been unanimous on this point. In a case with facts very much like those just described, in which the plaintiff

---

39. An exaggerated example is Gulfway General Hosp. Inc. v. Pursley, 397 S.W.2d 93 (Tex. Civ. App. 1965) (no liability in suit against hospital by incoming emergency patient who slipped on ice at emergency entrance).

40. Howard v. Poseidon Pools, Inc., 72 N.Y.2d 972, 975, 530 N.E.2d 1280, 1281, 534 N.Y.S.2d 360, 361 (1988).

41. Erickson v. Muskin Corp., 180 Ill. App.3d 117, 125-126, 535 N.E.2d 475, 480 (1989).

had been in the particular pool before and knew which end was shallow, a Michigan appellate court reflected the emotionally wrenching aspect of a quadriplegia-causing injury with this comment: "[A] simple act of pleasure on a hot summer's day, a dive into a pool, can result in a lifetime of heart-ache, frustration, pain and loss."[42] The plaintiff had testified that although he "knew serious injury could result from diving into shallow water," " 'just exactly what type of injury would result from it, I couldn't have said at the time.' " On that evidence, the court refused to uphold an "open and obvious" defense, opining that "[n]othing in the appearance of the pool itself gives a warning of the very serious consequences to which a mundane dive can lead."[43]

Even in that case, however, a majority of the Michigan Supreme Court reversed the appellate court, stressing that an "above-ground swimming pool is a simple product," with "nothing deceiving about its appearance, nothing enigmatic about its properties." The supreme court embodied its behavioral assumptions in its conclusion that "[t]he danger involved in div-ing into shallow water is obvious to the reasonably prudent user of such a product."[44]

Insights and intuitions. The litany of obviousness runs through many product categories, capturing a set of insights tied up with the concept of defect, with the consumer expectations test, and with societal beliefs con-cerning appropriate consumer conduct. The Sixth Circuit, for example, found the exposure of motorcyclists to accidents to be a prime case of "ob-viousness," saying that "a motorcycle is a light-weight, non-enclosed vehi-cle offering no protection in the event of collision."[45] In a very different product context, the Minnesota court of appeals applied an "obvious dan-ger" defense to a case in which the operator of a riding lawnmower tried "to reattach a belt while a drive pulley [was] running, when the user [could not] see his hand or the pulley."[46]

A quantitatively important set of applications of the obviousness defense appears in the industrial setting. In a Massachusetts case, the operator of a press brake sued unsuccessfully when he had several fingers crushed in the

42. Glittenberg v. Wilcenski, 174 Mich. App. 321, 324, 435 N.W.2d 480, 482 (1989).

43. *Id.* at 326, 435 N.W.2d at 482. The appellate court's characterization of the plain-tiff's knowledge appears in 174 Mich. App. at 324, 435 N.W.2d at 481. The "just exactly" quotation from the plaintiff appears in the supreme court's decision, 436 Mich. at 677, 462 N.W.2d at 350.

44. Glittenberg v. Doughboy Recreational Indus., Inc., 436 Mich. 673, 695-696, 462 N.W.2d 348, 358 (1990).

45. Shaffer v. AMF, Inc., 842 F.2d 893, 898 (6th Cir. 1988).

46. Mix v. MTD Prods., Inc., 393 N.W.2d 18, 20 (Minn. Ct. App. 1986).

machine. The court emphasized the plaintiff's testimony that it was "obvious" to him "that if a person placed any part of his body between the movable ram and the press brake bed, and the foot pedal was pressed, that person would be injured."[47] The Alabama Supreme Court offered this compressed generalization when it rejected the argument that a lubricant manufacturer should have warned about the hazards of lubricating exposed moving gears: "The use of certain products is so firmly grounded in common sense as to require no specific instructions or warnings."[48]

The concept of obviousness provides courts the opportunity to express, in a concise verbal package, a range of intuitions that capture the justice of particular situations. At the root of these intuitions is a sense that when there is no confusion in one's bargain with his or her environment, the law should enforce that bargain even if it turns out to be a harsh one. One might also infer a special use of the concept with respect to conduct that courts might hesitate to call outright foolishness, sometimes out of deference to the severity of particular injuries. In some such cases, "obviousness" is a polite mask for a judgment that a seriously injured person's conduct was so foolhardy as to bar recovery on moral grounds.

Behavioral issues. Yet even in cases where "obviousness" springs to the judicial pen, it is worth analyzing factual situations from the point of view of what we are coming to know of human behavior. For example, we might want to ask about the position on various cognitive scales of particular groups of consumers, targeted for the sales of certain products. In certain cases, we could ask where the group of which a particular consumer is a member ranks with respect to "cognitive complexity" or "cognitive personality."

One case that demonstrates the potential significance of this sort of question dealt with the electrocution of a man who flew a model plane with a control wire and metal accessories near exposed electric wires. In denying recovery, an Illinois appellate court referred to "readily apparent and well known dangers."[49] This may well have been a just result on the particular facts of the case. However, one might wish to inquire whether the seller knew that it was marketing its plane to a group of consumers who would be so likely to become wrapped up in the novelty of the product that their cognitive capacity might be strained to perceive even the "obvious" deadly connections between hand-held metal and electric wires. Were that so, there might be room for a difference of opinion about what "obviousness" truly meant in that factual setting.

---

47. Bell v. Wysong & Miles Co., 26 Mass. App. Ct. 1011, 1013, 531 N.E.2d 267, 269 (1988), rev. denied, 404 Mass. 1101, 536 N.E.2d 612 (1989).
48. Entrekin v. Atlantic Richfield Co., 519 So.2d 447, 450 (Ala. 1987).
49. Holecek v. E-Z Just, 124 Ill. App. 3d 251, 256, 464 N.E.2d 696, 699 (1984).

It is also useful to note that non-obvious dangers may coexist with obvious hazards. A North Dakota case that teaches this lesson involved an inner tube, called a Super Tube, that was equipped with handles and a harness so it could be attached to water-ski towropes. The plaintiff using the tube "skimm[ed] along the shoreline for a distance and then slammed into a boat" that was resting partly in water and partly on land. The defendant argued that it was "apparent to everyone of common intelligence that there is danger in colliding with a fixed object," but the court focused on some different aspects of the situation. It held that it was for the jury to decide whether the defendant should have warned that the tube "should not be towed above a certain speed," that it "would accelerate and arc around corners," that riders would not be able to control its speed or direction, and that spray from the tube would impair visibility.[50]

This result implies issues on at least two levels of consumer cognition: of what hazards was the plaintiff aware at the time of buying the product? And what were the realistic possibilities, in the actual act of skiing with the tube, that the plaintiff would recognize the dangers involved? As to the first question, besides being skeptical of a buyer's ability to visualize such hazards at the time of purchase, a court might think that sellers should take into account the relative adventurousness of the sort of consumer who would acquire such a product. As to the second, with or without help from experts in cognition, judges would have to make guesses about the ability of particular groups of consumers to absorb and assess the risk profile of a fast-moving activity.

We may refer, by contrast, to an admiring hyperbole by the teammate of a professional football quarterback, famous for his ability to see game action unfolding on the field in a particularly wide frame of vision. By this writer's recollection, the teammate said, "Bernie not only knows where all the receivers and defenders are, he can tell you about the guy who's selling Cokes in the stands." Not everyone, however, has the peripheral vision or the quickness of response in emergent situations of a National Football League quarterback. The law has to deal with consumer averages, and the relevant average may be that of a target group that has relatively low cognitive capacity.

Not Knowing What to Ask

One reason that the sophistication, information levels, and cognitive abilities of consumers are so important is that in some cases, people may be

---

50. Butz v. Werner, 438 N.W.2d 509, 512 (N.D. 1989).

so ignorant or intellectually unskilled that they do not know what to ask in the first place. This point is implicit in the fact that the doctrine of "assumption of risk," often used to support products liability defendants, will bar a claim only if the plaintiff voluntarily and unreasonably confronted a *known* risk. In one case, in which a farmer sustained fatal injuries when he bypass started his tractor, the court held that a showing that he "should have known" that the tractor "could be bypass started in gear" was insufficient to uphold an assumption of risk defense.[51] The decision helps to make the point that people who have insufficient information about a risk will be unable even to formulate the question of whether the risk exists.

Reliance and Expectations

The "Right to Rely"

The question of whether a consumer had a "right to rely" on certain product qualities recurs in many contexts. Technically, the roots of the idea of a "right to rely" in products liability law appear most directly in fraud doctrine, and, to an extent, under the heading of express warranty. The idea also appears, however, in the background of a large number of cases that do not involve express representations. In those cases, the notion of a right to rely becomes entwined with the concept of consumer expectations.

One of the principal requirements of the legal formula for fraud or deceit is that the buyer's reliance be justified.[52] This sort of terminology "reflects a kind of fiduciary notion of the obligations that those with superior information have to those who lack knowledge." It applies to cases where a party with superior knowledge, typically a seller, tries to take advantage of the impression of another party, typically a buyer, that the more knowledgeable party "knows the quality of goods."[53] At the same time, the law fosters a "right to rely" on grounds that it would be economically wasteful for consumers to search for information for which it seems reasonable and customary that they ought to be able to trust their sellers.[54]

Under the doctrine of express warranty, there has been some controversy about whether or not a buyer must show "particular reliance" on a specific representation. There is language in the express warranty section of the

---

51. McMurray v. Deere & Co., 858 F.2d 1436, 1441 (10th Cir. 1988).

52. *See, e.g.,* Fowler V. Harper, Fleming James & Oscar S. Gray, 2 The Law of Torts § 7.1 at 381 (2d ed. 1986).

53. M. Shapo, The Law of Products Liability ¶ 2.02[5], at 2-5 (1990).

54. *See id.* at 2-5 - 2-6.

Uniform Commercial Code and its comments that would support either position.[55] Critics of the erosion of the requirement of specific reliance, though conceding that the requirement "may disappear altogether," have inquired, somewhat plaintively, "Why should one who has not relied on the seller's statement have the right to sue?"[56] The comments to the Code respond that "[i]n actual practice affirmations of fact made by the seller about the goods during a bargain are regarded as part of the description of those goods; hence no particular reliance on such statements need be shown in order to weave them into the fabric of the agreement."[57]

Consumer Expectations: Illustrative Applications

While discussion proceeds under representational doctrines of products liability about the reliance requirement and its rationales, we should remember that reliance is rooted in expectations throughout this branch of the law. We now turn to analyze more generally the role of consumer expectations in products liability, especially in situations where there is no direct representation from buyer to seller. In this discussion, we keep in mind that product portrayal largely generates expectations, and we retain a heightened awareness of the way that sellers confect product images.

Comment i to section 402A of the Second Restatement of Torts retails the idea that in order to be "unreasonably dangerous," and therefore defective, a product "must be dangerous to an extent beyond that which would be contemplated by the ordinary consumer who purchases it, with the ordinary knowledge common to the community as to its characteristics."[58] There have been dissents as to the effectiveness of this test, including a very recent commentary in a Reporters' study for the American Law Institute,[59] under whose aegis section 402A was born. Many courts, however, have found this a persuasive standard. Let us consider some of the most evocative judicial ventures in the definition of consumer expectations.

One of the plainest approaches to the question has focused on risks that are part of the "common knowledge" of consumers. In an early decision under the strict liability doctrine, the Illinois Supreme Court refused to impose liability against a seller of shoes that became slippery when wet, holding as a matter of law that the shoes were not defective. Presumably from

---

55. For a summary of this language, *see id.*, ¶ 3.09, at 3-13–3-14.
56. *See* Robert Summers & James White, Uniform Commercial Code 339 (1980).
57. Uniform Commercial Code ¶ 2-313, comment 3 (1962).
58. Restatement (Second) of Torts § 402A, comment i (1965).
59. *See* 2 Reporters' Study, Enterprise Liability for Personal Injury 44-47 (A.L.I. 1991).

its own experience, the court invoked the "common knowledge" of consumers about the increased slipperiness of wet shoes.[60]

The same attitude has prevailed about other slipperiness hazards. In a case that involved a car that skidded during a snowstorm, the court insisted that "[s]kidding on ice is a phenomenon necessarily known to anyone after he first walks or rides on it" and spoke of a "common propensity of the product which is open and obvious."[61]

One finds similar declarations about the dangers inherent in glass, and sharp-pointed or sharp-edged objects. In one case, a nine-year-old lost an eye while he was playing with a glass bottle of cola, left on the front entrance of his house in a marketing campaign by the soft drink maker. The Nebraska Supreme Court opined that bottles "[a]s a matter of law . . . are not so inherently or potentially dangerous that a manufacturer could be found to be negligent for marketing its product in glass bottles."[62] We already have noted how a federal appellate court declared that the danger of lawn darts "should be obvious even to children of the tender age of eight,"[63] and how a state appellate court told a plaintiff injured by the decorative slots on a wheel cover that "the world is full of rough edges."[64]

The "Ought" and the "Is" of Consumer Expectations

The discussion so far has emphasized that there are many aspects of product portrayal, including the very appearance of the product, that are likely to influence judicial decisions. At this point, we should emphasize the difference between the "ought" and the "is" of consumer expectations, and the roles that judge and jury play in those determinations. In a relatively early products liability decision, Justice Goodwin of the Oregon Supreme Court sketched an interesting distinction. The case involved the separation of the rim of a truck wheel from the interior portion of the wheel when it hit a rock in the highway. Justice Goodwin distinguished the question of "what reasonable consumers do expect from the product," which he said was a "basically factual question" for the jury, from the question of

---

60. Fanning v. LeMay, 38 Ill.2d 209, 211-12, 230 N.E.2d 182, 185 (1967).
61. Zidek v. General Motors Corp., 66 Ill. App. 3d 982, 985, 384 N.E.2d 509, 512 (1978).
62. Gruenemeier v. Seven-Up Co., 229 Neb. 267, 271, 426 N.W.2d 510, 513 (1988).
63. First Nat'l Bank v. Regents Sports Corp., 803 F.2d 1431, 1437 (7th Cir. 1986), *see supra*, chapter 4, text accompanying note 30.
64. Tibbetts v. Ford Motor Co., 4 Mass. App. 738, 741, 358 N.E.2d 460, 462 (1976), *see supra*, chapter 4, text accompanying note 27.

"how strong the product *should* be," which he said that courts—that is, judges—had decided was "strong enough to perform as the ordinary consumer expects."[65]

In the particular case of the wheel separation, Justice Goodwin decided for the defendant because the record lacked evidence on what consumers expected. He stressed that to allow the case to go to the jury would be to permit jurors to give their opinion about "how strong the product *should* be."[66] The Oregon court's defect standard has evolved since then, with the court moving to impose on defendants "constructive knowledge of the condition of the product,"[67] but the case of the truck wheel still provides a useful benchmark on philosophy and fact.

As we previously noted,[68] the Washington Supreme Court has taken a somewhat different tack in strict liability cases, emphasizing that "[t]he jury does not evaluate the seller's actions," but rather "only determines whether the product is dangerous to an extent beyond that which would be contemplated by the ordinary consumer."[69] In saying this in a case involving a cracked truck wheel, the Washington court held that it was not error to refuse an instruction that created a presumption that a manufacturer knows "of the harmful characteristics of that which it makes." The court said that this formula, which it characterized as a "seller-oriented standard," would conflict with its own "buyer-oriented" test.

Whichever of these formulations is most appealing, we must stress that the doing of justice in products liability cases requires analysis of a progression of events that includes the generation of images by sellers, the *resulting* development of expectations, and the fabric of reliance that thus arises. This is not, in technical terms, a contractual fabric. But it is one that appears to control cases. The reason for that, no matter how much judicial focus there may be on the expectations themselves, is that the hinge of the legal relationship is the process of creating the expectation.

65. Heaton v. Ford Motor Co., 248 Or. 467, 474, 435 P.2d 806, 809 (1967).
66. *Id.*
67. *See, e.g.*, Phillips v. Kimwood Mach. Co., 269 Or. 485, 525 P.2d 1033 (1974).
68. *See supra*, chapter 4, text accompanying note 22.
69. Ryder v. Kelly-Springfield Tire Co., 91 Wash. 2d 111, 118, 587 P.2d 160, 164 (1978).

6

The Divided Soul of the
American Consumer

Our analysis of assumptions about the mind-set of consumers leads us to an examination of several interlinked fields of argument featuring ethical and economic ideas. In these battles, both sellers and injured consumers try to claim the high moral ground. Even more interestingly, consumers find themselves internally at war over the definition of their own best interests. In some respects, indeed, products liability law represents a struggle within the divided soul of the American consumer.

Tensions Between Moral Judgment and Economic Doctrine

In analyzing these tensions, we examine a few basic ideas and some conflicts that inhere within them. The ideas we scrutinize include consumer sensitivity to prices, the relativity of safety, and the notion that there are certain products that the public "needs."

Prices, market choice, and moral choice.   A fundamental economic tool lies in the premise that as a product becomes more expensive, consumers will buy less of it. Because the converse is generally true, a seller can expect to sell more of a product as the price falls. A modifying idea appears in the notion of elasticity of demand. In the case of products with relatively little demand elasticity, consumers will continue to purchase even as price climbs steeply. The concept of substitution enters here. An insulin-dependent diabetic would continue buying insulin even if its price took a steep runup. By comparison, in the case of products that have close substitutes, consumers are not likely to stand still for much of a price rise. They will flock to the most attractive alternative. The character of need and desire enters here, too. Even chocoholics confronted with a chocolate monopoly and no desirable surrogate would stop buying chocolate long before the diabetic leaves the insulin market.

Because people do tend to respond to price changes, marketplace actors play a complicated game with respect to consumer product safety. We have noted that in the terminology almost perversely favored by the economics profession, sellers will "bribe" consumers in various ways. They may, for example, provide incentives to purchasers to be more careful, or to search out information that as consumers they may more cheaply acquire, by offering them a lower price for a dangerous product. Consumers, on their part, may tender bribes of their own for more safety features.

In this arena, there arises a rich set of legal problems. Some of the most interesting issues appear when the defendant does not place an available safety device on a product. An illustrative set of cases involves power mowers. Assume, as an example, that for $250, one can buy a mower that will shut off when the user is not gripping the handle. The practical result of this is that it is impossible for a consumer—at least one who has not taken willful steps to defeat the shut-off feature—to try to free matted grass from the mower blades while the machine is running. The consumer could also buy for $200 a mower, made by the same firm, that does not have the shut-off feature. The consequence of purchase of many such mowers has been thousands of mangled fingers.

Those are the basic economic details. Now we must turn to interpretation. One might say that the market for less safe mowers produced an optimal result: consumers got exactly the measure of safety for which they bargained. By contrast, one might say that the cooperative enterprise represented by the bribe of the lower price—some economists have spoken of the seller "hir[ing] the consumer" to acquire information or to behave more safely[1]—did not work out. This casting of the problem highlights the skewered linguistics of the optimality interpretation, since the consumer is as much being paid to take a chance as to behave more safely.

An opinion of the Maryland Court of Appeals, previously discussed,[2] captured concisely the economic choices that confronted Harold Myers, a homeowner who sustained gruesome injuries from the rotating blade of a mower. Given that it was "apparent" when the plaintiff bought the machine

---

1. *See, e.g.*, McKean, Products Liability: Trends and Implications, 38 U. Chi. L. Rev. 3, 30 (1970)(focusing on acquisition of information). For prior discussion of this concept, see *supra*, pp. 60-61.

2. *See supra*, chapter 2, text accompanying note 47.

that it lacked safety devices, the court said that "in a free market, Myers had the choice of buying a mower equipped with them, of buying the mower which he did, or of buying no mower at all."[3]

One does not usually find the point put so starkly, but the Maryland court did analysts a favor by defining the issue that way. The decision effectively indicated that courts must make a choice between a straight takes-your-chances approach and one that declares a minimum standard for safety, which admittedly has the effect of making a choice for both seller and consumer. A pejorative way to label the choice of a minimum standard is to call it "paternalistic." That solves very little.

A judicial tradition with a distinguished pedigree has made clear that courts have maneuvering room to declare that a firm or person has not built enough safety into a product or activity. Judge Learned Hand issued the most famous pronouncement of this kind in the case of *The T.J. Hooper*: since "a whole calling may have unduly lagged in the adoption of new and available devices," "[c]ourts must in the end say what is required."[4] To be sure, Judge Hand was also the principal judicial parent of the idea that one judges negligence by whether injury costs have exceeded the costs of avoiding an accident.[5] However, the message of *The T.J. Hooper* is as stark and broad as that of the Maryland court in the lawn mower case. At the least, it allows judges to make a social judgment about minimum—not only optimum—levels of safety.

This is not to deny that such decisions might have some undesirable fall-out. What are the objections to detaching the standard of care from economic optimality? They include concerns about total effects on the level of accidents and effects on low-income consumers—these concerns sometimes being joined together. It is argued, for example, that judicial decisions that effectively demand more safety devices than "the market" would require will deprive low-income consumers of useful goods, because the safer models will be too expensive. Secondary effects might include the following: more consumers will suffer wrenched backs from mowing with push mowers than would those who would have hands mangled by power mowers without guards. Or low-income consumers will be driven to acquire older models of power mowers without safety devices, which statistically will be less reliable and thus will cause more injuries than would relatively cheap new mowers that lack safety devices.

This statement of the problem highlights the kinds of moral choices that courts must make in many products cases when there is a paucity of hard

---

3. Myers v. Montgomery Ward & Co., 253 Md. 282, 297, 252 A.2d 855, 864 (1969).
4. 60 F.2d 737, 740 (2d Cir.), cert. denied, 287 U.S. 662 (1932).
5. United States v. Carroll Towing Co., 159 F.2d 169, 173 (2d Cir. 1947).

information about consumer price sensitivity as it relates to the desire for safety. At this point, we simply emphasize the unavoidable moral content in judicially set definitions of unreasonable seller conduct or unreasonable danger in products.

The relativity of safety.   A related point concerns something that everyone knows at some level of thought and that sophisticated people like to think they understand very well. This is that safety is a relative matter. In our search for lives that are richer in various ways, few of us truly desire safety above everything else.

We are always making tradeoffs. We may drive substantial distances to relatively lucrative or stimulating jobs instead of accepting work within walking distance from our homes. Though wishing to avoid "second collision" injuries, we may drive cars rather than trucks—or tanks—because the cars are cheaper, or more stylish, or more maneuverable. As a young scholar, Dean Calabresi turned an evocative phrase when he spoke of the "decision for accidents."[6] Aaron Wildavsky has observed that "[s]afety is relative" and that there are opportunity costs in risks foregone.[7] Focusing on torts as a teaching subject, I wrote more than twenty years ago of "the kinds of weighing that torts has always taught the best."[8] Everyone knows that accidents arise from balancings and calculations of competing goals, and that the legal judgment of accidents similarly requires a calculus that permits relative valuation of ends and means.

The law of products liability provides an especially sharp reflection of the relativity of safety. Some of the most poignant examples of this recognition appear in cases in which claimants have been infected by AIDS virus from blood products used in transfusions. In one such case, involving a plaintiff transfused with a blood factor designed to combat hemophilia, the court refused to impose liability on the manufacturer in the following situation: On January 31 and February 3, 1983, a homosexual man donated contaminated plasma used to make the product. An internal memorandum of the defendant first mentioned a policy of questioning "high risk" donors on February 8 of that year, and an FDA document dated March 24 provided "[t]he earliest firm evidence" of that agency's position on the subject. Upholding a judgment notwithstanding the verdict for the manufacturer, the Tenth Circuit conceded that "[i]t may appear that to dispute over a matter of days is to split hairs." However, the court said that at a time when

---

6. Guido Calabresi, The Decision for Accidents: An Approach to Non-fault Allocation of Costs, 78 Harv. L. Rev. 713 (1965).

7. Aaron Wildavsky, Searching for Safety 209 (1988).

8. Marshall Shapo, Changing Frontiers in Torts: Vistas for the 70's, 22 Stan. L. Rev. 330, 340 (1970).

"[k]nowledge about the causes and transmission of AIDS" was growing "rapidly," "those few days are crucial to a finding of negligence."[9] It is manifest in such decisions that in cases where the plaintiff must confront two deadly risks—in this situation the Scylla of AIDS and the Charybdis of hemophilia—safety is very much a relative thing.

Where the Tenth Circuit in the AIDS-transfusion case dealt with negligence theory, a federal district court made the point explicit under Louisiana's version of strict liability, in a case involving injuries attributed to an anti-convulsant drug. The court noted that the effects of the product on "some individuals can be devastating, indeed fatal, especially where interaction with other prescription drugs is a factor." Yet in a situation where "[t]he quantitative risk evidence [was] very scant," and there were "very clear, frank and comprehensive" warnings "about the dangers of the drug," the court refused to find "that this highly utile medicine is unreasonably dangerous per se."[10]

We could multiply examples of this judicial recognition of the relativity of safety. The point is that courts decide products cases with a constant awareness of the statistical nature of accidents associated with risky activities, and an understanding that they must balance statistical risks with the benefits that products confer. This may seem simply an instance of economic reasoning, to be chalked up under headings like "risk-benefit analysis" or "risk-utility calculations." However, an observation that we previously made about consumers and prices has its analogue here.

Courts are society's moral agents, pro tem. When they are asked to determine whether conduct is "negligent"—according to the traditional definition, unreasonable in the circumstances—or whether a product is "unreasonably dangerous," they necessarily are making a moral judgment. How should people act? How safe should products be? Courts answering these questions speak—interstitially to be sure—from the pulpit.

Products the public "needs."   We may further highlight the tension between moral judgment and economic analysis by reference to a comment to section 402A of the Second Restatement of Torts, source of the most influential definition of strict liability for products. Comment c to that section justifies strict liability, in part, on the basis "that the public has the right to and does expect, in the cases of products for which it needs and for which it is forced to rely upon the seller, that reputable sellers will stand behind their goods."[11] There are many reasons to argue that consumers "have the right to do expect . . . that reputable sellers will stand behind their goods."

---

9. Jones v. Miles Laboratories, Inc., 887 F.2d 1576 (11th Cir. 1989).
10. Williams v. CIBA-Geigy Corp., 686 F. Supp. 573, 577 (W.D. La. 1988).
11. Restatement (Second) of Torts § 402A, comment c (1965).

But many economists would be scandalized by the notion that one of those reasons is that the public "needs" products, and the consumers are, *as a consequence,* "forced to rely upon the seller."

Perhaps consumers of sophisticated products do rely on sellers for safety. But that is not because they "need" those products. It may well be because the seller has generated a belief in the safety level of its product. That is one of the central arguments of this book. However, it is interesting that comment c reached for the idea that there are products that the public "needs" and for which consumers therefore must rely on sellers. The principal drafter of section 402A, Professor William Prosser, was a hard-headed lawyer, whose treatise on tort liability has been a standard reference work for two generations of law students, lawyers, and judges. This language, presumptively coming from the pen of so unsentimental a commentator, is symbolic of the strong strain of moral authority—vigorously independent of theories about the level of accidents that market transactions would dictate—that runs through our tort law.

An Attempted Reconciliation of Moral and Economic Factors: The Pivotal Element of Access to Information

Further examination of the tension between economic analysis and moral judgment leads us to a factor that may provide some reconciliation. The key lies in relative access to information. From the early years of the modern development of products liability law, judges have referred to this factor. For example, in a concurring opinion to an Arizona appellate decision in 1970, Judge Jacobson placed first on his list of "public policy considerations" supporting strict liability the notion that "[t]he manufacturer can anticipate some hazards and guard against their recurrence, which the consumer cannot do."[12] Judge Jacobson attributed that rationale to comment c of Restatement section 402A, which we have just quoted,[13] but if that idea appears in the comment, it is there only by implication. What is interesting is the idea itself, and the primacy of it in Judge Jacobson's own ranking system.

Allied to this, in the same judge's catalog of reasons for strict liability, is the proposition "[t]hat the consumer does not have the ability to investigate

---

12. Lechuga, Inc. v. Montgomery, 12 Ariz. App. 32, 37, 467 P.2d 256, 261 (1970) (Jacobson, J., concurring).

13. *See supra,* text accompanying note 11.

for himself the soundness of the product."[14] Taken together, these declarations add up to the view that there are data about products that are beyond the reach of most consumers, but are potentially, and often actually, available to sellers. This data includes knowledge of design and manufacturing processes, statistics on test performance, and information about performance on the market. This difference in relative access to information is a major foundation stone for a form of liability that tilts toward consumers.

Halcyon days. A parallel point relates to an historical image, one with almost mythic qualities but also one with substance. In this tale, once upon a time, things were simple: products were uncomplicated and so was the chain of distribution. The New Hampshire court drew on this chapter in the legal storybook in a case in which an automobile's lights failed, causing injuries to the driver and damaging his car. The court posited that the rule requiring that a consumer prove seller or manufacturer negligence "evolved when products were simple and the manufacturer and seller generally [were] the same person." This had implications not only for the consumer's ability to judge a product but also for the opportunity to prove his or her case in litigation: "Knowledge of the then purchaser, if not as complete as the seller's, was sufficient to enable him to not only locate the defect but to determine whether negligence caused the defect and if so whose."[15]

One example of the contrast between those fabled halcyon days and our own is the problem of the invisible defect. The California Supreme Court focused on that problem in a decision in which it flung out one of the farthest salients of strict liability. The plaintiff, a route salesman for a bakery, suffered injuries when the impact of a collision broke an aluminum safety hasp that held bread trays in place behind the driver's seat. When the hasp failed, the loaded trays "struck the plaintiff in the back and hurled him through the windshield." An expert for the plaintiff testified that the hasp "was 'extremely porous and extremely defective,' " being filled with "holes, voids and cracks." Although the defendant argued that "the hasp was not intended to be used without inspection and repair," the court emphasized that the defects were "not visible to the naked eye."[16]

The able consumer. We should note, by comparison, that courts are not likely to be as sympathetic to a consumer that possesses its own corps of experts. Thus, in one case, Scandinavian Airlines could not recover against

---

14. Lechuga, *supra* note 12, 12 Ariz. App. at 38, 467 P.2d at 262, (Jacobson, J., concurring), citing Santor v. A & M Karagheusian, Inc., 44 N.J. 52, 207 A.2d 305 (1965).

15. Buttrick v. Arthur Lessard & Sons, 110 N.H. 36, 39, 260 A.2d 111, 113 (1969).

16. Cronin v. J.B.E. Olson Corp., 8 Cal. 3d 121, 127, 501 P.2d 1153, 1157, 104 Cal. Rptr. 433, 437 (1972).

the United Aircraft Corporation for a defect in an engine that was alleged to have damaged the engine itself and the plane as well. In affirming a trial judge's decision that United could not employ the doctrine of strict liability, the Ninth Circuit said that the airline "had the expertise and personnel to inspect the engines for defects," as contrasted with the "lack of technical knowledge and expertise which would burden members of the general public in designing or manufacturing... engines."[17]

The ignorance is mutual.   To be sure, sometimes the ignorance is mutual. As the New Hampshire court pointed out in the case of the auto headlamps, "[h]ow the defect in manufacture occurred is generally beyond the knowledge of either the injured person or the marketer or manufacturer."[18] In that situation, what is the morality of strict liability, let alone the economic justification for imposing liability without negligence? In part, the case for strict liability lies in the inability of the consumer to prove his or her claim. But the courts also seem to be responding to other factors, especially in the case of relatively sophisticated products. One such consideration is the ability of product makers, at every step in the process of manufacture and distribution, to gather information about risk and to make adjustments that will reduce risk. A related element of decision lies in the notion of "technology forcing": the premise that manufacturers, under the pressure of liability rules, will come up with new and safer ways to do things.

Perhaps neither of these ideas, especially the idea of technology forcing, fits comfortably within traditional conceptions of negligence. But they do not necessarily conflict with a negligence-centered view of products liability. The doctrine of strict liability compensates for the frequent inability of consumers to dig into the complex mix of motive and self-justification that lies behind both the design of products and the choice of quality control levels. Many cases in which courts apply strict liability may involve negligence of an unprovable variety. The law thus struggles to mold doctrine to reality, trying to focus on policy concerns and not theoretical labels.

Unknowable risks.   There remains the problem of the truly unknowable risk. First, we should note that what is probably the biggest controversy over the imposition of liability for an unknowable risk is essentially a tempest in a teapot. The principal subject of the tempest was the asbestos case of *Beshada v. Johns-Manville Products Corp.*,[19] in which the New Jersey Su-

---

17. Scandinavian Airlines System v. United Aircraft Corp., 601 F.2d 425, 429 (9th Cir. 1979).
18. Buttrick, *supra* note 15, 110 N.H. at 39, 260 A.2d at 113.
19. 90 N.J. 191, 447 A.2d 539 (1982).

preme Court declared it appropriate to impose strict liability "for failure to warn of dangers which were undiscoverable at the time of manufacture."[20]

The *Beshada* court was fully cognizant of the argument that it was "unreasonable to impose a duty . . . to warn of the unknowable,"[21] but its answer was a pure strict liability answer. "Failure to warn of a risk which one could not have known existed," the court conceded, "is not unreasonable conduct." But that formulation, the court said, was "based on negligence principles." The court stressed that it was "not saying what defendants should have done. That is negligence." Rather, it was saying only "that defendants' products were not reasonably safe because they did not have a warning."[22] It might seem a contradiction in terms to establish a duty based on failure to warn of something about which one could not have known, or warned. But the point was that, regardless of the defendant's fault, "users of the product were unaware of its hazards and could not protect themselves from injury."[23]

The starkness of the rule announced by the *Beshada* court produced shock waves. But at least in the environment that generated the case, the crucible of asbestos litigation, observers need not have been shocked. The frequent imposition of liability based on fault for asbestos-caused illness, including decisions that impose punitive damages for exceptionally culpable conduct,[24] indicates that *Beshada's* seemingly pure version of non-fault liability was rooted in a factual foundation that generally included plenty of fault.

This is not to deny that there is a strain of strict liability that may entail liability for conduct that is in fact faultless. In chapter three we discussed a landmark decision of this sort, the transfusion hepatitis case of *Cunningham v. MacNeal Memorial Hospital*,[25] in which the Illinois Supreme Court declared that the defendant's inability to discover the virus in blood was "of absolutely no moment."[26] The fact that the Illinois legislature overruled *Cunningham*, and the probability that strict liability for products often attaches to conduct that was actually negligent, does not blur the reality that when challenged by particular cases, courts are sometimes willing to impose a truly strict form of liability.

20. *Id.* at 205, 447 A.2d at 547.
21. *Id.* at 204, 447 A.2d at 546.
22. *Id.* at 209, 447 A.2d at 549.
23. *Id.*
24. *See, e.g.*, Simpson v. Pittsburgh Corning Corp., 901 F.2d 277 (2d Cir. 1990).
25. 47 Ill.2d 443, 266 N.E.2d 897 (1970), *see supra*, chapter 3, text accompanying note 15.
26. *Id.* at 455, 266 N.E.2d at 903.

A principal conceptual foundation for this willingness lies in the notion that "[s]trict tort liability shifts the focus from the conduct of the manufacturer to the nature of the product."[27] Reinforcing that language from a Colorado appellate decision is the declaration by the North Dakota Supreme Court that under strict liability, "the reasonableness of the defendant's conduct is not at issue."[28]

Even those conceptual premises, however, do not imply an absolutist view of safety. Plaintiffs still must prove a product "unreasonably dangerous." Moreover, the purest of the strict liability decisions respond to imbalances in the market for information—access to information after an injury as well as before it. Additionally, even "technology-forcing" strict liability may have some negligence flavor, conveying a hint that the defendant could—efficiently—have done better.

All that being said, we must stress that moral choices lie behind liability judgments. We already have identified a set of judicial choices of this sort, embodying a sense that there are some risks, perhaps even some market-supported risks, to which consumers should not be subject. At least two other "shoulds" color the legal background. We turn, briefly, to profit as a basis for liability and then to the ethic of "spreading."

Profit

One foundation on which courts could base liability is that of profit alone: a firm should have to compensate just because it made money from a product that caused injury. If we put aside all the background factors we have identified, such as the nature of product portrayals and the deliberate character of manufacturers' design choices, this becomes a difficult case to make. A firm makes money from selling a product that fortuitously hurts a consumer, who bought the product at the market price for its perceived value to her. If we have no reason to believe that imposing liability on the firm would push it to make safer products, what is the economic rationale for imposing liability? And if the accident was truly fortuitous, what is the moral basis for requiring compensation? If an employee of the same firm unavoidably injures someone while driving the company truck, most people would think it wrong to say that the firm must pay simply because its employee drove.

Of course, one might argue that such focusing of liability has administrative advantages. It would tend to produce more certainty in business

---

27. Hamilton v. Hardy, 37 Colo. App. 375, 383, 549 P.2d 1099, 1106 (1976).
28. Mauch v. Manufacturers Sales & Serv., Inc., 345 N.W.2d 338, 346 (N.D. 1984).

budgeting and insurance arrangements. However, that sort of rule might influence behavior in undesirable ways. For example, one might argue that if consumers believed that they would be compensated for any injury that occurred during their use of a product, they might elect to take more chances than they would under a more restrictive set of liability rules. Scholars chalk up this idea under such labels as "moral hazard." The notion that the prospect of compensation will significantly cause people to increase physical risk to themselves may seem preposterous to ordinary people, but the economic intuition is one that deserves consideration when we assess the case for liability based on profit alone.

Spreading

There is another concept that provides a justification for liability without fault in the absence of other background factors, although in real life it is impossible truly to eliminate those other factors. This concept, the subject of fierce dispute, is that of "loss spreading." The basic idea is simple. A firm hopes to sell a product to one million consumers for one hundred dollars apiece. The product, through no fault of anyone, predictably will cause disabling injuries to one person in that million, who would suffer a million dollars in losses. If we could prospectively "spread" that cost around to all consumers who would benefit from the product without injury, each would pay just about one dollar extra. This would ensure compensation for the one injury victim, and all the other 999,999 consumers would reap their product satisfaction at the added cost of one dollar.

This rationale has more moral force than one based only on profit; it involves in the calculation the large body of persons who benefited from the product. The New Jersey Supreme Court in its *Beshada* decision defined one normative feature of the case for spreading in its declaration that "as between ... innocent victims and ... distributors, it is the distributors— and the public which consumes their products—which should bear the unforeseen costs of the product."[29]

The contention that producers can serve as loss spreaders for individual misfortunes caused by their products has particular intuitive appeal when a seller is a large firm. It is less persuasive with respect to small enterprises. Taking up this point in a decision as long ago as 1971, the New Mexico court of appeals noted that only eleven of 400 manufacturers in Albuquerque employed 250 persons or more, and thus properly questioned the as-

---

29. Beshada v. Johns-Manville Prods. Corp., 90 N.J. 191, 209, 447 A.2d 539, 549 (1982).

sertion that product injuries were "increasingly attributable to large-scale enterprise."[30]

There are other arguments that oppose the spreading rationale. One of these inheres in the idea that redistribution of wealth is a job for social legislation, not judicial decisions in personal injury cases. In that connection, we observe that tort law must always be sensitive to the trap of Robin Hood-ism: requiring one person to compensate another just because the first person is richer.

An analogous argument is that judicial reliance on spreading "represents an unprincipled use of the judicial process to achieve a no-fault insurance system for products."[31] This seems an overstatement, since there is a universal requirement that plaintiffs in products cases must prove defect and causation, and since every defendant may offer defenses based on the unreasonable behavior of plaintiffs.[32]

The real question about the propriety of a spreading rationale is whether it contributes to a fair allocation among consumers of the social costs of useful products, especially in situations in which the producer is as morally innocent as the injured person. This is a close question, but given the way that producers generate product portrayals, and given the benefits that most products provide to the many who use them without injury, there is a strong case for spreading the losses of the few. As controversial as it is, the spreading rationale may help to resolve the tension between moral judgment and economic precepts. It may serve as an arbiter between our instincts about what is fair among consumers and our commitment to a system of market prices. In building into prices the costs that products inflict on society, it advances fairness among the members of the community by proportioning the burden of injury to their use of society's goods.

---

30. Stang v. Hertz Corp., 83 N.M. 217, 221, 490 P.2d 475, 479 (Ct. App. 1971).
31. *See* 1 M. Shapo, The Law of Products Liability, ¶ 7.05[7][c][ii], at 7-29 (1990).
32. *See id.*, at 7-30.

7

Theories of Liability

Recently I heard a distinguished philosopher declare, "I hate doctrine." At some level of discussion, anyone trained in law would agree with that statement. Doctrines can imprison our thoughts if we let them do so. A major task of lawyers, indeed, is to cut below the mask that doctrine provides and to get at "reality." But in doing that, we always must be mindful of two things.

First, doctrines emerged from "reality." They did not spring up by themselves. They emerged as a shorthand classification scheme to facilitate lawyers' reactions to a variety of situations.

The second point grows naturally from the first: properly used, doctrine is a tool, a conceptual tool. It provides a concise, although admittedly sometimes cryptic, way to slice through complex fact situations and competing intuitions about what our legal reaction should be to those situations. It is thus unproductive to be dismissive of doctrine. What we must do is to use it as a tool, to make sure that we control it and that it does not rule us.

In earlier chapters, we built up a base of history and policy—the "reality" underlying suits about product-caused injuries. Let us now examine some major categories of liability theory to see how they reflect reality.

Inaccurate Representations

I will classify the first set of theories under a new kind of terminology, that of "inaccurate representations." I have selected this term deliberately instead of, for example, the label "misrepresentations." The reason is that the latter term can carry misleading connotations about some statements to which the law has applied it.

Fraud. To be sure, the common connotations of the word "misrepresentation" extend to situations in which a seller deliberately misstates the qualities of its product. We call that "fraud," or "deceit," and courts have applied those terms not only to the most conscious kinds of misstatements, but also to assertions by those who are reckless as to the truth or falsity of what they say. Lord Herschell enunciated that test for fraud in the 1889 English decision in *Derry v. Peek.*[1] That case arose from what today we would call allegations of securities fraud, centering on statements in a prospectus for the sale of stock. The plaintiff alleged that the defendant had misrepresented a company's legal right to use steam or mechanical power, instead of horses, for operating a tramway. In his opinion, Lord Herschell extended the definition of fraud beyond false statements made knowingly or "without belief" in their truth to include the recklessness standard.

Negligent misrepresentation. Decisions over the years have fought out the essentially factual question of whether a defendant has behaved culpably enough to satisfy the test of *Derry v. Peek.* Courts also have imposed, relatively infrequently, liability for conduct they call "negligent misrepresentation."[2] We should note that although there are not many cases directly under this label, there are battalions of decisions under negligence theory that implicitly condemn what is, after all, culpable behavior in the presentation of the product to the market.

The law of fraud corresponds very directly with reality. Fraud rules provide a remedy for conduct that is, by conventional standards, quite culpable and even immoral. It also makes real life sense to provide relief for those who show injury from careless representations; this is in line with the more general idea, embodied in both law and ethics, that victims of negligence deserve compensation.

Faultless misstatements: Express warranty. Seemingly more difficult are the questions of whether and when one should have to compensate for misstatements that are not in any conventional sense culpable, and what the theory of recovery for such statements should be. The fact is that the law has given recovery for faultless misstatements for a long time, under the roof of commercial law doctrine. The principal theory has been "express warranty." Under that doctrine, the buyer need show only that the seller made an "affirmation of fact or promise . . . which relates to the goods and becomes part of the bargain."[3] Not only is this a non-fault type of liability,

---

1. 14 App. Cas. 337 (H.L. 1889).
2. *See* 1 M. Shapo, The Law of Products Liability, ¶ 2.03 (1990).
3. UCC § 2-313(1)(a) (1978).

but the law seems to be turning to the view that the plaintiff need not show reliance on the warranty in a particular transaction.[4]

The practical meaning of this doctrine is that whenever a buyer can show that a seller's factual assertion about a product has turned out not to be true, the buyer may at least get his or her money back. Commercial ethics, as well as good business, seems to require no less.

Faultless misstatements: A tort theory.   An offshoot of the first quarter century of products liability development has been a small group of decisions that use a tort theory to impose a non-fault liability for misstatements. As a matter of stated doctrine, this is a theoretical extension.

To hold merchants to their bargains under the label of contract or commercial law sounds business-like enough. By contrast, the imposition of a non-fault liability in tort has overtones not simply of contracts broken but of injuries inflicted. Yet some courts have done precisely that in accepting the theory retailed in section 402B of the Second Restatement of Torts. That section imposes liability for "physical harm . . . caused by justifiable reliance upon [a] misrepresentation" without regard to fault—either fraud or negligence.[5] A few decisions, centered mostly in the Tennessee courts, even extended that brand of liability to pecuniary loss, an idea that was proposed for inclusion in the Restatement but did not appear in the final version.[6] However, the Tennessee Supreme Court recently recanted its decision imposing this sort of liability.[7]

An important feature of section 402B, yoked with its theory of liability for misrepresentations without fault, is its explicit declaration that the plaintiff does not have to show that he or she "bought the chattel from or entered into any contractual relation with the seller." We should note that even under the doctrine of express warranty, which tends to invoke images of face-to-face transactions and direct sales, this is not a novel idea. As far back as 1958, the Ohio Supreme Court applied an express warranty to a consumer's products claim against a manufacturer. The plaintiff in this case asserted that a "Very Gentle" Toni Home Permanent set had been anything but gentle, causing her hair to "[fall] off to [w]ithin one-half inch of her scalp."

---

4. *See, e.g.*, 1 M. Shapo, The Law of Products Liability ¶ 3.09 (1990).

5. Restatement (Second) of Torts § 402B (1965).

6. *See, e.g.*, Ford Motor Co. v. Lonon, 217 Tenn. 400, 415, 398 S.W.2d 240, 246-247 (1966), referring to tentative draft of proposed section 552D in Restatement (Second) of Torts, Council Draft No. 17 at 76 (1963).

7. *See* First Nat'l Bank of Louisville v. Brooks Farms, 821 S.W.2d 925, 931 (Tenn. 1991).

Opposing the then "prevailing view . . . that privity of contract is essential in an action based on a breach of an express or implied warranty," the Ohio court emphasized how manufacturers "make extensive use of newspapers, periodicals, signboards, radio and television to advertise their products."[8] The court declared that "[t]he warranties made by the manufacturer in his advertisements and by the labels on his products are inducements to the ultimate consumers," and concluded that manufacturers should "be held to strict accountability to any consumer who buys the product in reliance on such representations."[9]

A path toward justice.   The sum of the combination of express warranty law in the Ohio home permanent case and tort liability in section 402B is this: a seller who makes a statement in advertising, or otherwise, is liable for injuries attributable to that statement if it turns out to be untrue in fact, even if it is made without fault.

It may well be that this integrated rule accords with the normal expectations of sellers who advertise. At least at the retail level, the express warranty doctrine corresponds with that behavioral premise. But the emergence of a tort theory indicates that this rule also accords with a broader sense of justice. It is particularly interesting, in this connection, that the law has moved toward a relatively minimalist set of requirements with respect to buyer reliance as well as seller intent.

In evaluating the basis in reality of this rule, we might judge it as economically efficient. We could, for example, see it as optimizing the costs of searching for information about products. We might even view the law as a handservant of economic optimality by virtue of its promotion of trust in the consumer market.

Yet there appears another idea, rooted in the reality of common ethical precepts, through which the law exerts its moral authority all across the area of misstatements about products. Especially in situations where there may not be much repeat business in a short period, and in markets where it may take a long time for adverse product information to permeate to most consumers, the law of inaccurate representations—including all kinds of misstatements, not just deceitful ones—finds its foundation in a social sense of ethical conduct and fair dealing. Page Keeton captured the moral core of this concept more than a half century ago in an article on nondisclosure, in which he said that "it would seem that the object of the law . . . should be to impose on parties to the transaction a duty to speak whenever justice, equity and fair dealing demand it."[10]

---

8. Rogers v. Toni Home Permanent Co., 167 Ohio St. 244, 248, 147 N.E.2d 612, 615 (1958).

9. *Id.* at 249, 147 N.E.2d at 615-616.

10. P. Keeton, Fraud: Misrepresentations of Opinion, 21 Minn. L. Rev. 643, 669 (1937).

Negligence

The concept of negligence occupies the broadest zone of tort law. The most cited theory of recovery in personal injury complaints, it represents a substantial wedge of our views about proper conduct, literally as a matter of law but surely also as a matter of what is right.

Doctrine. The basic idea of negligence law is that one should have to pay for injuries that he or she causes when acting below the standard of care of a reasonable, prudent person participating in the activity in question. This standard of conduct for actors relates to a belief that centers on potential victims: that people have a right to be protected from unreasonable risks of harm.[11] A fundamental aspect of the negligence standard of care resides in the concept of foreseeability. In one of the most famous of torts opinions, in what today would be called a products liability case, Judge Brett wrote that there is a duty "to use ordinary skill and care to avoid . . . danger" when "one person is by circumstances placed in such a position with regard to another . . . that every one of ordinary sense who did think would at once recognize" the risk of danger "if he did not use ordinary care and skill."[12] It is interesting that in this nineteenth-century opinion, long before the coinage of the term "products liability," this formulation emerged from a case dealing with a ship painter's allegation that the failure of a rope on a scaffold caused him to fall.

Rationalizations: Economic analysis. Since negligence law must deal with most of the range of risky human conduct, it is not surprising that it evokes a wide spectrum of rationalizations. One substantial body of academic opinion focuses on the question of whether negligence law produces efficient outcomes, and indeed some scholars are convinced that it does.[13] These commentators are drawn to the notion of a legal system that responds, at levels often undefined by its arbiters, to a standard that theoretically will produce for consumers exactly the package of risks and benefits that they truly desire. Economic analysis forces legal scholars to think about a set of factors that both sellers and buyers must take into account, at various strata of consciousness, throughout the processes of making marketing, buying, and using products. Those considerations principally boil down to costs and benefits, with the category of costs further subdividing into the cost of injuries and the expense of injury avoidance.

---

11. *See, e.g.,* the definition in Restatement (Second) of Torts § 282 (1965).
12. Heaven v. Pender, [1883], 11 Q.B.D. 503, 509.
13. *See, e.g.,* Posner, A Theory of Negligence, 1 J. Legal Studies 29 (1973).

Regulation as the standard.   Yet the world as it is impinges on the models of those disposed to tease questions of what constitutes negligence into a purely economic framework. For that structure will not account for a substantial, and increasing, wedge of decisions. In an increasingly statutory society, one would have to consider the many cases in which the applicable standard of care appears in a government regulation. In that regard, we must note that although sometimes regulators seek to capture efficient solutions, governmental safety rules frequently reflect a social choice that emphasizes moral concerns at the expense of economic optimality.[14]

The morality of judges and juries.   Beyond the moral component of regulation, and apparent in regiments of decisions of both new and old, is the fact that neither judges nor jurors check their moral training at the door of the courthouse. This is surely a principal piece of intellectual baggage that jurors bring to their deliberations, and indeed many rules of law that judges enforce on juries effectively rein in the tendency of jurors to engage in moralizing.

But, quite as importantly, judges bring their own sets of moral "oughts" to decision making. It is here that we confront the breadth of mind of Learned Hand. We have noted that that great judge presented tort lawyers with two famous pronouncements of seemingly very different stripe. In one, he formulated a negligence test based solely on cost considerations. In the other, he opposed the use of industry custom as a defense, declaring that since an entire industry "may have unduly lagged," it is ultimately for courts to "say what is required."[15]

It might be contended that there is no necessary contradiction between the two declarations—that "what is required" is what is cost-justified. But the tone of Judge Hand's insistence that courts must say what is required weighs against that argument. It implies a measuring of many competing considerations, including notions of what is morally proper in the circumstances. We often must speculate about the motivations of judges as they thread their way through cases that present the question of what negligence is. But one reasonable hypothesis is that they ask themselves how they would wish to be treated in the same situation, not knowing in advance on which side of a controversy they would find themselves. This is a variation on John Rawls's definition of the principles of justice.[16] More anciently, it resonates with the essential idea of the Golden Rule.

---

14. Dean Calabresi captured this point in his discussion of what he calls "specific deterrence" in The Costs of Accidents (1970), *e.g.* at 100-102.

15. *See supra*, chapter 6, text accompanying notes 4-5, summarizing United States v. Carroll Towing Co., 159 F.2d 169, 173 (2d Cir. 1947), and The T.J. Hooper, 60 F.2d 737 (2d Cir.), cert. denied, 287 U.S. 662 (1932).

16. *See* J. Rawls, A Theory of Justice (1971), e.g., at 136-142, 255-257, on the "veil of ignorance" and the "original position."

A case of AIDS contamination of a blood product provides a poignant example. An expert testified for the plaintiff that the defendant should have employed a heat-treating method to test for viruses. But since this testimony was "entirely in opposition to . . . the standard of care as established by the conduct of the pharmaceutical community" at the time the plaintiff became infected, the court would not permit him to establish a standard of care by "hindsight."[17]

One might view this as simply a latter day rehearsal of the industry custom defense. The explanation, however, seems at once simpler and deeper. It involves a weighing of competing expectations within each of us about how we would expect to be treated in the same circumstances. One part of our minds, drawing on the ideas of product portrayal set out previously in this book, would react that someone in the position of the plaintiff would feel betrayed by the infusion of the protein of a fatal illness. Another part of us, however, would respond to the fact that an industry that was actively struggling with a unique problem, newly spotlighted, had not yet chosen a solution. Thus, the deeper explanation is that the question is one of notice, and that notice in such a case equals fairness. Different judges might cast the balance differently on which party was primarily entitled to notice: the plaintiff of the peril of illness, if it were known or knowable, or the defendant of the risk of liability when it believed it was doing the best that anyone could do.

What is important for the legal process is not the result in this tragic, close case. It is how negligence law works to provide a way that judges, and sometimes juries, may translate basic principles of jurisprudence into a legal standard for injury cases. The operational definition of reasonable care in particular cases answers the question of how people might fairly expect to be treated.

Strict Liability

The idea that one should not be held under a standard to which one could not previously refer provides a bridge to our discussion of the now well established, but still controversial, theory of strict liability. It is useful to give a thumbnail sketch of the history and rationales of that theory.

Some history.   A narrative of modern products liability law, written as history alone, would consume more than a thick volume. For our purposes, it is appropriate to rehearse in very capsulized form some events of the pe-

---

17. McKee v. Miles Laboratories, Inc., 675 F. Supp. 1060, 1064 (E.D. Ky. 1987).

riod beginning in 1958. In that year the Ohio Supreme Court applied the doctrine of express warranty, well established for face to face transactions, to a national advertiser in a suit for a product injury.[18] That decision's breach in the "privity" rule, which had required consumer plaintiffs to show a contractual relation with the selling defendant, was an especially important ingredient in the background of a series of judicial decisions and proposed rules in the early 1960s.

The judicial pronouncements—including decisions by the highest courts of New Jersey, California, and New York—employed different formulations of a strict liability rule, under the terminology of both tort and commercial law.[19] But the most widely accepted rule that emerged from this seminal period was that embodied in section 402A of the Second Restatement of Torts.[20] This provision, adopted by the American Law Institute, imposed liability on sellers of "any product in a defective condition unreasonably dangerous to the user or consumer or to his property" even when they had "exercised all possible care in the preparation and sale of [the] product," and even though there was no direct purchase or contractual relation between the parties.[21]

Rationales.   Courts and commentators have presented diverse reasons for favoring strict liability as a basis for deciding products cases. In 1965, in a case involving the failure of brakes on a tractor unit that collided with a bus, the Illinois Supreme Court invoked a collection of rationales that included "public interest in human life and health, the invitations and solicitations to purchase the product and the justice of imposing the loss on the one creating the risk and reaping the profit."[22] In a notable article published in the same year, Professor Thomas Cowan referred to the terminology of quality control that describes as "consumer's risk" the chance that a test procedure will lead to bad results, and said that the imposition of liability in those circumstances amounted to "compensation for a loss resulting from a deliberately assigned risk."[23]

---

18. *See supra*, text accompanying notes 8-9.

19. For a fairly detailed description of this development, see Shapo, A Representational Theory of Consumer Protection: Doctrine, Function and Liability for Product Disappointment, 60 Va. L. Rev. 1109, 1128-1150 (1974). A contrasting interpretation appears in Priest, The Invention of Enterprise Liability: A Critical History of the Intellectual Foundations of Modern Tort Law, 14 J. Legal Studies 461 (1985).

20. Restatement (Second) of Torts § 402A (1965).

21. *Id.*

22. Suvada v. White Motor Co., 32 Ill.2d 612, 619, 210 N.E.2d 182, 186 (1965).

23. Cowan, Some Policy Bases of Products Liability, 17 Stan. L. Rev. 1077, 1091-1092 (1965).

We already have adverted to the controversy about the legitimacy of spreading as a basis for products liability.[24] We refer specifically to spreading here because, however one feels about the intellectual merit of the idea, it appears to be a significant factor in judicial willingness to impose strict liability. We have noted that critics lament the spreading rationale as facilitating an end-run toward a system of no-fault liability. Whether or not that is a valid concern, it no longer comes as a surprise to defendants that this is an idea that influences courts. There is notice to potential litigants not only about the trend of the law, but the reasons that fuel the trend.

Doctrines compared.   An important practical question concerning the use of doctrine in products cases is how much difference it makes.

In some situations, the choice of theory may significantly influence results. This is especially true, for example, if the plaintiff can show that the defendant engaged in fraudulent misrepresentation. Among other consequences, this may entitle the plaintiff to punitive damages, which might not be available without a showing of fraud or similarly reprehensible conduct.

When we move to the other end of the culpability scale, we encounter an interesting parallel among non-fault theories of liability. We have noted the existence of theories, old and new, that impose a strict form of liability for representations: the commercial law doctrine of express warranty and the newly invented tort theory of non-fault liability for misrepresentation. The tort version of strict liability for product defects lines up doctrinally with these theories. Under both sets of strict liability theories, the question is not whether the defendant behaved with fault. It is only whether its representation turned out to be false in fact—or whether its product turned out, in fact, to be defective. The law thus confronts sellers with a broad facade of liability theories that technically do not require the plaintiff to show fault.

One might well ask, does not this set of theories diverge wildly, and unjustly, from the basic principle that one should be held liable only if one has behaved culpably? One pragmatic answer is that the doctrine of express warranty has imposed a strict form of liability for a long time—and that under the unsentimental banner of commercial law.

Another response is that there is not such a gulf as one might imagine between "negligence" and "strict liability." At the dawn of the invention of strict liability for products, Dean Prosser—the principal drafter of section 402A—opined that it "might very well be that there is not one case in one hundred in which strict liability would result in recovery where negligence does not."[25] Moreover, as Prosser showed, the tort doctrine of strict liabil-

---

24. *See supra*, chapter 6, pp. 103-104.
25. Prosser, The Assault Upon the Citadel (Strict Liability to the Consumer), 69 Yale L.J. 1099, 1114 (1960).

ity could simply be viewed as a frank statement of a trend that already had developed under the commercial law-rooted doctrine of implied warranty of merchantability.[26]

This comparison of doctrines draws forth the point that strict liability allows running room for a plaintiff whose injury has in fact been caused by negligence, but cannot prove it. The theory reduces claimants' need to rely on the proof of negligence doctrine known as res ipsa loquitur, which permits plaintiffs to prove fault circumstantially from nothing more than the happening of an accident. Strict liability does not eliminate the necessity, on many occasions, to prove a products case circumstantially. It does, however, reduce the intellectual turmoil that accompanies the question of whether lay jurors may fairly infer fault from a product failure alone. One should add that this is not to say that the sensible instincts of jurors will often fail on such issues. When a brand-new machine catches fire after only a half day's use, both judges and jurors are likely to agree that it was defective, and that the defect originated with the maker. Courts are as likely to render that kind of judgment under implied warranty labels[27] as under circumstantial theories serving the tort rubric.[28]

Our principal point is that strict liability sometimes does the job that negligence theory cannot do, or cannot do convincingly, although a defendant has, in fact, been negligent. This does not exhaust the possible missions of strict liability. Another explanation is that strict liability is a kind of super-negligence theory, effectively ratcheting up the standard of care for certain activities distinguished by their degree of peril or their public involvement. The general tort law has held that certain enterprises, for example the transmission of electricity and the ownership of common carriers, entail particularly high standards of care.[29] An historical invocation of a strict liability principle that paralleled such especially rigorous fault standards occurred in the decades before 1960, when courts applied a warranty theory of liability to food producers.[30]

Pure strict liability.   If the decisional troops of strict liability frequently appear as support forces for negligence, we must then ask, what are the

---

26. *See id.*, e.g., at 1103-1114.

27. *See* Nerud v. Haybuster Mfg., Inc., 215 Neb. 604, 340 N.W.2d 369 (1983).

28. Cf. Nash v. General Elec. Co., 64 Ohio App. 2d 25, 27-28, 410 N.E.2d 792, 794-795 (1979)(toaster oven; five years of normal use did not negate inference of defect when there was expert testimony that specific defect caused fire, and circumstantial evidence that defect existed "when the product left the hands of" the maker).

29. *See, e.g.*, Prosser & Keeton, Law of Torts 208-209 (5th ed. 1984).

30. *See, e.g.*, discussion of Mazetti v. Armour & Co., chapter 2, text accompanying notes 4-10.

cases of pure strict liability? In the main run of cases, it may be practically impossible to isolate such decisions from those with at least some hidden component of "fault."

Certainly, some of the most controversial applications of strict liability have involved conduct that arguably was quite culpable, and concerning which plaintiffs invoked strict liability for tactical reasons. Some important asbestos litigation falls into that category.[31] Moreover, many applications of strict liability theory to general design defect litigation— another use of the theory that has engendered a lot of argument— rest on judicial analyses that closely parallel negligence law.[32]

We have discussed at least one hard-core strict liability decision, that in the Illinois transfusion hepatitis case,[33] which was itself legislatively abrogated. But apart from a few such decisions, and cases in which the defendant's portrayal of its product has created an aura of warranty—if not specified a warranty—there may not be very many pure strict liability cases. Thus, it would appear that a principal vocation of the doctrine is to bolster claims that are, in substance, claims for negligence, but for which it is difficult to pinpoint the culpable aspect of the defendant's conduct.

Given the definition of fairness we have developed for products litigation, we would have to conclude that, as an abstract doctrine, strict liability is a fair theory. It provides notice of its rather modified strictness. As much as negligence theory, it enables manufacturers to plan for exposure to litigation, from the angles of both risk management and insurance. Moreover, many decisions applying strict liability implicitly communicate to potential defendants the importance of how they project their products' images to the public. Finally, in practice, strict liability has represented a response to injuries that in fact have been caused by elusive acts of negligence.

The most difficult question for decision is not whether to subscribe to the abstract theory of strict liability, as contrasted with technically "fault"-based negligence law. It is whether a product is "defective." For it is the concept of defect, the subject of the next chapter, into which the law packs so many of our hopes and fears about the goods that we buy and the chance that they will cause us harm.

---

31. *See, e.g.,* chapter 6, text accompanying note 24.

32. *See* Birnbaum, Unmasking the Test for Design Defect: From Negligence [to Warranty] to Strict Liability to Negligence, 33 Vand. L. Rev. 593, e.g., at 618-636 (1980).

33. Cunningham v. MacNeal Mem'l Hosp., 47 Ill.2d 443, 266 N.E.2d 897 (1970), discussed *supra,* chapter 3, text accompanying note 15, and chapter 6, text accompanying notes 25-26.

8

The Meanings of Defect

At the heart of products liability law is the requirement that a plaintiff show that a product had a defect. The requirement is central to all versions of strict liability, and something very like it inheres in the law on breach of warranty. It is also crucial, sometimes implicitly, to efforts to prove that a seller has been negligent.

It is frequently the concept of defect, rather than the precise theory of liability, that reflects the beliefs, policy preferences and intuitions that drive decision makers in one direction or another in products cases. This chapter focuses on characteristics that inhere in the physical unit of the product itself. In the next chapter, we analyze issues arising from alleged deficiencies in the printed or symbolic information that accompanies the product—the so-called "warnings" problem.

A Spectrum of Problems

As we shall see, there are many competing definitions of "defect." We begin with a descriptive conclusion: a defect is a dangerous characteristic of a product unit that causes injury in a way that requires a seller to pay for the injury.

As we proceed, it is well to keep in mind a range of different kinds of hazards that inhere in products. Consider four types of cases:

• A cherry pit in an otherwise succulent pie, which breaks a consumer's tooth.

• An automobile, made exactly according to its design, that has insufficient strength to withstand a collision at relatively low speeds.

• Tobacco that is agriculturally up to standard but causes lung cancer.

• A unit of blood that transmits the AIDS virus, which cannot be detected by pretransfusion testing.

The products in these cases differ from one another functionally, and these differences may result in legal distinctions. The cherry pit is a leftover from the "natural" state that is a low probability statistical artifact of cherry pies. The seller of the pie does not want the cherry to have a pit. The auto maker, by contrast, wants the car to be just as it is marketed, and the collision risk is one associated with a use that is not intended for the product—frequently involving the culpable act of a third person—although it is one that is quite expectable statistically. The tobacco, like the car, is exactly what the grower hoped it would be, and it carries a high statistical frequency of illness; by contrast with vehicle injuries, the illness would occur as a result of the usually intended use for tobacco. The hypothetical unit of blood carries a statistically knowable risk, but one that cannot be discovered before consumption. Statistically, this case is rather close to the cherry with the pit; but the seller of the pie could, theoretically, check every cherry to see if it were pitted.

Despite these differences, the products share at least one set of characteristics: they all disappoint consumers to a point that if you asked someone beforehand whether she would buy the product for a particular use or encounter it in a particular way, identifying the sort of injury associated with that use or encounter, she would have serious misgivings. And, human nature being what it is, if you asked the consumer after the injury whether she would buy, use or encounter the product if she had a second chance, she would very likely protest that she would not do so at all.

Of course, law, like life, does not always provide succor for the injured. Specifically in our present area of inquiry, the way that our law defines a defect does not always line up with our prospective misgivings or our hindsight judgments about our consumption decisions. We should observe, in this connection, that one of the benefits the law provides us is a way to get outside ourselves and to judge our cases objectively.

A Range of Relevant Factors

The task of objectifying these judgments is a difficult one. The question of whether a product is "defective" depends on many factors. Some of these are in the main socially derived; some require a focus, with varying degrees of intensity, on the consumer. While defenses based on the consumer's conduct center principally on the particular person—her individual mindset, her ability to make a personal choice—judicial definitions of defect tend to strike an average among consumers. We examine here some factors that frequently attract analytical attention in the effort to define defect.

Acceptable risk.   At one rather abstract level, the decision of whether a product is defective is essentially a social determination of whether a risk is acceptable. The concept of "acceptable risk" increasingly has appeared in legal literature, although we find explicit references to it more in the avowedly policy-oriented discussions associated with public regulation of product hazards[1] than in decisions on single-injury controversies under products liability law.

Yet, if courts do not usually make specific reference to this concept in deciding products cases, it implicitly underlies much of their analysis. A list of factors formulated by Dean John Wade to test the question of whether a product is defective, now much cited, demonstrates how the issue turns on social judgments of the acceptability of risk. Wade's first factor, for example, fixes on "[t]he usefulness and desirability of the product—its utility to the user and to the public as a whole."[2] Two other factors, in Wade's list of seven, refer to "[t]he availability of a substitute product which would meet the same need and not be as unsafe," and "[t]he manufacturer's ability to eliminate the unsafe character of the product without impairing its usefulness or making it too expensive to maintain its utility."[3]

One thing that may strike the reader about these factors is that they concern matters that in a perfectly free marketplace should be left to the consumer. Isn't it up to each member of the public to decide about "[t]he usefulness and desirability of the product"? Shouldn't it be the consumer, and not a judge, who does the weighing implicit in the question of whether there is a substitute product that meets "the same need"? If the product is not oversold, why should the "manufacturer's ability to eliminate" its "unsafe character" be a factor in determining whether it is defective?

The answer is that it is society, principally through its courts, that makes the decision of whether a product is defective. And that judgment is one that usually embodies a determination of whether a risk is *socially* acceptable. That is why, for example, courts tend to be kinder to medical products than to other goods. That is why they occasionally sound like avenging angels with respect to other kinds of products. Consider, for example, the language of a federal decision on a child's claim for disfiguring injuries caused by a drain cleaner. The court declared that the product had been "proven defective in that it was negligently designed to include an unreasonably caustic chemical in unnecessarily high concentration so as to render it inherently and unreasonably dangerous for its intended use."[4]

---

1. For two studies focusing on the concept, *see* William Lowrance, Of Acceptable Risk (1976); Pascal J. Imperato and Greg Mitchell, Acceptable Risks (1985).

2. Wade, On The Nature of Strict Tort Liability for Products, 44 Miss. L.J. 825, 837 (1973).

3. *Id.*

4. Drayton v. Jiffee Chem. Corp., 395 F. Supp. 1081, 1084 (N.D. Ohio 1975), *modified*, 591 F.2d 352 (6th Cir. 1978).

This language is particularly interesting because of the way it commingles the terminology of negligence with the locutions of strict liability. Restatement section 402A employs the phrase "unreasonably dangerous" as a modifier for the term "defective condition." Although the most widely accepted conception of strict liability emphasizes that that theory focuses on the product, rather than the conduct of the seller, this court did not make such a fine distinction.

How can we account for the court's technically unorthodox combination of the language of two different doctrines? Confronted with a little girl who had been terribly scarred by a common household product, it made a social judgment about what society would, and should, tolerate. How does one determine what is an "unnecessarily high concentration" of an "unreasonably caustic chemical?" Those are judgments that the court makes, in a specific factual context, on behalf of society. And, inescapably, they are in significant part moral judgments.

Consumer expectations.   We discussed in previous chapters some behavioral aspects of the formation of consumer expectations, centering specifically on the commonness of product dangers as a factor in products liability judgments.[5] Here, we will employ the case of cigarettes to illustrate the variety of issues associated with a focus on expectations.

Especially until recently, the record of cigarette plaintiffs in court has been almost uniformly unsuccessful. An extraordinary early case involved the suit of Edwin Green, who sued the American Tobacco Company for lung cancer that he attributed to smoking Lucky Strike cigarettes. This prolonged litigation could be the subject of a book by itself. Here, we fix on a couple of key arguments in the case, which after many years of legal infighting concluded in the defendant's favor.

The manufacturer won an initial skirmish in 1962, convincing a jury that the company could not reasonably have known of the danger of lung cancer and persuading a majority of a Fifth Circuit panel that there was no implied warranty based on justifiable reliance on the seller's skill and judgment.[6] In dissenting against this holding, Judge Cameron viewed the applicable Florida law as saying that, in effect, Green had entered a contract with the company that "cover[ed] every package of cigarettes purchased by him." This hypothesized agreement, he thought, guaranteed that the defendant's cigarettes were "fit to be used by [the] purchaser," that they did "not contain any harmful or deleterious substance," and that the company would "in-

---

5. See *supra*, chapter 5, text accompanying notes 60-64. See also chapter 4, text accompanying notes 27-30.

6. Green v. American Tobacco Co., 304 F.2d 70 (5th Cir. 1962).

demnify the user against any injury, loss or damage which may result from the smoking of said cigarette."[7]

Judge Cameron's characterization of the problem was influential to another Fifth Circuit panel that held, six years later, that Mr. Green "was entitled to rely on the implied assurance that the Lucky Strike cigarettes were wholesome and fit for the purpose intended."[8] But the defendant then won a rehearing before the full court of appeals, which reversed its panel and held for the company. The *en banc* court relied on a dissenting opinion to the panel decision, in which Judge Simpson had insisted that the product was "in no way defective." The defendant's cigarettes, he said, "are exactly like all others of the particular brand and virtually the same as all other brands on the market."[9]

This view drew a stern, but ultimately futile, dissent from Judge Coleman, who had been the author of the panel decision favoring Green that the full court reversed. On a technical level, Judge Coleman argued that the court should leave the question to a determination by the Florida Supreme Court on that state's law. But his opinion also rang with moral indignation. The effect of the majority's holding, he wrote, was to leave to juries "the law on the sale of cancer producing products"—a determination that "no court would ever" make "if it were dealing with any other known poison."[10]

Judge Coleman's line of argument simply highlighted the fact that the issue in the cigarette cases embraces competing sets of moral concerns. Two decades later, in another cigarette suit, the Sixth Circuit replicated the Fifth Circuit's final result in the Green litigation. The Sixth Circuit noted that the plaintiffs before it had "offered no proof that these cigarettes were 'improperly manufactured' or contained 'dangerous impurities.' " That court concluded that because there was "no evidence whatever that the use of the defendant's cigarettes presents risks greater than those known to be associated with smoking," a jury could not find them "defective."[11] With the court's notation that "[t]he normal use of cigarettes is known by ordinary consumers to present grave health risks," the core of this holding seems to lie in a morality of expectations.

Litigants have fought several battles over an extended front of fact and concept in the cigarette cases. There is the problem of whether a product that duplicates the qualities of every other product of its line ("good to-

---

7. *Id.* at 81-82 (Cameron, J., dissenting).

8. Green v. American Tobacco Co., 391 F.2d 97, 106 (5th Cir. 1968).

9. *Id.* at 110 (Simpson, J., dissenting), subsequently accepted by majority of court en banc, 409 F.2d 1166 (5th Cir. 1969).

10. *Id.* at 1168 (Coleman, J., dissenting).

11. Roysdon v. R.J. Reynolds Tobacco Co., 849 F.2d 230, 236 (6th Cir. 1988).

bacco") can be held defective. There is the issue of whether one can weigh the risk of a product like cigarettes against its "utility," a question that bedeviled several tribunals in the much-publicized litigation over the death from lung cancer of Rose Cipollone.[12] And, tucked inside the "risk/utility" discussion, is the question of what people reasonably might expect from smoking cigarettes. In one edition of the Cipollone litigation, Judge Sarokin of the federal district court in New Jersey said he was bound by the idea "that products such as cigarettes cannot be deemed defective because the alleged risks of these products have been part of the common knowledge of consumers for years."[13]

In the case of cigarettes alone, we might isolate at least three positions about the ingredients of justice: (1) that implied representations of fitness accompany any product intended for ingestion or inhalation; (2) that the legal standard embodies an average of the common expectations of consumers; (3) that the issue depends on the actual understanding of a particular consumer. An important aspect of the Cipollone litigation was the latter factor: the jury found Ms. Cipollone eighty percent responsible for her illness because she had smoked the defendant's cigarettes. The Third Circuit, however, reversed a holding for the defendant on a failure to warn claim because the trial court had not asked the jury to differentiate between Ms. Cipollone's smoking before and after 1966, the effective date of the first federal cigarette labeling legislation passed in 1965.[14]

The particular understanding of a consumer plaintiff will bear strongly on the defenses available to a manufacturer. But our focus in this chapter is on the question of what a defect is, and here the battle is between a moral judgment about the sale of a highly dangerous product and the morality of resting a decision on the general understanding of most consumers.

To link together concepts we have discussed thus far, the question that lurks behind the judicial choice between moralities is how far courts may go in making judgments about the acceptability of the risk posed by a particular product. Cigarette makers advanced the argument that the federal cigarette legislation of 1965, and its 1969 successor, had made that choice

---

12. *Compare, e.g.*, Cipollone v. Liggett Group, Inc., 649 F. Supp. 664, 671 (D. N.J. 1986) (refusing to dismiss claims based on design defect theory) *with* Cipollone v. Liggett Group, Prod. Liab. Rep. (CCH) ¶ 11,637 (D. N.J. Oct. 27, 1987) (holding that plaintiffs could not recover under a risk/utility theory) *and* Cipollone v. Liggett Group, Inc., 893 F.2d 541, 578 (3d Cir. 1990) (unconvinced that "there was sufficient evidence . . . that the 'inherent[ly] [dangerous] characteristics of cigarettes were known to the ordinary consumer or user,' prior to 1966," when the federal cigarette labeling legislation became effective).
13. Cipollone v. Liggett Group, Prod. Liab. Rep. (CCH) ¶ 11,637 (D. N.J. Oct. 27, 1987).
14. *See* Cipollone v. Liggett Group, Inc., 893 F.2d 541, 556-559 (3d Cir. 1990).

for the nation as a whole. Both statutes featured provisions requiring specified warnings on cigarette packages; the 1969 statute substituted the words "is dangerous" for the words "may be hazardous." Both statutes contained "pre-emption" provisions, forbidding any other legal requirement dealing with "smoking and health," with the 1969 legislation broadly prohibiting any "requirement or prohibition based on smoking and health" from being "imposed under State law with respect to the advertising or promotion of any cigarettes the packages of which are labeled in conformity with the provisions of this Act."[15]

Writing for two different sets of justices of the United States Supreme Court on an appeal by Rose Cipollone's family, Justice Stevens partially accepted and partially rejected the defendant's argument that the legislation effectively barred products liability claims for cigarette-caused illness. In a part of his plurality opinion joined by six other justices, he held that the relatively narrow language of the 1965 legislation did not bar state law damages actions, but rather only pre-empted state and federal lawmaking bodies from "mandating particular cautionary statements" on labels and in advertisements.[16] In another part of his opinion, however, Justice Stevens declared that the 1969 legislation pre-empted the Cipollone claims on failure to warn theories to the extent that they alleged that the defendants' "post-1969 advertising or promotions should have included additional, or more clearly stated, warnings."[17] He spoke only for three other justices on this point.

A substantial majority of the court came together on the proposition that the plaintiffs could bring claims based on intentional conduct, including specific misstatements, by the defendants. The plurality said that the legislation did not preempt the plaintiffs' "claims based on express warranty, intentional fraud and misrepresentation, or conspiracy."[18] Since three other justices argued that Congress had not intended to preempt *any* common-law damages actions under state law,[19] seven members of the Court thus agreed that cigarette plaintiffs could at least claim for affirmative statements that turned out to be false or for conspiracy.

The Supreme Court's decision settled a question of great importance about the division of lawmaking authority concerning the health hazards of cigarette smoking. But even the smoke of battle on this question could not obscure the centrality of the social determination of what a defect is. It

---

15. Pub L. 91-222, § 5(b) (1970).

16. Cipollone v. Liggett Group, Inc., 112 S. Ct. 2608, 2619 (1992).

17. *Id.* at 2621-22.

18. *Id.* at 2625.

19. *Id.* at 2626-32 (concurring and dissenting opinion by Blackmun, J.).

is now clear, whether one focuses on consumer expectations or acceptability of risk, that one may not facilely answer that question by saying that it is defense enough that a cigarette was made from "good tobacco."

Alternative design. Another factor to which courts often refer is the availability of alternative designs for the product that caused the plaintiff's injury.

It lightens the plaintiff's burden to be able to show an alternative design. A graphic example appears in a case in which the driver of a refrigerated meat trailer claimed that the way meat was hung in the vehicle made it unreasonably unstable on curves. Experts testified for the plaintiff about feasible alternatives for hanging meat. One method was to tie the meat to the floor; another was to put partitions in the trailer to "restrict the swinging motion of the meat." Since the defendant did not show that these alternatives would not keep the meat from swinging wildly or that they were economically unfeasible, the court concluded that a jury could have found that the "special dangers" of the vehicle "constituted an unreasonable danger."[20]

Not only may it be desirable for plaintiffs to show an alternative design; frequently courts will require them to do so. In a case in which the gas tank on a car burst into flames after a rear-end collision, in which the Alabama Supreme Court ultimately upheld a "crashworthiness" claim, the court emphasized the need for plaintiffs to prove a safer alternative design. To hold otherwise, the court said, would make auto makers "insurers of their products' safety."[21]

Moreover, although some courts have said that plaintiffs do not have to prove that an alternate design is "efficient on a cost/benefit basis,"[22] others have required claimants to show that "in terms of costs, practicality and technological possibility, the alternative design was feasible."[23]

We can discern a strong strain of fairness in judicial insistence on proof of a feasible alternative design, in the sense that it is arguably unfair to hold someone to a standard that did not exist when he acted. Yet it would seem that this begs the question of what is unreasonable danger, or at least pushes us into other inquiries about acceptability of risk. For the logical outcome of this insistence would be that a manufacturer could make an extremely dangerous product and then claim it was not defective simply because no one had made a better one.

---

20. Mitchell v. Fruehauf Corp., 568 F.2d 1139, 1144-45 (5th Cir. 1978).
21. General Motors Corp. v. Edwards, 482 So.2d 1179, 1189 (Alab. 1985).
22. Marchant v. Dayton Tire & Rubber Co., 836 F.2d 695, 700 (1st Cir. 1988).
23. Oberst v. International Harvester Co., 640 F.2d 863, 865 (7th Cir. 1980), quoting Lolie v. Ohio Brass Co., 502 F.2d 741, 744 (7th Cir. 1974).

Perhaps in some cases courts should hold such a manufacturer blameless, if the consumer fully understood and unreasonably encountered the risk. However, in the absence of a showing that the plaintiff has behaved unreasonably, the courts have not been sympathetic to the notion that consumer knowledge of a risk equals a lack of unreasonable danger in the product. For example, in the case just described involving the meat trailer, the court preceded its favorable reference to the evidence about design alternatives by adverting to the testimony of five truck drivers about the unpredictability and extreme hazardousness of hanging meat trailers. With respect to that testimony, the court declared that "[k]nowledge on the part of skilled operators of the dangerous character of a product should not prevent a jury from deciding that an unreasonable danger exists." This was especially so in the case before it, the court said, where the knowledge "did not ensure that reasonable care would defeat the dangerous character of the product, since a crucial aspect of the danger is unpredictable handling in emergencies." The court epitomized the problem as being that "the risk of injury is highest when the utility of knowledge of the dangerous qualities is lowest."[24]

It would thus appear that a proposition widely accepted as part of the test for defect is substantially flawed. Proof of a feasible alternative design should not necessarily be a component of the defect standard. The argument that there was no notice of standards at the time of manufacture is not dispositive. In that connection, we should note that a defendant's competitors at that time may have been formulating safer designs about which the defendant may not have known. In any event, a key inquiry is how strongly the defendant was on notice about the hazardous character of its own product, irrespective of the level of safety achieved by its competitors or even by other models of its own product.

One reason for this is the fact that the existence of any product, even a very dangerous one, has market-creating capacities. The presence of the product on the market may create an irresistible inclination to use it, a situation especially likely to create unjust impacts on employees. It is here that the demand for novelty generates effects that may require legal constraint. The requirement that plaintiffs show an alternative design arguably may stimulate producers to be first rather than safe.

The role of experts.   It is well to say a word about the role of experts in products litigation. In matters involving scientific knowledge, experts play an especially significant role, for example, in testifying on questions of causation. But they also may contribute to decisions about the meaning of

---

24. Mitchell v. Fruehauf Corp., 568 F.2d 1139, 1143 (5th Cir. 1978).

defect. Illustrative is a California case in which the plaintiff attributed toxic shock syndrome to the defendant's tampons. Experts for the plaintiff not only testified as to causation but opined that the tampon was defective in design. They cited, among other things, the highly absorbent quality of the defendant's tampon and its "radial expansion feature," the effect of which was to "occlude[] the vaginal canal and become[] a 'plug' which is analogous to an abscess."[25] The defendant apparently argued that the plaintiff should not be able to employ a consumer expectations test because the experts had testified, but the court rejected that contention. Indeed, the court said that the expert evidence would support a jury finding "that the tampon had failed to meet consumer expectations as to its safety."[26]

A noteworthy aspect of this holding is that it permits the plaintiff to use experts not only to establish a basically empirical proposition—a causal relationship between product and disease—but also in support of what is essentially a set of normative propositions, translating into what a defect is. When the court approvingly cites expert testimony that such features as absorbent quality and radial expansion are each "a defect," it seems to be relying on the experts' "oughts" and not only on their views of what happened. It is also interesting that the expert testimony that the court found relevant to consumer expectations focused on opinions about defectiveness rather than the "fact" of what those expectations are.

Trade-offs.   Another important aspect of defect analysis is one familiar in everyday decision making. Practically everything we do—from my choice of typing speed for this sentence to your decision about whether to have a pat of butter or to ask the waiter for margarine to your sister's decision to drive 65 where the speed limit is 55—involves judgments that combine a search for personally defined goods with an effort to limit risk. If I can, on average, type 60 words per minute with five mistakes, but only 50 words per minute with one mistake, I must calculate where I will wind up in terms of typing production, on balance, at the end of my workday.

Product makers must make the same kinds of calculations, at varying levels of concreteness and consciousness. One of the most serious types of these decisions occurs when one must decide how much safety to build into a product. Issues involving vehicle "crashworthiness" arise from such choices by producers. In the early days of products liability development, a California trial court defined the boundaries of the argument with its statement that although automobile manufacturers were not required to con-

---

25. West v. Johnson & Johnson Prods., Inc., 174 Cal. App. 3d 831, 849-850, 220 Cal. Rptr. 437, 446-447 (1985).

26. *Id.* at 867, 220 Cal. Rptr. at 458.

struct a "Sherman tank," it would not be acceptable if they built cars out of "papier mache."[27]

Given the statistical fact that many motor vehicles will, over the course of their useful lives, collide with other objects, this use of word pictures captures a general intuition. The difficult questions arise from allegations of design defects in situations where there is a substantial range of choice for the manufacturer. Consider, for example, the Colorado Supreme Court's response to a motorcyclist's claim that injuries to his leg would have been reduced if the cycle maker, Honda, had put crash bars on the vehicle. The court considered the defense-oriented argument that the case should turn on consumer contemplation, but found that test insufficient by itself. To rely completely "upon the hypothetical consumer's contemplation of an obvious danger," the court said, "diverts the appropriate focus and may thereby result in a finding that a product is not defective even though the product may easily have been designed to be much safer at little added expense and no impairment of utility."[28] The court rejected the manufacturer's motion for summary judgment on the question of defective design, referring to evidence "that Honda could have provided crash bars at an acceptable cost without impairing the motorcycle's utility or substantially altering its nature."[29]

Some implications of these statements deserve comment. First, as we have noted,[30] courts do take into account the metaphysics of products. Where an automobile need not be as well-protected as a Sherman tank, a motorcycle does not have to be as cushioned against collisions as an automobile. Second, the court's reference to utility, like any judicial use of "risk-utility" language, recognizes the need for trade-offs in product design.

Perhaps most interesting, however, is the court's insistence that a design may be defective even though it does not violate a consumer contemplation standard. There seem to be two economic ideas at war here. The court's reference to the "acceptable cost" of crash bars implies that the design may not have met the Learned Hand test—that is, the accident costs associated with the design might exceed the expense of including crash bars. And yet

---

27. Badorek v. Rodgers, Prod. Liab. Rep. (CCH) ¶ 5899 (Cal. Super. 1967). Compare a New York Times editorial, "Safety Gets Into Gear," March 8, 1966, at 36M, quoted in Judge Kiley's dissenting opinion in Evans v. General Motors Corp., 359 F.2d 822, 827 (7th Cir. 1966). The editorial declared that a crashworthy car would not have to "look or drive like a Sherman tank. Safety and style need not be enemies."

28. Camacho v. Honda Motor Co., 741 P.2d 1240, 1246 (Colo. 1987), (en banc), *rev'g* 701 P.2d 628 (Colo. Ct. App. 1985) (danger "within the contemplation of the ordinary consumer," *id.* at 631).

29. *Id.*

30. *See* chapter 5 *supra*, pp. 79-81.

it is a basic philosophical element of the economic lexicon that people should be able to choose risky products, so long as they are aware of the risk. We might thus view the Learned Hand test, though couched in hard-headed economic terms, as interfering with free consumer choice.

In any event, it would seem that even if it subscribed to the Learned Hand test, the court would be making a normative judgment about acceptable levels of risk. After all, a statement that efficient outcomes are preferred outcomes represents an opinion about what is just as well as about what is economical. An alternative justification for the decision may lie in the notion that in placing on the market a product with risks that could easily be eliminated, the manufacturer is imposing unfairly on purchasers. Some might think it internally contradictory to say that about a product whose risks were within the contemplation of ordinary consumers. But whether or not the case is cast in terms of imposition or cost-effective outcomes, it certainly appears to be governed by a judgment about what is morally right between the parties.

There are competing angles of analysis, to be sure, and they become evident as one introduces new facts into the problem. Just two years before the cycle decision, the Colorado Court of Appeals denied recovery to a tractor driver for injuries that occurred when a dead tree fell across the machine when he was using it to clear debris. In this case, the manufacturer derived legal ammunition from its provision of ninety different equipment options, including overhead protective structures. Stressing that the plaintiff "best knew the environ and the uses he intended for the tractor when he purchased it," the court concluded that because he "was in the best position to evaluate and eliminate the danger by purchasing an overhead protective safety option, he should accordingly bear the loss from his failure to do so."[31] This is thus a case where the specificity of the consumer's choice at least matches the deliberate character of the manufacturer's choice.

We may pose the question another way, relative to trade-offs. A recurrent issue in tort law is, who is trading for what against whom? In the case of the cycle crash bars, the court apparently saw a situation in which the defendant controlled the relevant choices; it was gaining in economy of construction at the expense of the rider's safety. Of course, we could characterize the case another way: we could say that the rider was trading off his safety in favor of his pocketbook. That argument is more powerful, as in the case of the tractor, when the consumer has viable choices among levels of safety.

"Polycentric" features of design.   The relatively simple case of the motorcycle crash bars leads us into the much more complex legal problems that

---

31. Davis v. Caterpillar Tractor Co., 719 P.2d 324, 327 (Colo. Ct. App. 1985).

arise with the design of more complicated machines. Professor James Henderson presented an interesting definition of the problem in an article that fixed on the "polycentric" nature of design. Borrowing the term from a use by Professor Lon Fuller in another context, Henderson emphasized the many choices and trade-offs that designers of complex products must make in trying to maximize their usefulness.

Henderson put the question rhetorically: "What if . . . all of the issues in cases typically brought to courts for decision were related to one another in such a way that it was impossible for a litigant to address himself to any one issue apart from a consideration of all the others?"[32] The problem in permitting a plaintiff to focus on a single design feature in a product like a car, Henderson suggested, is that it does not allow for the "spider web" character of the problem—pull on one strand, and "a complex pattern of readjustments will occur throughout the entire web."[33] The difficulty inherent in allowing courts much leeway in auto design cases was analogous to "the task that would face a court called upon by a coachless football team to assign positions to the players in a principled fashion."[34]

Henderson, who played the line for Princeton, and who this writer can testify inspires confidence as a doubles partner in tennis, had focused on an important point. But his analysis seemed strained when he insisted that courts that held for plaintiffs in design cases were doing so "only in the most obvious cases of marketplace breakdown producing the clearest examples of unreasonably safe design."[35]

An example of the gap between analytical premise and reality was Henderson's principal citation to the case of *Larsen v. General Motors*,[36] in which the Eighth Circuit had upheld a crashworthiness claim in favor of a plaintiff who was injured when a head-on collision thrust the steering mechanism on his car into his head. When one considers the date of manufacture of the plaintiff's 1963 Chevrolet Corvair—more than two years before the effective date of the National Traffic and Motor Vehicle Safety Act—it is highly arguable to call the steering mechanism on that vehicle an example of "marketplace breakdown." One could, perhaps, fit the case

---

32. Henderson, Judicial Review of Manufacturers' Conscious Design Choices: The Limits of Adjudication, 73 Colum. L. Rev. 1531, 1536 (1973).

33. *Id.*

34. *Id.* at 1537.

35. *Id.* at 1571-72, focusing on automobile design. More generally, *see id.* at 1573 ("By and large, judicial review of product design has occurred only in a few product categories and only in cases conforming remarkably closely to patterns involving marketplace breakdowns and widely recognized design alternatives").

36. *See id.* at 1572 n.166, referring to Larsen v. General Motors Corp., 391 F.2d 495 (8th Cir. 1968).

within a "polycentricity" analysis by saying that this was a design feature that could be changed without making over the rest of the plaintiff's Corvair.

A partial antidote to *Larsen* appeared in a case in which the Fourth Circuit turned down a claim that asserted, in the words of the trial judge, that a Volkswagen microbus had insufficient "energy-absorbing materials or devices or 'crush space' " to save the plaintiff from injuries that occurred in a collision with a telephone pole. Accepting the characterization of the plaintiff's van as "a van type multipurpose vehicle," the court noted that the design had been "uniquely developed in order to provide the owner with the maximum amount of either cargo or passenger space in a vehicle inexpensively priced and of such dimensions as to make possible easy maneuverability."[37] This focus on the character of the vehicle, which supported the appellate court's reversal of the trial court's judgment for the plaintiff, brings the metaphysics of products into play. The rule of this case strongly favors a manufacturer that has filled a niche occupied by a product category with a specific, complex set of characteristics. The Fourth Circuit observed in its opinion that there was no evidence "that there was any practical way of improving the 'crashability' of the vehicle that would have been consistent with the peculiar purposes of its design."[38]

To an extent, the decision represents both a vindication of the "polycentricity" argument and a recognition of trade-offs. But these features of the case cannot obscure the fact that courts are making a social judgment, not only an economic one, any time they resolve disputes involving the strength of products to withstand predictable shocks. That point, capable of broad generalization, applies with particular force to the crashworthiness cases. Congress has been careful to preserve the domain of courts over that form of judgment, despite judicial lamentations,[39] in the National Traffic and Motor Vehicle Safety Act. In that legislation, Congress made explicit that "[c]ompliance with any Federal motor vehicle safety standard . . . does not exempt any person from any liability under common law."[40]

The federal motor vehicle legislation was an act of social conscience, driven not by concerns of economic balancing but by revulsion to carnage on the highways. Since there is a strong component of judicial conscience in the common law of crashworthiness, the legislation in effect gives consumers two shots at arguing that particular auto designs are socially unacceptable.

---

37. Dreisonstok v. Volkswagenwerk, A.G., 489 F.2d 1066, 1073- 1074 (4th Cir. 1974).
38. *Id.* at 1074.
39. *See, e.g.*, Dawson v. Chrysler Corp., 630 F.2d 950 (3d Cir. 1980), cert. denied, 450 U.S. 959 (1981).
40. 15 U.S.C.A. § 1397(c) (West 1982).

The cost of safety.   For anyone who reads a lot of appellate decisions in products liability cases, it is striking how infrequently courts focus on the actual dollar cost of avoiding plaintiffs' injuries.

We should mention two implications of this fact. First, however much commentators and even judges talk about negligence in terms of a comparison of the costs of accidents and accident avoidance, neither lawyers nor courts focus on this idea, at the point of decision, with much precision.

The second implication has broad application throughout the law of personal injury. It is that much—perhaps most—of the law of torts is a series of short stories about how cheap it is to avoid an accident. The low cost of avoidance often lines up comfortably with the Learned Hand formula, but the equation will not always favor a claimant if one calculates the cost of a safety measure across a product line.

First, assume a narrow focus on a single product unit that causes a million dollar injury that could have been avoided by a one-dollar safety feature. We can easily say, with that tight focus on one victim and one product unit, that the maker of the product should have employed that feature on that unit. Now, more realistically, we can consider the case in which three people would suffer million dollar injuries in a time period during which the manufacturer of the product sold one million products. If the manufacturer employed the one-dollar safety feature, it would save three million dollars of injury costs at the cost of a million dollars. Clearly, it would seem, the manufacturer in this situation also should have adopted that feature. Now assume, by contrast, that there were three million units of the product, and only one would cause a million dollar injury. It would not then be cost-effective to employ the one-dollar safety feature, which would require a three million dollar expenditure to save injury costs of one million dollars.

Having observed the different results that the mathematics of cost comparisons may produce, we elaborate the first point: courts do not usually make that kind of calculation, and it would appear that defendants are hesitant to suggest it. The reason derives at least partly from the fact that tort cases necessarily focus on the individual accident. Courts often refer to broad policy rationales for tort law, but there still is a lot of I-and-thou thinking when judges get down to decision making.

To be sure, there are some decisions in which courts have specified the costs of remedial measures. One example is an Oregon case in which the plaintiff was injured when an automobile hood flew up on the highway. In affirming a judgment for the manufacturer of the vehicle, the Oregon Supreme Court referred to testimony by a product quality engineer for the defendant, who was called as a witness for the plaintiff. This witness said that there had been reports of only six or seven inadvertent hood openings in a period of seven or eight years, and a design engineer said that a preventive design proposed by a plaintiff's expert would have cost five to ten dollars a car.[41] The court did not spell out the relevant calculations, but one can guess at its arithmetic: say the company makes a million cars a year. It will cost at least five million dollars to keep hoods from flying up once a year. Assume an average cost of $250,000, or even one million dollars, for one injury, which is essentially the annual figure. From this it appears that it would be economically irrational—"unreasonable"?—to impose liability for failure to use the safer design.

By comparison, specific cost-counting aided claimants in a First Circuit case where the plaintiffs attributed a fire that consumed their home to the inadequacy of markings on a chimney pipe that was installed upside down. The court vacated a directed verdict for the defendants when there was evidence that if they had added tabs on the pipe, costing about one tenth of a cent per pipe, it "would have substantially reduced the likelihood of inadvertent upside down installation."[42] In another decision that mentions a dollar cost of safety, the Maryland Court of Appeals must have had in mind the severity of the harm—the death of the plaintiff's decedent from multiple injuries in a case involving the design of a front-mounted snowplow hitch on a colliding vehicle. Reviewing a $2,500,000 verdict for the plaintiff, the court affirmed, given evidence that the cost of an attachment that might have prevented the accident was about seven dollars. The court noted that this attachment was "very common in the trade generally" and that the defendant itself had used it on some vehicles.[43]

It is a commonplace in the law that one must separate the liability issue—whether there are facts to justify recovery under a viable legal theory—from the damages question: if there may be a recovery, how much should it be? However, the cases we have just discussed teach us that the severity of a particular injury may influence the liability issue when the cost of preventing that one injury, viewed relative to it, is comparatively small. This phenomenon is likely to occur even when the costs of preventive measures, spread across the defendant's entire product line, might be very large.

One might interpret this state of affairs as indicating that courts are only interested in the justice of the case as between two individuals. Recently, Professor Ernest Weinrib has powerfully advanced the argument that this should be the case.[44] But one might also view the court as playing an inter-

---

41. Roach v. Kononen, 269 Or. 457, 467, 525 P.2d 125, 130 (1974).

42. Duford v. Sears, Roebuck & Co., 833 F.2d 407, 411 (1st Cir. 1987).

43. Valk Mfg. Co. v. Rangaswamy, 74 Md. App. 304, 317, 537 A.2d 622, 628 (1988), *rev'd on other grounds*, 317 Md. 185, 562 A.2d 1246 (1989).

44. *See* Weinrib, Legal Formalism: On the Immanent Rationality of Law, 97 Yale L.J. 949, *e.g.*, at 1005-08 (1988).

stitial policymaking role, sometimes responding to the probability that the kind of accident at issue will occur again. In that mode, courts choose from a menu that ranges from notions of optimizing deterrence to a more moralizing view of accident prevention.

A Smorgasbord of Tests

Courts dealing with the defect question resort to a range of analytical frameworks. Some try to isolate the principal aspects of the case that seem most compelling and to rationalize their decisions in terms of those factors. Other courts, and commentators, have sought to define the concept in a more encompassing way. The variety of these efforts mirrors the human and technological complexity of the cases. There follows a brief catalog of several of these definitions.

The Learned Hand test. We have referred to Judge Learned Hand's negligence formula, with its focus on comparison of accident costs and the expense of avoiding accidents.[45] For cases pleaded under the negligence label, this test may be the functional equivalent of the standard for defect. Although courts may not often equate the concepts, a finding of no negligence often is the equivalent of a judgment that a product was not defective.

The Calabresi-Hirschoff test. In 1972, two scholars using the lens of economic theory ventured a definition of strict liability that also overlaps substantially with the defect concept. These authors, Guido Calabresi and Jon Hirschoff, suggested that the court should determine which party is "in the best position to make the cost-benefit analysis between accident costs and accident avoidance costs and to act on that decision once it is made."[46]

Glosses on section 402A. Section 402A of the Second Restatement of Torts, the most-cited general formula on strict liability for products, provides only an extremely compressed reference to defect. It declares that strict liability will apply to a product "in a defective condition unreasonably dangerous to the user or consumer or to his property."

It has remained for scholars and judges to flesh out this concept. One of the most-cited commentaries came from Dean John Wade, one of the most respected veterans in the field of torts scholarship, who succeeded William

---

45. *See supra,* chapter 6, text accompanying note 5, and chapter 7, text accompanying note 15.

46. Calabresi & Hirschoff, Toward a Test for Strict Liability in Torts, 81 Yale L.J. 1055, 1060 (1972).

Prosser as reporter of the Second Restatement. Wade offered a list of factors "which seem of significance in applying the [unreasonable dangerousness] standard."[47] We referred earlier to several of these factors, which include the utility of the product, the availability of substitutes and the practicality of making the product safer.[48] Wade's catalog also mentioned the likelihood that the product would cause injury combined with the seriousness of potential harm, and the feasibility of producer loss spreading "by setting the price of the product or carrying liability insurance," as well as factors related to the user's awareness of danger and ability to avoid injury.[49]

Wade's synthesis was a progenitor of several factor-oriented approaches. Judge Edward Becker, then on the federal trial bench in Pennsylvania and now a member of the Third Circuit, offered an analogous list in a 1977 opinion focusing on the design of an automobile fuel tank.[50] Interestingly, where Dean Wade had said that ordinarily the judge should not place such factors before the jury unless there was one element with "especial significance,"[51] Judge Becker included his list of factors in instructions to a jury about the meaning of "unreasonably dangerous."[52]

Several commentators have weighed in with other lists of the elements that seem most important in the determination of defectiveness,[53] and many courts have referred to such catalogs, especially to Dean Wade's list of factors.[54]

Courts and commentators also have essayed more general definitions. Probably the most abstract was the California Supreme Court's 1970 attempt, in effect, to define "defect" by itself,[55] an effort that ultimately the court recognized as inadequate.[56]

The Pennsylvania Supreme Court, developing its rule through several decisions' worth of intramural argument, arrived in 1974 at the broad formulation that the manufacturer is "effectively the guarantor of its product's safety."[57] It spelled out this idea in 1978 to include the proposition

---

47. Wade, On the Nature of Strict Tort Liability for Products, 44 Miss. L.J. 825, 837-38 (1973).

48. *See supra* this chapter, text accompanying notes 2-3.

49. *See* 44 Miss. L.J. at 837-38.

50. Bowman v. General Motors Corp., 427 F. Supp. 234 (E.D. Pa. 1977).

51. Wade, *supra* note 47, at 840.

52. *See* 427 F. Supp. at 243-244.

53. One summary appears in 1 M. Shapo, The Law of Products Liability, ¶ 8.04[3], at 8-11 - 8-12 (1990).

54. Shepard's citations lists well over one hundred judicial references to the article.

55. Cronin v. J.B.E. Olson Corp., 8 Cal. 3d 121, 501 P.2d 1153, 104 Cal. Rptr. 433 (1972).

56. *See* Barker v. Lull Eng'g Co., 20 Cal.3d 413, 143 Cal. Rptr. 225, 573 P.2d 443 (1978), discussed *infra*, text accompanying notes 60-62.

57. Salvador v. Atlantic Steel Boiler Co., 457 Pa. 24, 32, 319 A.2d 903, 907 (1974).

that the jury "may find a defect where the product left the supplier's control lacking any element necessary to make it safe for its intended use or possessing any feature that renders it unsafe for the intended use."[58] The Pennsylvania court emphasized its hostility to the "unreasonably dangerous" concept, saying that that phrase had "no place in the instructions to a jury as to the question of defect"[59] in a case involving the design of an industrial machine.

Also in 1978, the California court refined its stark "defect" test with a bifurcated definition of the concept. Under this formula, announced in the case of *Barker v. Lull Engineering Co.*,[60] the plaintiff could succeed in one of two ways. He could show that a product failed to perform "as safely as an ordinary consumer would expect when used in an intended or reasonably foreseeable manner."[61] Or, even if the product satisfied ordinary consumer expectations, the plaintiff could win if the "design proximately caused his injury" and the defendant could not prove that "on balance, the benefits of the challenged design outweigh the risk of danger inherent in such design."[62]

The different definitions of defect we have reviewed represent a variety of perspectives, some anchored in traditional legal theory and others in economics. Some employ factor analysis and others attempt to formulate a single definitional tool. Some overlap substantially with others, and some tend to be in opposition with one another. What links them is their participation in an effort to capture an idea of the justice of cases involving product injuries. As the variation in theories implies, that idea is a hard one to pin down. This is not surprising, given the diversity of fact situations and the multiplicity of relevant factors among the cases. Yet as we describe this complex landscape of theoretical disagreement, and as our own analysis unfolds, we should stress this: each decision that courts mold into the framework of the overall definition of defect will itself represent a cultural benchmark, something that helps to define our attitudes about ourselves and the products that are so much part of our lives.

Defect and a Concept of Justice

In analyzing the concept of defect with respect to the question of what justice is in products liability cases, we must first note our assumption that

---

58. Azzarrello v. Black Bros. Co., 480 Pa. 547, 559, 391 A.2d 1020, 1027 (1978).
59. Id.
60. 20 Cal.3d 413, 573 P.2d 443, 143 Cal. Rptr. 225 (1978).
61. Id. at 429, 573 P.2d at 454, 143 Cal. Rptr. at 236.
62. Id. at 432, 573 P.2d at 456, 143 Cal. Rptr. at 238.

justice in this arena is in significant part an individualized concept, applicable to particular litigants. This does not imply that justice does not have "instrumentalist" implications—that courts should not concern themselves with policy goals, or with the broader social and economic consequences of their decisions.[63] But it does mean that, in the first instance, judges will not give primacy to such factors as the potential effect of their decisions on such institutions as insurance markets.[64] To repeat, this is not to say that such matters will not affect our final formulation of what justice consists of in products cases. It is only to highlight one of the implications of the mundane observation that products liability law emerges from cases between and among individual disputants.

With that point in mind, we may refocus this discussion of defect to some of the principal concerns that have sensitized courts to consumer claims in products cases.

The comments to section 402A of the Second Restatement of Torts provide an important background for this discussion, not only because they carried a distinguished professional imprimatur but because they have frequently been cited by courts. An important feature of those comments was their insistence "that the seller, by marketing his product for use and consumption, has undertaken and assumed a special responsibility toward any member of the consuming public who may be injured by it."[65]

A parallel rationale depends on the notion of a "powerless" consumer, for whom Justice Traynor expressed particular concern in his influential *Greenman* decision when he spoke of placing the costs of injuries on manufacturers "rather than . . . the injured persons who are powerless to protect themselves."[66] One might read Justice Traynor as focusing in that sentence on financial "powerlessness," but other statements in the same paragraph imply general concerns about the consumer's relative lack of marketplace ability, in the context of the representational image of the product.[67] Further linked to these views of what is just in the circumstances of consumer product injuries is the Illinois Supreme Court's declaration

---

63. For a powerful argument against the instrumentalist position, see Ernest Weinrib, The Monsanto Lectures: Understanding Tort Law, 23 Valp. L. Rev. 485 (1989).

64. One commentator who has focused on this concern is George Priest, The Current Insurance Crisis and Modern Tort Law, 96 Yale L.J. 1521 (1987).

65. Restatement (Second) of Torts § 402A, comment c.

66. Greenman v. Yuba Power Prod., 59 Cal.2d 47, 27 Cal. Rptr. 697, 701, 377 P.2d 897, 901 (1963).

67. See id. ("[I]t should not be controlling whether plaintiff selected the machine because of the statements in the brochure, or because of the machine's own appearance of excellence that belied the defect lurking beneath the surface, or because he merely assumed that it would safely do the jobs it was built to do").

that "[t]he public interest in human life and health demands all the protection the law can give,"[68] which parallels an assertion in the Restatement comment quoted above that "the consumer . . . is entitled to the maximum protection of the hands of someone," namely the seller.[69]

Behind such pronouncements we may discern a conviction that typically it is sellers, especially manufacturers, who effectively have the whip hand: it is they who make unilateral decisions about design and quality control; it is they who fashion advertising campaigns; it is they who monitor accident reports.

From this view of the world, there emerges a sense that in products liability, a central component of justice is the vulnerable position of consumers. A related element of justice lies in the moral innocence of the claimant, when that is a factual element of the case. It is true that under the reigning conception of strict liability, the seller is not morally at fault either. But the moral innocence of the plaintiff takes on special significance because of its joinder with his or her vulnerability and with the very fact of injury itself.

---

68. Suvada v. White Motor Co., 32 Ill.2d 612, 619, 210 N.E.2d 182, 186 (1965).
69. Restatement (Second) of Torts § 402A, comment c (1965).

9

Warnings

Our focus on the moral aspects of consumer transactions in the defect context logically leads to the questions of when a seller must warn consumers of product hazards, and when warnings are adequate.

The warnings issue naturally follows from the defect question for this reason: The defect concept deals in a general way with the character of the danger. But if the plaintiff shows that a hazard rises to the level of defect, or to a comparable level of danger that would place the onus on one who did not mention it, often the defendant still may escape by showing that it has communicated the hazard to the plaintiff. Although it is not always the case, in many situations the moral choice then becomes the plaintiff's. That is why the warnings issue frequently overlaps with the question of whether the plaintiff should be barred from recovery because of his or her own conduct, which is the subject of chapter ten.

Doctrine and Policy

Theoretical overlaps

An important technical aspect of the law of warnings in products liability lies in its doctrinal complexity, a complexity that reflects the underlying policy struggles in the law. Besides its frequent association with the contributory fault issue, the question of whether there is a duty to warn overlaps substantially with the issue of whether there is a defect, which we discussed in the last chapter. We shall discuss below the commerce between the warnings issue and the concept of obviousness. And we must mention here that there is theoretical warfare between negligence and strict liability on the question of which doctrine shall reign in the warnings area, although we shall not treat that controversy in detail.

Instructions and warnings.   Having identified these theoretical over-laps, we should also speak of a significant distinction, that between "in-structions" and "warnings." Some observers might say that the ideas are indistinguishable: a warning is simply a cautionary instruction. But the dis-tinction can be real and the labels can stand for something. One who in-structs without warning, where warning is required, may be liable.

On this subject, a Virginia case from the 1950s is a classic. The label on an orchard spray called Tag contained the statement, "Do not use this product on bearing apple trees later than two weeks following petal fall or the first cover spray, whichever comes first." McClanahan, who owned an orchard, apparently used Tag some time after the designated period. He seems to have done this on the recommendation of a salesman for the de-fendant, a fact that in itself may have been sufficient to turn the case for the plaintiff, although the Virginia Supreme Court did not focus on that. The result, he alleged, was significant damage to his trees.

The supreme court dealt directly, and unsympathetically, with the trial judge's view that, as the supreme court summarized it, "the defendant had exhausted its duty to the plaintiffs by giving directions for use [and] that the plaintiffs had not followed the directions." The supreme court viewed the label as in effect saying, "Here is a way to use this product which we guarantee will kill the weeds infesting your lawn or the scab infesting your orchard." Yet, the court opined, the instructions for use could not be taken as saying, "This is the only safe way to use our product." The McClanahan plaintiffs had, in fact, used great care in applying the chemical, and indeed evidently had followed the "customarily recognized safe practice in their locality" about spraying. The nub of the case was that even if the plaintiffs did not follow the directions, "This is not a case of a plaintiff acting in de-fiance of a warning. Here there was no warning."[1]

Analogous holdings appear when a seller uses a laconic observation with euphemistic qualities instead of a "clear cautionary statement" about a substantial hazard. Consider, for example, a case in which the plaintiff sus-tained injuries from the blow-off of a bottle cap. The maker of the bottle capping machine argued that it should be absolved because of a statement in the owner's manual that "[l]eakage or closure blow-off at lower pres-

---

1. McClanahan v. California Spray-Chemical Corp., 194 Va. 842, 862-864, 75 S.E.2d 712, 724-725 (1953).

sures can occur when closure application is improper." A Texas appellate court thought that a jury could have found this statement inadequate to describe the hazard, stressing that "no mention is made of the serious nature of personal injuries which can result from a bottle cap blow-off."[2]

Information and moralisms. At one level, questions of this sort, and indeed most questions involving the duty to warn, are essentially problems in the economics of information. One way to put the issue is, how much would it cost to provide the necessary information about a hazard, and how would that compare with the cost of the accidents that the lack of a warning would likely cause? Plaintiffs relying on warnings theory will usually contend that the expense of giving the information would have been trivial as compared with the cost of their injuries.

But the flavor of the decisions often does not convey a concern with dollar signs. Rather, the tone is sometimes moralistic, even didactic: "Here there was no warning."

The saturation problem. Even given that the warnings problem cannot neatly be reduced to dollar values, however, we must consider the potential problem of saturation of warnings. In a case in the Court of Appeals for the District of Columbia, the plaintiff contended that propane cylinders lacked a sufficiently explicit warning about the "explosive, as well as flammable" nature of the product. The defendant had placed what Judge Williams characterized as "a brief message on the canisters themselves and a more detailed one" in a pamphlet which went to the plaintiff's employer. In holding that a jury could not reasonably have found a breach of the duty to warn, Judge Williams observed that while plaintiffs frequently argue that it is very cheap to include extra bits of information in a warning, "[t]he primary cost is, in fact, the increase in time and effort required for the user to grasp the message." Each extra item, he said, "dilutes the punch of every other item," and pieces of cautionary information "get lost in fine print."[3]

User discernment. A familiar paralleling of ethical and economic concerns appears in the question of what effect the discernment of the product user should have on the duty to warn. In one sense, we might view the question strictly as one of economics: who could most cheaply acquire the relevant knowledge about the hazard that caused the injury? In another sense, however, the law seems to aim at a subjective individualizing of the justice of situations.

---

2. Alm v. Aluminum Co. of America, 753 S.W.2d 478, 480-481 (Tex. Civ. App. 1988), further appeal, 785 S.W.2d 137 (Tex. 1990).
3. Cotton v. Buckeye Gas Prods. Co., 840 F.2d 935, 938-940 (D.C. Cir. 1988).

One may consider, in this regard, a case involving fireworks kits, originally sold by mail order to a child. The young purchaser abandoned part of the kits in a bottle in a park. Six children were injured, two fatally, two days later when someone threw a match in the bottle. In a suit against a manufacturer of chemicals used by the sellers of the kits, the Third Circuit reversed a defendant's judgment. Not only did the court find a duty to warn of the danger of mixing the defendant's chemicals with other chemicals in fireworks; it rejected the defense that the subsequent "misuse" of the kit was beyond the ambit of the defendant's liability. The court declared that because the duty to warn arose "from the probability that the chemicals would be misused," the "misuse would not be a superseding cause" of the injuries, "nor an unforeseeable use."[4]

One might rationalize this doctrinal view simply on an information cost basis in regard to the youthful original purchaser. But with respect to how the consequences of the failure to warn visited themselves on the children in the park, an important factor in the decision appears to be the superior position of one who unleashes dangerous products into a community. The purchaser's act of abandoning the kits was a near causal event to the injuries, but the court's judgment for the plaintiffs goes beyond any information imbalance between the purchaser and the manufacturer. Recognizing the control over the safety of third parties inherent in the defendant's failure to warn, the decision seeks to do justice between a non-purchaser and a seller. It is useful to view the case as one involving an especially dangerous characteristic of the product, untied from its informational content. From this perspective, the decision represents more of a concern with power and control than with information theory.

Yet even if one hesitated to view the fireworks case as being controlled by a power-based analysis, other decisions make clear that courts will respond sympathetically to the product user whose personal limitations prevent comprehension of warnings. An illustrative Mississippi case involved injuries to an employee who "slipped or misstepped" while he was working on a salt bath furnace, sustaining burns that led to the amputation of a leg. The plaintiff admitted that he knew that the furnace " 'contained very hot liquid,' " but he also asserted that he had "absolutely no knowledge that the liquid . . . was hot enough to cause me to lose my leg." The plaintiff's employer testified, in the court's characterization, that the plaintiff's "level of intelligence inhibited his full understanding of the relative danger," saying that "he's a great person, but it's hard to guard against ignorance."

As is the case with many decisions in this area, we might classify the case doctrinally in various ways. We could define the pivotal issue as whether the

---

4. Suchomajcz v. Hummel Chem. Co., 514 F.2d 19, 29 (3d Cir. 1975).

plaintiff "assumed the risk." With respect to that theory, the Mississippi court's reversal of a summary judgment for the defendant referred to conflicting evidence on whether the plaintiff "fully appreciated the dangerous nature of the product with which he dealt on a daily basis." But we might also view the case as centering on a question of design defect; the particular bath where the plaintiff was hurt had no catwalk, although two other salt baths in the plant did. On that point, too, the court denied summary judgment, noting evidentiary conflict on "the extent of the danger involved and whether it may be attributed to a defect in . . . design." Moreover, as the court also noted, we could phrase the issue as "whether the danger . . . was 'open and obvious,' " or as one primarily concerned with lack of warning.[5] The salient point is that the court bends in favor of a user with serious difficulty in comprehension.

The "sophisticated user" doctrine. Across the liability fence from the consumer who is incapable of absorbing a warning stands the "sophisticated user." The products liability defense with that label finds its principal application in the workplace. In our earlier discussion of expertise under the heading of consumer desires and preferences, we described two Fifth Circuit cases that permitted defendants to use versions of the "sophisticated user" concept.[6] These cases merit elaboration under our discussion of warnings doctrine. In one of these decisions, the court rejected a claim by a worker who was overcome by fumes while he was stripping a barge that had carried a chemical product laden with benzene. The court held that knowledge of the dangers of the chemical was "well within the scope of the . . . professional expertise" of the crew of which the plaintiff was a member, and found, indeed, that the crew had actual knowledge of the cargo.[7] To rationalize such a result, one may not have to go beyond the notion that the burden should fall on the person in the position to avoid injury at the least cost.

The other case dealt with the specialized knowledge of a worker with a second-grade education, a full-time tire serviceman who was hurt when he overinflated an agricultural tire. Noting that this claimant "could read and understand the meaning of the word 'warning,' " the court pointed out that he had mounted "perhaps thousands" of tires that had warnings against inflating them above 35 pounds. The court insisted that the plaintiff's "argument that he did not pay attention to these warnings does not excuse his ignorance." Melding its response to issues involving contributory negli-

5. Pargo v. Electric Furnace Co., 498 So.2d 833, 834-835 (Miss. 1986).

6. *See supra*, chapter 2, text accompanying notes 42-43.

7. Martinez v. Dixie Carriers, Inc., 529 F.2d 457, 466-467 (5th Cir. 1976).

gence as well as the duty to warn, the court concluded that, "Because [the plaintiff] should have known the maximum recommended inflation level for this tire, Firestone had no duty to warn him of the dangers of inflating the tire above 35 psi."[8]

One might view this case like that of the benzene residue on the barge, as simply an exercise in least cost avoidance. However, the decision also exhibits strong moral content. Although some may disagree with the result, the accent appears to be on individual responsibility.

Individualization may sometimes vindicate claimants in the face of the "sophisticated user" doctrine. Illustratively, a plaintiff's familiarity with a general class of goods will not support the application of the defense to a specific kind of product that falls within the general class. An example is a case in which an employee fell from a scaffold. The court rejected the defense when the president of the window cleaning firm for which the plaintiff worked knew about "fist clips" but had "virtually no experience" with "U-clips."[9] This is another example of how the individualization of justice follows the degree of particularized knowledge, a principle that in turn benefits both plaintiffs and defendants.

Obviousness

The facts of cases involving alleged duties to warn often stimulate judicial appeals to intuitions about the justice of situations. A frequent companion of these appeals is a concept we have introduced above,[10] that of "obviousness." There are several avenues for use of the "obviousness" defense. It may provide a way to argue that a product was not designed defectively. It may support a finding of contributory fault. And, under our present lens, it may create a defense against a claim of duty to warn.

To supplement our earlier discussion of the overlap among such concepts as duty to warn, the "sophisticated user" defense and the doctrine of "assumption of risk," we may refer to two cases. In one, a trucker continued to drive although he knew that his vehicle's brakes were grabbing. Affirming a judgment notwithstanding the verdict that the trial judge gave in favor of the truck maker, the Fifth Circuit held that the defendant did not have a

---

8. American Mut. Liab. Ins. Co. v. Firestone Tire & Rubber Co., 799 F.2d 993, 995 (5th Cir. 1986).

9. McNeal v. Hi-Lo Powered Scaffolding, Inc., 836 F.2d 637, 642-43 (D.C. Cir. 1988).

10. *See supra*, chapter 5, pp. 84-87.

duty to warn.[11] In the other case, an experienced tree cutter suffered injuries when a chain saw kicked back. A federal trial judge, ruling for the manufacturer from the bench, referred to the "sophisticated purchaser doctrine" while employing the obviousness defense against a duty-to-warn theory.[12] In both of these cases, "obviousness" may be a surrogate for a determination of the party who can process and use information most cheaply. Especially when made by the judge in a way that effectively takes the case away from the jury, this kind of decision conveys a primarily economic timbre.

Jury issues. There are other cases, in which the court leaves the "obviousness" question to the jury, where the definition of the issue appears to focus more on moral responsibility than on the comparative availability of information. This is the tenor of a Fifth Circuit decision in a case in which a teenager's eyeglasses shattered during a basketball game. The trial court directed a verdict for the manufacturer of the glasses. As the appeals court characterized it, the trial judge

> likened the duty to warn [the plaintiff] about the eyeglasses shattering while playing volleyball to the necessity to warn in a case of the manufacturer of knives telling the purchaser not to put his fingers under the knife or not to stick your fingers in boiling waters when preparing food in plastic containers for eating, or to warn a person not to point a loaded gun at himself when he buys one.[13]

Refusing to accept this set of analogies, the appellate court said tartly that the trial court had taken "it upon itself to decide that it was not a requirement for a manufacturer or seller of eyeglasses to tell a teenager or anybody 'if you wear glasses and get hit while you've got them on, they might break.' " The Fifth Circuit implicitly inserted a moral ingredient into the procedural issue of whether there should have been a directed verdict, saying that "[t]he trouble was that [the trial judge] was not the trier of fact. He should have allowed the jury to decide this issue from the evidence that had been presented."[14]

It may seem ironic that it was the trial judge in this case who most straightforwardly engaged in moralizing with his analogies about knives, boiling water and guns, and that the appellate court concluded the issue on the ground that what seems at base to be a moral question was an issue of fact. Yet the necessarily procedural cast of this solution does not obscure

---

11. Scott v. White Trucks, 699 F.2d 714, 724-25 (5th Cir. 1983).

12. Poland v. Beaird-Poulan, 483 F. Supp. 1256, 1264-65 (W.D. La. 1980).

13. Boudreaux v. Jack Eckerd Corp., 854 F.2d 85, 87 (5th Cir. 1988).

14. *Id.* at 87-88.

the fact that the basic issue was what the manufacturer *ought* to have done about the risks associated with its glasses.

An analogous lesson appears in a decision by the Indiana court of appeals, in a case in which a woman sustained back and neck injuries and became epileptic from an accident involving a lawn chair. In setting up the chair, the plaintiff unfolded it and opened its legs until she met resistance while the legs were in a vertical position. She then turned the chair upright and tried to sit in it. The chair collapsed. An expert testified for the plaintiff that people generally know about the dangers of not opening a lawn chair properly, but that "they believe there is a safe way to do it, namely, by unfolding the legs to a vertical position until resistance is encountered." The court concluded that "[i]f people do in fact generally hold such a belief," it could not rule "as a matter of law" that the danger of injuries like the plaintiff's was "open and obvious."[15]

Analysis of the lawn chair case should focus initially on the image that the product presented to consumers about safe use, but ultimately the question is one of "oughts." In and among the delicate empirical questions of what people do expect, there are mixed factual and philosophical issues about what product sellers have a right to believe about people's expectations and their actions, and fundamentally normative questions of how much cushion sellers must provide for what may seem to them consumers' inattention to detail.

The obvious and the ordinary.   One of the best illustrations of the obviousness problem is a case from a generation ago, the decision of the Court of Appeals for the District of Columbia in *Jamieson v. Woodward & Lothrop*.[16] The case is fascinating because it drew forth the fiercest legal argument on a most commonplace product—"an ordinary rubber rope, about the thickness of a large lead pencil, about forty inches long, with ropes on the ends." As Judge Prettyman described the article, which was called a "Lithe-Line," "[i]t was a simple elastic exerciser," accompanied by "eight silhouette sketches of exercises . . . with a summary description of each exercise." The plaintiff, Ms. Jamieson, suffered a detached retina as she was doing a muscle strengthening exercise. While she was lying down with the rope tight against the soles of her feet, the rope slipped and struck her in the eye.

In his majority opinion upholding a summary judgment for the manufacturer, Judge Prettyman chanted a litany of products whose perils "truly" could be called " 'inherently dangerous', because they might slip": "A

---

15. Kroger Sav-On Store v. Presnell, 515 N.E.2d 538, 544 (Ind. Ct. App. 1987).

16. 247 F.2d 23 (D.C. Cir. 1957), cert. denied, 355 U.S. 855.

tack, a hammer, a pane of glass, a chair, a rug, a rubber band." He attached a reserve class of "myriads of other objects." The simple gist of his argument was that one could not impose liability for failure to warn of the elasticity of a rubber rope. The product was analogous to a rubber band, which adults knew would snap back; even small boys used the principle in making slingshots. Moreover, although one could visualize "a cut lip, bloody nose, or black eye" from a "mishap" with the Lithe Line, it was not reasonable to foresee a detached retina. The issue was for the court, wrote Judge Prettyman, rather than one to be exposed "to the possible prejudices, sympathies or whims of a lay jury."[17]

Judge Washington, dissenting, focused in part on the beguiling statements in the leaflet that came with the product — "[g]iven enough of this ingenious little elastic rope it is possible for *any* body to prune the hips, sleek the legs, carve the waistline ... And do it pleasantly!" Given the aura created by this language, he thought it a jury question whether a purchaser "would be warranted in assuming that an exercise, prescribed without qualification by a well-known and reputable manufacturer ... could be performed ... without injury," and argued that a jury could find "a duty to warn or otherwise protect."[18] Judge Washington's response to Judge Prettyman's catalog of assertedly minor injuries, if arguably sexist, could well be de-genderized: "It would be a rare woman indeed who would willingly use an exerciser which, without fault on her part, could give her a black eye or a cut lip or any facial injury."[19]

This case shows the stresses and strains that a simple fact situation, involving a mundane product, can place on courts; the vote on this distinguished tribunal was five to four. Part of the problem arises from the tendency of a liability rule to force manufacturers into a saturation mode for warnings; it seems so simple to require an extra printed line on a leaflet, but after a while, people grow numb to baskets-full of warnings. The central issue, however, appears to be one of what image the product presented to the consumer, and what someone in the position of the manufacturer should have figured out about the consequences that could flow from that image. There seems no particular reason why judges would be better at that judgment than juries.

Let us now ask whether a decision for the plaintiff in the Lithe Line case would likely establish a mindset in other manufacturers that would cause them to be more cautionary about ordinary products. Such a decision probably would communicate a message with that effect, and the signal would

---

17. *Id.* at 26, 28, 29, 33.
18. *Id.* at 38-39 (Washington, J., dissenting).
19. *Id.* at 35.

be clear enough that it would seem to establish a fair rule, at least prospectively. The question then becomes simply one of who should pay the loss in this particular case. Although the individual case is a difficult one, I would be inclined to favor Ms. Jamieson, primarily because of the gloss that the manufacturer's representations attached to the product.

A rather colloquial description of a rule favoring the plaintiff would run this way: Was the danger obvious? Yes. Was the manufacturer negligent in not pointing out the obvious danger? Maybe, in the context of the advertising. Who should decide? The jury, since the negligence issue was disputed. It is true that if Ms. Jamieson had thought up the Lithe Line idea on her own, she could have bought a rubber rope at the hardware store and used it in self-invented exercises. It is also almost certain, though, that the hardware salesperson would not have told her, as the leaflet did, that she would "marvel at the supple way your body responds with new lines of rhythm and beauty as you stretch yourself into shape and gain the grace and poise that you've coveted all your life!"[20]

Materiality

The justice problems embedded in warnings issues require a mixture of objective and subjective analysis when the question is whether the lack of a warning was material to the plaintiff's decision to encounter a product. An alternative to casting the problem as one of materiality is to view it as a causation question, since one way to state the issue is whether the giving of a warning that was not given would have significantly influenced the plaintiff's choice.

One application of a relatively objective standard appears in a rabies vaccine case, in which the plaintiff received an injection in preparation for her husband's assignment to Buenos Aires, a place where there were few potential rabies contacts. In holding for the plaintiff, the court said that if there had been disclosure of the risk of side effects in the context of the relatively low need for prophylaxis, a person situated like the plaintiff would reasonably have decided to decline the treatment.[21]

A very different profile of vaccine litigation triggered the Arizona Supreme Court's refusal to accept a plaintiff's argument that a particular consumer would have chosen to avoid a risk that practically everyone else seemed willing to take. Rejecting a claim for the fatal polio that a father

20. *Id.* at 37 (quoted by Washington, J., dissenting).
21. Anderson v. McNeilab, Inc., 831 F.2d 92, 93 (5th Cir. 1987).

contracted from his two-month-old child, who had taken a dose of Sabin vaccine, that court referred to the fact that "millions of Americans gave the vaccine to their children." Where the plaintiff widow could not testify that she would not have let her child take the vaccine under any circumstances, and where the risk factor was one in five million, the court would not presume that the parents would not have allowed the vaccination if they had been told of the risk factor.[22] This decision makes a legal judgment of what is reasonable on the basis of an almost universal social practice.

Courts have mixed particular facts with an objective standard in other products contexts with great quantitative importance. For example, in an asbestos case, Judge Newman wrote for the Second Circuit that where "[t]here was no evidence that [the plaintiff] was aware of asbestos hazards, and they were not obvious," it was for the jury to decide "what a worker, alerted to the hazards, would have done."[23] An analogous set of holdings appeared in the most-publicized cigarette litigation. In denying a manufacturer's motion for directed verdict, Judge Sarokin referred to the idea that the jury could have found that the defendant's portrayal of its product "fostered" a smoker's belief that "the cigarette companies would not market a dangerous product."[24] In another opinion in the same case, premising that "[t]he adequacy of warning depends upon all of the risks encountered by the average consumers," he had concluded that "[a] plaintiff may well argue that had she or he been warned of all the risks, cigarettes would have been avoided."[25]

A case dealing with fuel tank crashworthiness evinces a more particularized concern with the plaintiff's state of mind. In this case, a Texas appellate court referred to the testimony of a Mustang purchaser that having received a recall letter on Pintos, he "called the Ford dealership and was informed that the recall letter did not apply to Mustang II vehicles." The court appeared to give weight to the purchaser's assertion that his daughter would not have driven the Mustang if he had been warned of the fire hazard associated with rear-end collisions.[26]

The need to focus on the specificity of the plaintiff's information may cause courts to superimpose issues associated with the doctrine of assumption of risk upon the materiality question. In a Pennsylvania case, the plaintiff attributed electrocution injuries to the arcing of current between power

---

22. Sheehan v. Pima County, Ariz., 135 Ariz. 235, 238, 660 P.2d 486, 489 (1982).

23. Raney v. Owens-Illinois, Inc., 897 F.2d 94, 96 (2d Cir. 1990).

24. Cipollone v. Liggett Group, Inc., 683 F. Supp. 1487, 1496 (D.N.J. 1988).

25. Cipollone v. Liggett Group, Prod. Liab. Rep. (CCH) ¶11,637, at 33,086-33,087 (D.N.J. Oct. 27, 1987).

26. Ford Motor Co. v. Durrill, 714 S.W.2d 329, 33 (Tex. Ct. App. 1986).

lines and a trailer made by the defendant. Although the plaintiff admitted that he was "aware of the danger from *contact* between the trailer and the power lines," the court discerned no evidence "that he was aware of the danger in allowing the trailer to be operated *near* the power lines." It thus found a fact question as to whether a warning of the danger of operating the vehicle near the lines "would have caused [the plaintiff] to act differently."[27]

The more relevant a plaintiff's particularized knowledge is to a risk, the more likely it is that courts will view that knowledge as dispositive against a duty to warn. For example, one court denied recovery in a case involving injuries attributed to use of a birth control pill because the plaintiff had not disclosed to her physician that she had had an episode of toxemia.[28]

One message that comes through from these cases is that courts will expect people to do their best when they engage in a risky course of conduct. In that connection, judges appear to reserve to themselves a significant part of the task of deciding whether parties have done their best, or at least whether what they have done is good enough. This appears to be a judicial determination on the moral question of what people deserve.

Disclaimers Compared

It is useful to compare the commercial law-based rules on disclaimers and limitations of liability with the tort law of duty to warn. The disclaimer rules, now rooted in the Uniform Commercial Code, permit a seller to "exclude or modify" implied warranties under certain conditions. For example, the Code allows a seller to disclaim the implied warranty of merchantability, although it requires that the seller "mention merchantability" and declares that if the disclaimer is written, it must be "conspicuous."[29] In accord with the longstanding practice of both merchants and casual sellers, the Code permits the exclusion of all implied warranties "by expressions like 'as is', 'with all faults' or other language which in common understanding calls the buyer's attention to the exclusion of warranties and makes plain that there is no implied warranty."[30] A parallel set of Code provisions

---

27. Books v. Pennsylvania Power & Light Co., 362 Pa. Super. 100, 109, 523 A.2d 794, 799 (1987).

28. Seley v. G.D. Searle & Co., 67 Ohio St. 2d 192, 200-201, 423 N.E.2d 831, 838-839 (1981).

29. U.C.C. § 2-316(2) (1978).

30. U.C.C. § 2-316(3)(a).

allow sellers to "limit or alter the measure of damages," for example, by saying that the buyer's remedy will be no more than the "return of the goods and repayment of the price or ... repair and replacement."[31]

A significant contrast between the tort law and the Code is that where the tort warnings rules require the manufacturer to take active steps associated with the product itself to avoid liability, the Code permits a general avoidance of, or limitation of liability. This relative ease of exculpation helps to explain the fact that, in products litigation, most successful defenses based on disclaimers apply to cases involving economic loss, but not personal injury.

A landmark denunciation of a defendant's effort to utilize a disclaimer for personal injuries appeared in *Henningsen v. Bloomfield Motors, Inc.,*[32] one of the decisions that inspired the development of strict liability for products a generation ago. That case, which involved personal injuries suffered by the owner of a new car when it ran off the road, arose in a market context that may be difficult for younger readers to imagine. Today, with many auto manufacturers in the field and a variety of warranty extensions available to consumers, it may be hard to realize that General Motors, Ford, and Chrysler accounted for 93.5 percent of passenger car production in the United States in the year 1958. But it was against that background that Judge Francis wrote for the New Jersey Supreme Court in *Henningsen* that the standardized auto warranty used by the Big Three manufacturers was "imposed on the automobile consumer. He takes it or leaves it, and he must take it to buy an automobile."[33] It was in the context of this "gross inequality of bargaining position"[34] that the court declared that Chrysler's disclaimer was "so inimical to the public good" that it must be struck down.[35]

In its treatment of limitation or exclusion of consequential damages, the Uniform Commercial Code announces a general rule that overlaps substantially with the *Henningsen* holding. The Code declares that "[l]imitation of consequential damages for injury to the person in the case of consumer goods is prima facie unconscionable."[36] The language of unconscionability may seem strong stuff for a "commercial code," but we must stress that this rule applies only to consumer products. We may observe, in this connection, that the New Jersey court's decision in *Henningsen* employed the theory of implied warranty of merchantability rather than strict liability for

---

31. U.C.C. § 719(1)(a).
32. 32 N.J. 358, 161 A.2d 69 (1960).
33. *Id.* at 390, 161 A.2d at 87.
34. *Id.* at 391, 161 A.2d at 87.
35. *Id.* at 404, 161 A.2d at 95.
36. U.C.C. § 719(3).

products, a doctrine that awaited its formal invention a couple of years later.

A lot of currents come together here, but much of the judiciary's hostility to disclaimers for personal injury may be summed up in the ideas of portrayal and power. In the liability section of its decision, the *Henningsen* court referred to "the ordinary layman . . . responding to the importunings of colorful advertising."[37] Besides focusing these considerations of product promotion in a particularly sharp way, the disclaimer issue in *Henningsen* accents the contrast that warnings law provides with respect to the use of seller power. When a consumer is warned about a specific hazard, she can take self-protective measures to avoid injury. But a consumer against whom a disclaimer is effective can protect herself only against the financial consequences of injury, even physical injury, and can do that only by the purchase of insurance or the prior accumulation of wealth. Thus, a disclaiming seller takes advantage not only of its creation of demand but its ability to enforce an anti-liability rule in situations where bargaining may not be an effective option.

Practical Justice

Leading precedents on warnings and disclaimers, taken together, add to our stock of ideas about practical justice in products liability law. Our consumer law is highly individualistic, as befits a set of rules applicable to a free market. One starting point is the model of the consumer who is able to take care of herself, being well-informed about all relevant characteristics of the product, with modifications being made to accommodate factual departures from that model. When hazards inherent in a product make themselves known to the consumer, courts view the model as being fulfilled.

The "obviousness" defense presents a particularly interesting manifestation of individualistic thinking. The effect of "obviousness" in cases brought under the warnings rubric is to eclipse completely the plaintiff's cause of action, rather than to serve as an affirmative defense. This version of the obviousness concept has an ethical basis that relates to the voluntariness of the consumer's conduct in encountering the product. We should, however, draw a prospective distinction between this use of "obviousness" and the doctrine of "assumption of risk," discussed in the next chapter, which requires that the consumer's choice be not only voluntary but unreasonable.

---

37. 32 N.J. at 384, 161 A.2d at 83.

When the product's hazard does not figuratively announce itself to the consumer, courts leave the metaphor of obviousness and focus directly on duty to warn. One might try to cast this duty in economic terms, focusing on the seller's comparative advantage concerning relevant information about risk. But it appears that the imposition of such duties depends more on judicial notions about proper exercises of sellers' power in their relations with consumers. To be sure, it also may depend on the individual knowledge of particular consumers. Judicial consideration of the "sophisticated user" doctrine reflects this individualizing tendency in decisions favoring plaintiffs as well as defendants.

Standing behind decisions in duty to warn cases is an ethic that builds on notions of self-reliance, founded on the ability to choose. We should note that choice is a double-edged idea in this context, not limited to the consumer side of disputes. Usually at least implicit in the decisions that find duties to warn is the idea that the manufacturer had an opportunity to choose more consumer safety by including cautionary information. But typically more salient is the premise, whether articulated or not, that a warning would enable the plaintiff to make the sort of choice that comports with our notions of personal dignity.

The diverse faces of choice are quite as evident in the law on disclaimers. When a consumer buys a product "as is," or after having read a statement that denies the manufacturer's responsibility for making the product merchantable, the law imputes to him a choice, both as to the peril of primary harm and as to the risk that the seller will not have to compensate for that harm. However, it is for reasons that grow out of our special concerns for personal integrity that the law turns paternalistic with respect to disclaimers for personal injuries. The drafters of a business-centered document, the Uniform Commercial Code, crafted a rule for that situation that places ethical constraints on the enforcement of harsh bargains.

The law on disclaimers and warnings does operate on a sophisticated conception of how information drives the marketplace. But even more importantly, it is redolent of ideas, born of a thousand cases, about the subtle morality of choice.

10

Consumer Conduct

Our exploration of the lessons that products liability law teaches us about ourselves now turns to focus more closely on the consumer rather than the seller. Many of us are engaged in selling of one kind or another, but the role of consumer is a universal one, and in the consumer product context it is a role to which all of us can easily relate.

We already have viewed the consumer as a receptor of messages sent by the seller. In the last chapter, we analyzed cases in which the consumer claims that he or she is a victim of a lack of messages, or inadequate messages. The seller in such cases often will contend that the consumer had sufficient information about the product but did not use it prudently. In that sense, the duty to warn issue serves as a bridge to our present analysis of the role of the consumer as an actor in his or her own right. In this chapter we ask what effect particular kinds of consumer conduct should have on liability judgments. And we inquire how the law on that subject reflects society's views about the relevant elements of the human condition.

The cases represent a wide range of behavioral models. In various situations, we as consumers are free actors who are usually rational, in knowing our own best interest and acting in accord with it; we are sometimes careless; on occasion we try to extend our bargain with the seller beyond what it will fairly bear; and not infrequently we find ourselves trapped by circumstance.

General Summary of the Doctrines

In probing the social significance of the law, we begin with the law itself. First, we treat sellers' defensive theories based on consumer conduct.

Contributory Negligence

The basic definition of contributory negligence is simple: it is the failure of a plaintiff to exercise reasonable care for his or her own safety. The defense is a relatively stringent one from the consumer point of view, because its theory is objective. The unvarnished doctrine of contributory negligence requires a claimant to live up to the standard of the reasonable, prudent person, whatever information or talents the plaintiff possesses. In its pragmatic morality, this rule sends a message. It says to the person who is below the community average in ability or intelligence that he or she must either avoid risk or accept the legal consequences of being unable to recover damages.

A straightforward example of the operation of this doctrine appears in a North Carolina case in which a worker suffered an amputation when he put his hand in a machine used in a yarn mill. The plaintiff said he had no idea that there were moving parts inside the machine when he put in his hand, which was struck by a cylinder covered with sharp, wire-wound teeth. In denying recovery to the plaintiff, the state supreme court emphasized that the contributory negligence doctrine would apply even though he was not "*actually aware*" of the unreasonable danger of injury," so long as the defendant proved that the plaintiff had ignored unreasonable risks that "would have been apparent to a prudent person exercising ordinary care for his own safety."[1]

There do exist ameliorating doctrines for the plaintiff who "should have known better." For example, some courts have allowed the "inadvertent" plaintiff to escape the contributory negligence defense, as in a case where a worker said that his hand came in contact with conveyor sprockets after he lost his balance.[2]

There are also decisions that allow claimants to invoke especially stressful circumstances against the defense of contributory negligence. In a Fifth Circuit case, the plaintiff suffered severe injuries from the explosion of a multi-piece wheel, which occurred in the emergency repair yard of a telephone company service center. The occasion was a crisis created by a tornado, and the plaintiff and his co-workers had been laboring 14 to 15 hours a day in response to the emergency conditions. In these circumstances, the court took into account the crowded conditions of the yard, the number of people standing around waiting for vehicles to be repaired, and the "degree of commotion in the yard on account of the urgency of the work."[3]

---

1. Smith v. Fiber Controls Corp., 300 N.C. 669, 673, 268 S.E.2d 504, 507 (1980).
2. Schell v. AMF, Inc., 567 F.2d 1259 (3d Cir. 1977).
3. Bowers v. Firestone Tire & Rubber Co., 800 F.2d 474, 477 (5th Cir. 1986).

Assumption of Risk

Courts thus engage in some individualizing of justice even under the relatively objective eye of the contributory negligence doctrine. But these subjectivizing tendencies become much clearer under the label of "assumption of risk." That theory, which most courts prefer to "ordinary contributory negligence" for the assessment of consumer conduct in products cases, allows the defendant to prevail only by showing that the plaintiff voluntarily and unreasonably encountered a known risk.

This idea stands in striking contrast to the traditional presentation of contributory negligence doctrine. Ordinary contributory negligence, which permits a defense against the plaintiff who "should have known" of a risk as well as the claimant who actually knew of it, appears through the lens of recent scholarship as classically economic in its objectivity. We may view the rule as utilitarian, seeking an arithmetical match between large numbers of persons and the products they use, with the purpose of achieving the greatest good for the greatest number.

A free market morality. By contrast, the theory of assumption of risk is an individualizing one, although the subjective features of the doctrine do not submerge its stark free market orientation. Some courts appear to view a plaintiff's actual knowledge of a risk as sufficiently coloring the character of his conduct to bar recovery. Thus, a worker's fear of losing a job if he or she refuses to do dangerous work will not keep the defense from its appointed work. In chapter two, we described the Sixth Circuit's denial of recovery to Perry Orfield, who was struck by a fifty-foot oak while he was using a bulldozer without a canopy to arrange uprooted trees in piles. We noted the court's technical insistence, under defect doctrine, that the machine was not dangerous beyond the contemplation of an ordinary consumer.[4] Under our present lens, the most relevant language is the court's declaration that the plaintiff was "fully aware of the dangers which would be incurred in conducting the windrowing operations without the canopy guard."[5]

One could slice this kind of rule on an economic carving board ("You pays your money and you takes your chance") but the emphasis seems moral. We have other common sense expressions that capture the sense of justice that inheres in such rulings: "You made your bed, now lie in

---

4. Orfield v. International Harvester Co., 535 F.2d 959 (6th Cir. 1976), discussed supra, chapter 2, text accompanying note 49.

5. *Id.* at 964.

it." The sum of it is that the law will hold you to your bargains, including harsh bargains.

Even an eleven-year-old child could not escape the defense, in a case where he was injured on a water slide ride. The Georgia court of appeals declared that this young claimant was "[f]ully aware of the ride's propensities and armed with the 'consciousness of the force of gravity' which makes every child who is old enough to be at large aware of the risk of falling."[6] Affirming the court of appeals, the Georgia Supreme Court tied the locution of "patent and obvious danger" to that of assumption of risk.[7] Perhaps the best explanation for such a holding is that the manufacturer was not negligent, or that the product was not, in the world of water slides, defective.

How free to choose? Beyond the doctrine, however, so long as the focus is on individual choice, the moral element is central to such cases. This is particularly obvious in those decisions—contrary to the holding in Orfield's case—that refuse to require the plaintiff to tie herself to a dangerous machine or else risk the loss of her job. In another case previously discussed, involving injuries that occurred on a press, Judge Garrity refused to accept as realistic the plaintiff's "option of quitting her job" when she "lacked a trade or college degree and had to help support a family." As we noted, he said that in those circumstances, "the facts strongly rebut voluntariness in the ordinary sense of the word."[8]

Moral considerations burst to the surface here, and on both sides of the dispute. On the one hand, the court refuses to accept the idea that such a plaintiff is free to be a moral actor. Indeed, it implicitly tells the product maker this: even if it is the employer who selects the machine and thus most directly chooses the level of risk, a manufacturer will be held to a recognition of who it is that will be using the machine and of how constrained her choice, in fact, will be.

We must not neglect the other side of the story. Some with an economic bent will contend that to allow the plaintiff's claim may have a socially deleterious effect on the manufacturer's incentives for the production of useful goods. (There is the further assertion that such decisions will skew workers' incentives to take care of their own safety, but in many situations—by def-

---

6. Abee v. Stone Mountain Mem'l Ass'n., 169 Ga. App. 167, 169-70, 312 S.E.2d 142, 145 (1983), aff'd, 252 Ga. 465, 314 S.E.2d 444 (1984).

7. *See* Abee, *supra*, 252 Ga. at 465-466, 314 S.E.2d at 445.

8. Downs v. Gulf & W. Mfg. Co., Prod. Liab. Rep. (CCH) ¶ 11,459, at 32,717 (D. Mass. 1987), previously discussed, chapter 2, text accompanying note 51.

inition fraught with peril—this seems far-fetched.) The economic argument posits that wage rates for dangerous jobs reflect their relative benefits and costs in a free market, and reasons that judicial reluctance to enforce assumption of risk type defenses will interfere with the market for safety. Beyond this we may glimpse a utilitarian notion that the greatest number of people will benefit from relatively low levels of safety and high levels of production. Today, advocates of the defense would add one more specialized rationalization: the need to minimize labor costs, including liability costs, to resist foreign competition.

Ethics of the relationship. These are serious arguments, in a system accustomed to looking toward policy considerations in the judgment of disputes between private individuals. Why have they not swayed the courts that refuse to enforce the assumption of risk defense? The reason is that a principal focus of such decisions is on the ethics of the relationship between seller and worker. This is not to say that this is the exclusive concern of courts, but only that in cases that present the issue so starkly, policy considerations like the alleged challenge from foreign competition lie in the background, perhaps to be used only as tiebreakers.

In focusing on the litigants, rather than trying to contain the litigants and the policy background in the same depth of field, some courts have effectively made an ethics-centered view the law. We introduced in chapter three the New Jersey Supreme Court's elimination of the contributory fault defense, even in the version called assumption of risk, in cases involving industrial machines. In one of these decisions, in which the New Jersey court abrogated the defense as to strict liability cases in the workplace, the court said that "[t]he defendant manufacturer should not be permitted to escape from the breach of its duty to an employee while carrying out his assigned task . . . when observance of that duty would have prevented the very accident which occurred."[9] In the later of a brace of cases, in which the court barred the use of the defense even for negligence claims, it referred to "[t]he practicalities of the workday world," where "in the vast majority of cases, the employee works 'as is' or he is without a job."[10]

These decisions are particularly interesting, coming as they do from the highest court of a heavily industrialized state, a court that implicitly must have considered the policy implications of its decisions and opted in favor

---

9. Suter v. San Angelo Foundry & Mach. Co., 81 N.J. 150, 168, 406 A.2d 140, 148 (1979), discussed in chapter 3, text accompanying notes 3-4.

10. Green v. Sterling Extruder Corp., 95 N.J. 263, 271, 471 A.2d 15, 20 (1984), discussed in chapter 3, text accompanying notes 5-6.

of a reading of the individualized realities of workplace behavior. In the background, of course, stand competing concerns of social justice and market incentives. But in such jurisdictions, employees house within themselves potentially competing desires: for jobs at wages the market will support, and for safety. This court's efforts to balance those desires culminated in a choice to do justice as defined by the position of the individual worker.

Misuse

A third defensive theory is rather peculiar to products cases: the doctrine of misuse. This is a legal chameleon that feeds on several locutions, including the language of "abnormal use" and the "intended use doctrine" as well as the contributory negligence and assumption of risk theories just discussed.

The quintessential "misuse" is "abuse" of a product. In one of the clearest cases, a beer manufacturer successfully defended a suit by a young person injured when someone threw a bottle of the firm's brew at a telephone pole.[11] And an elevator manufacturer defeated a claim for a death resulting from the failure of its product in a freshman dormitory, where students subjected the elevator to such punishment that it was said that they "systematically destroyed" the equipment.[12]

A more difficult case created some conflict among New York judges. The defendant was the maker of a "robot-like plastic figure"—"Voltron—Defender of the Universe"—designed as a toy "for children four years of age and older." An eight-year-old boy flung a sharp, detachable part of the toy toward a six-year-old neighbor, causing serious eye injuries. In affirming a denial of summary judgment sought by the manufacturer, a majority of the appellate division drew on expert testimony about images of the robot spinning a star-shaped weapon at his enemies, events depicted in TV shows and videocassettes.[13] A dissenter emphasized that no parts of the toy were "mechanically or electrically movable or projectible," and argued that the only possible conclusion was that the child who threw the toy "abused" it "by using it in a way never intended."[14] The court of appeals affirmed the appellate majority, saying that it was for the jury to decide "whether the

---

11. Venezia v. Miller Brewing Co., 626 F.2d 188, 190-191 (1st Cir. 1980).

12. Davis v. Reliance Elec. Co., 351 So.2d 1238, 1240-1241 (La. Ct. App. 1977), cert. denied, 353 So.2d 1334 (La. 1978).

13. Lugo v. LJN Toys, Ltd. 146 A.D.2d 168, 539 N.Y.S.2d 922 (1989), aff'd, 25 N.Y.2d 850, 552 N.E.2d 162, 552 N.Y.S.2d 914 (1990).

14. 146 A.D.2d at 176-177, 539 N.Y.S.2d at 928 (Sullivan, J., dissenting).

product was defective and reasonably safe for its intended use or a reasonably foreseeable intended use."[15]

Without its background of image creation, the case would not be as strong for the plaintiff, but that factor seems dispositive. It is the image that defines "intended use." An important, related strand of the case concerns the ethical position of the manufacturer, whose ad campaign defined the breadth of its duty to know the harmful potential of its product.

Conceptual Linkages and a Morality of Behavior

The relationship among these three doctrines—contributory negligence, assumption of risk, and misuse—deserves separate comment. For these theories relate to each other, and to several other legal concepts, in ways that reveal the moral bases of judicial concern with claimants' behavior. Indeed, courts are developing a morality of choice and personal responsibility under these various labels. In this section, we seek to define the common ground of the concepts that underlies the terminology.

Contributory Negligence and Assumption of Risk

As we indicated above, courts tend to distinguish the concepts of contributory negligence and assumption of risk. Contributory negligence, which is relatively unforgiving to consumer claims, employs an objective standard. It will bar, or reduce, liability to plaintiffs who have reason to know of a hazard, including knowledge that could be acquired through investigation. By contrast, assumption of risk requires both that the plaintiff behave unreasonably and that he or she have voluntarily confronted a known risk. In products liability cases, most courts allow defendants to use assumption of risk, but not contributory negligence, as a defense.

Viewed as an original matter, this distinction probably creates more trouble for courts than it is worth. The fundamental question ought simply to be, "Did the plaintiff behave with reasonable care or his or her own safety?" Given the background of imagery that accompanies products to market, it may well be that in most products cases, the only time the plaintiff acts with less than reasonable care is when he or she voluntarily encounters a risk about which he or she knows. In other words, because of the

---

15. 75 N.Y.2d at 852, 552 N.E.2d at 163, 552 N.Y.S.2d at 915.

image that sellers project for their products, the only contributory negligence is assumption of risk. Otherwise, since other kinds of tort claims will generally be barred or reduced by any form of plaintiff carelessness, it would be difficult to justify why products cases are different. The rest is embroidery.

Some fairly subtle rationales support defenses based on the plaintiff's conduct,[16] but it would seem that the central question is whether a claimant's carelessness presents a moral reason to deny recovery, with the degree of knowledge being one important factor in judging carelessness in particular contexts. It may be objected that a unitary contributory negligence standard presents an insufficiently delicate classification scheme. But the practical equation of contributory negligence with assumption of risk in an advertising-saturated product arena would seem to achieve the necessary refinement. What is important is not the artificial conceptual distinction, but rather the real-life correspondence of the theories in the products environment.

Misuse and Contributory Negligence

A similar analysis provides a frame for the relationship of both contributory negligence and assumption of risk with the doctrine of misuse. With respect to contributory negligence, many decisions that employ "misuse" terminology or its variations prove, on scrutiny, simply to involve findings that the claimant was not duly careful for his or her own safety. Illustrative is a case in which a mechanic suffered severe burns when he failed to disconnect ignition wires while working on an engine. In rejecting an appeal against a directed verdict for the auto maker, the Michigan Supreme Court said that as a qualified mechanic, the plaintiff "knew that unless certain steps were taken, his turning of the key would produce a spark which might cause a fire" and that he "was not deterred by his knowledge."[17] Although the court refers to "improper use" phraseology in a precedent, its ruling seems nothing more than a declaration that as a matter of practical morality, the plaintiff did not deserve to recover because of his carelessness in a context in which he brought specialized knowledge to a specialized job.

We analogize here our analysis of the prevailing judicial use of the doctrine of assumption of risk in products cases. In a comparable way, the principal employment of the concept of misuse appears to be to describe a foolish sort of conduct that should be defined as contributory fault in the

---

16. For one of the best discussions, see Schwartz, Contributory and Comparative Negligence: A Reappraisal, 87 Yale L.J. 697, 721- 726 (1978).
17. Crews v. General Motors Corp., 400 Mich. 208, 219, 253 N.W.2d 617, 620 (1977).

products context. An example of the constraints inherent in the misuse defense appears in an Illinois case in which the plaintiff drove a golf cart at full speed. Noting that the general use was for an intended purpose and that use at full speed was foreseeable, the court concluded that the plaintiff had not engaged in a "patent 'misuse.' " Declaring that "mere carelessness or negligence is not enough to bar . . . recovery,"[18] the court in effect established the limitations on conduct-based defenses in products cases. The total doctrinal set of that conduct appears to be comprised of the categories that most courts call "misuse" and "assumption of risk."

A Colorado case presents an interesting technical wrinkle, involving a distinction between the defenses applicable to negligence actions and strict liability claims. The plaintiff in this case suffered injuries on a woodworking machine when he reached under his workbench to make adjustments on the machine while it was operating, and his forearm touched the spinning blade. The court allowed that this conduct "could be considered as a defense to [the plaintiff's] negligence claim," but said that it did "not, as a matter of law, constitute misuse for purposes of his strict liability claim." It thus held that it was appropriate to charge the jury on comparative negligence on the plaintiff's negligence count, but that it was error to give a misuse instruction on his strict liability count.[19]

Parallel moralities of tort. This analysis reveals some parallel moralities of tort law. One may view basic negligence law as representing a combination of normative judgments about the rightness or wrongfulness of injurers' conduct and the objective rationality of victims' behavior. Strict products liability imposes against sellers a relatively stringent standard, based in theory on the hazardousness of the product, which more fully takes into account the realities of power and especially of image-making in the marketplace of consumer goods. In actions under that theory, the courts have tended to individualize their analysis of the plaintiff's conduct. I simply emphasize that it would be better, within the framework of those parallel moralities, if the courts cleaved to a single question with respect to the plaintiff's behavior: the question of what is reasonable in the circumstances, under the applicable products liability doctrine.

Assumption of Risk and Misuse

To complete the circle among the three major defensive doctrines, it seems appropriate to blend together misuse and assumption of risk as the

---

18. Sipari v. Villa Olivia Country Club, 63 Ill. App.3d 985, 992, 380 N.E.2d 819, 825 (1978).

19. Patterson v. Magna American Corp., 754 P.2d 1385, 1387 (Colo. Ct. App. 1988).

principal kind of conduct—perhaps the only kind of conduct—which constitutes contributory fault for products liability purposes. In an opinion that took the analysis part way, an Indiana appellate court characterized misuse as "part of assumption of risk when the user has knowledge of the defect." The decision, which is instructive both in its perceptiveness and its limitations, involved a tire blowout that led to the overturning of the plaintiff's tractor-trailer. Employing a "series of mathematical formulae and computations," the defendant argued that the plaintiff drove the truck an excessive distance after the blowout. Although evidently not quarreling with an instruction on contributory negligence, the court found it appropriate to refuse an instruction on misuse. The court declared that the concepts were "distinguishable," "[s]ince misuse involves a subjective determination of continuing conduct in the presence of a known defect, and contributory negligence presumes an objective determination of failure to find or guard against a defect when a duty to do so is present."[20]

Because the evidence did not "unerringly" establish that the plaintiff kept driving on the blown out tire with knowledge of the defect, the court did not think that the defendant deserved a misuse instruction. Under the analysis we have presented, the court was correct in functionally equating misuse and assumption of risk, although incorrect in apparently allowing a contributory negligence defense.

The Massachusetts Supreme Judicial Court viewed the subject from quite a different perspective. With Massachusetts clinging to implied warranty as its theory of choice in products liability cases, the court had to respond to a certified question as to whether, under that theory, the misuse defense applied to "foreseeable uses of the product as well as to unforeseeable uses." Declaring that "the defendant's ability to foresee the plaintiff's voluntary, knowing and unreasonable misuse of the product is irrelevant,"[21] the Massachusetts court emphasized its rejection of liability for breach of warranty when a defendant "should reasonably have foreseen that the plaintiff would *unreasonably* and voluntarily use a product, knowing it to be defective and dangerous."[22]

Moral judgment and intellectual efficiency. All this may seem an exercise in doctrines dancing on the head of a pin. But when we dig below the doctrinal talk, we discern that what the courts are seeking to find is an answer that is fair in the context of the way products are portrayed, and which respects the ability of informed consumers to make risky choices. Thus, seemingly technical legal classifications provide a pathway for courts to work out the moral bottom line of individual cases.

---

20. Fruehauf Trailer Div. v. Thornton, 174 Ind. App. 1, 11-12, 366 N.E.2d 21, 29 (1977).
21. Allen v. Chance Mfg. Co., 398 Mass. 32, 35, 494 N.E.2d 1324, 1326 (1986).
22. *Id.* at 35-36, 494 N.E.2d at 1326-1327 (1986).

It is true that the conceptual structure has become baroque, and that it would be wise to make it simpler. I would collapse assumption of risk and misuse into the general category of contributory fault, reducing the issue to whether the plaintiff behaved reasonably in the circumstances. The circumstances would include the way the product was portrayed, the plaintiff's ability to bargain, the plaintiff's actual knowledge, and the suddenness of the injury-causing occurrence. It appears that in most products cases, courts think that the only sorts of conduct that should bar or reduce liability are a subjectively unreasonable encounter with a known risk or a type of use that so egregiously departs from the product's evident function as to be subjectively foolish. To say that ordinarily it is only those kinds of behavior that can be contributory fault would be the most intellectually efficient way to deal with the problem of the plaintiff's conduct in products liability cases.

Duty to Warn

We shall now briefly explore some other conceptual linkages that bear on the issue of consumer behavior, and that also appear to fit into the judicial effort to package morality and law in a way that achieves practical justice. One of these linkages involves a subject we considered under its own doctrinal heading in chapter nine: the duty to warn.

An interesting joinder of warnings concepts and consumer conduct issues appears in a well-publicized case in which the Tenth Circuit upheld a large punitive award for a toxic shock fatality associated with the use of tampons. International Playtex, the manufacturer, claimed that Betty O'Gilvie had acted unreasonably in continuing to use super-absorbent menstrual tampons after developing symptoms that caused her to ask her doctor whether she had toxic shock syndrome. The manufacturer contended that Ms. O'Gilvie had been unreasonable in not seeking a second opinion when she was skeptical about her doctor's reassurance. Knitting the question of whether Ms. O'Gilvie was at fault to the warnings issue, the court observed that a jury had found the manufacturer's warnings inadequate and concluded that this finding was "dispositive of the comparative fault issue because failure to heed an inadequate warning is not unreasonable." The defense contained the seeds of its own destruction, inherent in what the court characterized as the manufacturer's contention that Ms. O'Gilvie was "at fault in disregarding a warning that did not properly apprise her of the very hazard to which she fell victim." This argument, wrote Judge Seymour for the court, was "simply without legal or logical support."[23]

---

23. O'Gilvie v. International Playtex, Inc., 821 F.2d 1438, 1444 (10th Cir. 1987).

Consumer Conduct and Causation

Folk wisdom tells us that there is more than one way to skin a cat. Another doctrinal approach to skinning the cat of the plaintiff's conduct involves the concept of causation. A fundamental requirement of tort law is that the plaintiff demonstrate that the defendant's product or conduct was the factual cause of the injury. In an Eighth Circuit case involving a tire that blew up, the defense argued that the plaintiff assumed the risk by overinflating the tire. The jury gave a verdict for the defendant under an instruction that asked whether the plaintiff "thereby caused his injury." Affirming, the appellate court said that the verdict necessarily implied a conclusion that the plaintiff had not proved "that the alleged defect caused the injury."[24]

A case involving an exploding Coke bottle provides an interesting parallel. In the incident that gave rise to this Louisiana litigation, the plaintiff tried to open the bottle with a basin wrench. He tried to use the circumstantial evidence of the explosion to prove that the bottler was negligent, but the court succinctly turned away this argument. Premising that "[o]ne who undertakes to open a bottle of coca cola with a basin wrench, breaking the bottle in the process, is negligent," the court declared that "the most plausible and, indeed, the inescapable inference as to the cause of plaintiff's accident is his own negligence and not that of the bottler."[25]

In such decisions, courts use plaintiffs' independent choices of how to deal with products to override the images of safety projected by sellers. As the courts perceive these cases, the locus of power concerning product use has shifted to the consumer. The concept of causation, superimposed on defenses based on the plaintiff's conduct, becomes the vehicle to translate that reality into law.

The Link to the Defect Concept

This chapter carries forth the theme of reciprocity between the process of making and selling products and the process of consumer choice and use. This reciprocity is particularly obvious in the way the defect concept links up with the conduct of the consumer.

Some of the doctrinal possibilities in this linkage, but also some potential for error, are evident in an Iowa case. Robert Aller, who worked for a cabinet-making firm, suffered injuries when a co-worker activated an indus-

---

24. Collins v. B.F. Goodrich Co., 558 F.2d 908, 911-912 (8th Cir. 1977).
25. Dugas v. Coca-Cola Bottling Co., 356 So.2d 1054, 1058 (La. Ct. App. 1978).

trial saw while Aller's hand was under the guard. Quarreling with the idea that consumer expectations should define whether a product is "unreasonably dangerous," Aller argued that this test "injects considerations of contributory negligence into a strict liability case." He contended that "if an ordinary buyer expected a machine to be in the condition received, the jury may tend to think that the buyer was contributory negligent by using the machine in that condition." The Iowa Supreme Court cast the case differently: "[O]nce a jury finds the ordinary buyer expected the machine to be in the condition received, it must find the plaintiff cannot recover on a theory of strict liability." In this view of the matter, "[s]uch a jury could not tend to consider contributory negligence at all."[26]

This presentation of the concepts, while perhaps technically persuasive, seems to ignore the plaintiff's conduct at the moment of the injury. Moreover, it may insufficiently take into account a somewhat divisible behavior that could have been conditioned by the character of the machine: the plaintiff's initial choice to place his hand under the guard. If the plaintiff's actions in either regard were not careless, the judgment that strict liability was not appropriate seems questionable; if his actions were careless, of course, he would have been contributorily negligent.

Another case, in which the claimant was a substantial business rather than an individual worker, shows how behavior that might be chalked up under defenses based on the plaintiff's conduct also ties into the concept of defect. The plaintiff was a railroad that sued another railroad that rebuilt a hopper car. The theory was that the use on such cars of solid bearings, rather than roller bearings, created an unreasonable risk of "hot boxes." The plaintiff claimed that a hot box caused an explosive and costly derailment, and won a substantial judgment.

In reversing this judgment, an Illinois appellate court rejected the plaintiff's argument that the design of the hopper car had created an unreasonably dangerous condition. The court emphasized that the plaintiff had repeatedly inspected all its trains for hot boxes, knowing "full well the risks and dangers of transporting freight cars equipped with solid bearings." Declaring that there was no "concealed physical flaw but purely a matter of design known to plaintiff," the court concluded that to impose liability on the defendant would make it an "insurer." Having effectively chalked up the plaintiff's conduct against it under the defect heading, the court also concluded that it had "assumed the risk" because its own evidence showed that it was "fully aware of the hazard of a hot box occurring on cars equipped with solid bearings."[27]

---

26. Aller v. Rodgers Mach. Mfg. Co., 268 N.W.2d 830, 836 (Iowa 1978).

27. Toledo, P. & W. R.R. v. Burlington N., Inc., 67 Ill. App. 3d 928, 933-934, 385 N.E.2d 937, 940-942 (1978).

The Commingling of Concepts: A Reprise

Complex relationships exist among the risks associated with designs and levels of warning, the knowledge of product users, and consumers' conduct. Employed judiciously in an effort to define the realities of product use, doctrines may throw into relief the justice of cases.

A case involving a hockey helmet provides a good example of how overlapping legal categories can contribute to sensible decisions. The helmet in question was designed in three sections to facilitate adjustment. The plaintiff, a prep school athlete, suffered injuries when a puck penetrated the gap of the helmet where the three sections joined together. In support of a judgment notwithstanding a jury verdict for the plaintiff on a negligence claim, the defendants argued that the plaintiff knew of the risk he ran because the gap was obvious. However, the Massachusetts Supreme Judicial Court disagreed, focusing on testimony by the plaintiff that he believed that the helmet "would protect his head from injury" and on the fact that it had been provided to him by his coach, "a person whose judgment the plaintiff had reason to trust."

In ordering reinstatement of the plaintiff's verdict on the negligence count, the court opined that "it was the function of the jury to balance the obviousness of the helmet design against the plaintiff's testimony and the circumstances in which he received the helmet in order to arrive at a conclusion as to what the plaintiff knew at the time of the injury."[28] The court stitched together this result with a holding that it was proper for the jury to find the defendants liable under a strict liability theory based on the design of the helmet. With respect to the design defect claim, the court noted that other manufacturers made one-piece helmets and that although they were more expensive than the three piece helmet, they had not been shown to be economically infeasible.[29]

The helmet case illustrates how courts mesh complicated facts and legal doctrines in an effort to get at the street-level facts of consumer life: the relationship among product design, the existence and availability of information about risks, and the probable intensity of the consumer's focus on the relevant risk in the context of a particular activity.

It remains to consider a case that initially would appear a clear loser for the plaintiff, and indeed did result in a defendant's judgment, but one that has an interesting twist. A woman crawled into a car trunk and closed the lid on herself in an effort to commit suicide. Somehow surviving after alleg-

---

28. Everett v. Bucky Warren, Inc., 376 Mass. 280, 289, 380 N.E.2d 653, 659 (1978).
29. *See id.* at 290-291, 380 N.E.2d at 660.

edly being locked in the trunk for nine days, she sued the Ford Motor Company because she could not get out. The federal district court in New Mexico was predictably unsympathetic. It rejected the plaintiff's strict liability and negligence claims, saying that "a manufacturer has a duty to consider only those risks of injury which are foreseeable." Among other theories proffered by the plaintiff, the court also turned down a count based on implied warranty of merchantability, saying that "[p]laintiff's use of the trunk was highly extraordinary, and there is no evidence that the trunk was not fit for the ordinary purpose for which it was intended."[30]

We could muster a lot of realities to support this decision: the unusual character of the plaintiff's act; the fact that, however desperate, it was *her* act; the fact that the trunk presumably was made like all, or many other, automobile trunks. But then we would have to consider one other question, which my son Nat, then sixteen, quickly offered when I put the case to him: Could one not argue that an unopenable trunk was a design defect for this plaintiff, because it would have been a defect for *any person who became inadvertently locked inside*? However the reader reacts to that question, what is now apparent is the subtlety of the relationship between defect and defenses based on the plaintiff's conduct. The question also underlines the need for courts seeking the justice of cases to consider reality in all its richness.

Symbol of Social Values

The fascinating legal character of the case law of consumer conduct in products cases matches the fascination of its human dimensions. It usually takes at least two to make an accident, and courts must fix legal responsibility, sometimes assigning it entirely to one party and sometimes dividing it. Judicial decisions in the more difficult cases on this issue help us to define our social contours. These cases force judgment, factual and legal, on a variety of matters with social content:

- The degree of power exercised by producers and sellers with regard not only to the design and manufacture of products, but the way in which they portray those goods to the public.
- The degree of moral responsibility that attaches to producers and sellers relative to their exercise of power over design, manufacture and portrayal.
- The existence of product images as metaphysical concepts in the consciousness of product users.

---

30. Daniell v. Ford Motor Co., 581 F. Supp. 728, 730-731 (D. N.M. 1984).

- The product user as a moral agent with personal responsibility for a variety of choices, including choice of the basic risk level associated with a product and choice of specific courses of action in product use.
- The competition between consumer dignities: the dignity associated with the right to make choices about risk, and the dignity associated with the physical integrity that is placed at risk by product hazards.
- The probable effect of legal rules on choices of design, portrayal, and use by producers and consumers.
- The specificity of notice that consumers should have of product hazards.
- The degree of meaningful knowledge that groups of consumers, and individual consumers, possess about product hazards.
- The degree of subjectivity with which the law should assess consumer behavior.

Products liability decisions in general, I have suggested, tell us a lot about ourselves as a society. Those decisions that focus on consumer conduct are sometimes especially revelatory. They confront us with the aphorism of Pogo: "We have met the enemy and he is us." They represent a studied effort to think through our beliefs about risk at the individual level, about the tradeoffs that life requires of us, about the degree of choice truly available to us, and about the power of others to shape our choices in both gross and subtle ways. They make the question of responsibility come alive on both sides of the fence between sellers and consumers. They clarify for us the high moral content of that question.

11

Critical Volleys

An astonishing number of major articles and book-length critiques on products liability has bridged the 1980's and the 1990's. This chapter provides critical sketches of a few of these works, to convey the flavor of the arguments that have fed into proposals for change in the law while contributing to the general debate on the subject.

First, we shall refer to two books aimed beyond technical audiences: one by a state court judge, Justice Richard Neely of the West Virginia Supreme Court, and one by Peter Huber, a lawyer based in the Manhattan Institute. Both of these authors wield purple pens.

Neely's Screed

The title of Justice Neely's 1988 book on the subject left no doubt about his assessment: *The Product Liability Mess*.[1] Neely's primary villain was "home cooking" by state courts — the tendency of those courts to favor "local individuals" in products actions against "out-of-state corporations."[2] In Neely's view, politically minded judges had cheerfully been engaging "in the business of redistributing wealth from out-of-state defendants to in-state plaintiffs."[3] Neely's high good spirits in writing this book are apparent in his description of many judges as "black-robed Magdalenes" who "devote the rest of their lives to doing penance for having been business whores when they were young."[4] "[T]hese guys and gals," he

---

1. Richard Neely, The Product Liability Mess (1988).
2. *See id.*, *e.g.*, at 15.
3. *Id.* at 45.
4. *Id.* at 59.

wrote, "are just a bunch of politicians who spend all day running a big chunk of America's government"; they "shar[e] many of the vices of ordinary political hacks."[5] As polemicized entertainment, these broadsides might be enjoyable even to a reader who did not share Neely's basic point of view. However, such language threw into question the seriousness of his broad assertion that "American courts . . . have said that everyone is liable if it strikes a jury to make him liable."[6] Confronted with such hyperbole, one who had read thousands of appellate decisions favoring defendants, and who reasonably believed that those decisions stood for tens of thousands of trial court cases with the same outcome, might have been entitled to ask where show time left off and analysis began.

Neely's specific solution was somewhat vague, but it appeared in general to be to make products liability law a more nationalized jurisprudence. He proposed a "unified, coordinated system" for dealing with products liability issues.[7] However, since he thought Congress was not likely to pass products liability legislation,[8] his remedy was for the Supreme Court to create "a new national common law of liability,"[9] or a federal common law of the subject,[10] or, in still another version, "a national law of products liability."[11]

To be sure, through the murk of these proposals there flashed important insights about the litigation system. Neely is at his best when he writes of the "balance of terror" in litigation, in which such strategic counters as the threat of punitive damages and the ability of defendants to delay trials, "when combined," tend to press parties toward settlement.[12] He is less convincing in his insistence that courts, undertaking a "major policy change," would "know enough about their own system to enable them to restructure all of the counterbalancing terrors at the same time."[13] He does not say why it is that the "federal courts"[14] would be better at "establish[ing] a national law of product liability" than the federal and state courts previously have been.

---

5. *Id.* at 131.
6. *Id.* at 84.
7. *Id.* at 66.
8. *See generally id.*, Chapter 4.
9. *See id.* at 6.
10. *See e.g., id.* at 117-119.
11. *See id.* at 169.
12. *See, e.g., id.* at 93.
13. *Id.* at 162-63.
14. *See id.* at 169.

A particularly telling aspect of Neely's proposal was his listing of the factors that federal courts should take into consideration in "craft[ing] the law." Most of the entries on this list, such as "insurance availability and cost," "the desirability of encouraging the manufacture of safe products" and "the desirability of spreading inevitable individual risks to society as a whole"[15] are slightly different names for the very factors that courts have consulted for more than two decades.[16] Lamentably and ironically, by making the Supreme Court the flagship of the reform effort, Justice Neely's proposal practically would guarantee more litigation: more squabbling over language and meaning, more cases in the federal system, more cases on the Supreme Court's overloaded docket.

Huber's Diatribe

One of the most publicized criticisms of products law came contemporaneously from Peter Huber, a senior fellow of the Manhattan Institute. His book, *Liability: the Legal Revolution and its Consequences*,[17] became a kind of popularized bible for would-be tort reformers. However, although the book advanced several fair criticisms of the evolving law, its very flashiness, its desperate striving for the turn of phrase, revealed its weaknesses.

Huber's bogeyman, rather than the state courts, were "the Founders."[18] These misguided interventionists were members of a platoon — sometimes it seemed a battalion — of law professors and judges. They created, from a melange of social engineering, economic theory and misplaced compassion, a system of liability laws that ultimately proved the folly of their meddling ways. Seeking to establish a regime of adequate compensation and proper incentives to safety, they instead created a climate that dampened innovation, took from consumers their ability to choose and often resulted in net losses in the quantum of safety available to society.

Huber deplored the "wholesale repudiation of the law of contract."[19] Under "the old tort law," "[i]f someone wanted to buy a fast horse, lightweight canoe, sharp knife, or strong medicine, that was her business and

---

15. *See id.* at 170.

16. *See, e.g.,* the catalog of factors in John W. Wade, On the Nature of Strict Tort Liability for Products, 44 Miss. L.J. 825, 837-838 (1973), summarized in chapter 8, text accompanying notes 2-3 and notes 47-51.

17. Peter Huber, Liability: the Legal Revolution and its Consequences (1988) [hereafter, "Huber"].

18. *Id.* at 6.

19. *Id.* at 7.

her risk."[20] Never mind that the new tort law—or any law, new or old—did not impinge on choice in any of these areas selected for their imagery, save perhaps "strong medicines." No matter that there was a broad legislative consensus, born of unfortunate experience, in favor of the regulation of "strong medicines." The problem was that "tort law" now overrode individual preference: a somewhat more modern-sounding catalog of these sins named "lawn mower design, vaccine manufacture, heart surgery, and ski slope grooming."[21]

The Founders, principal target of Huber's sallies, first took on a simian image. They viewed disclaimers, Huber wrote with a characteristic turn of phrase, "much as a pack of chimpanzees welcomes a python, with much hollering and chest pounding and waving of arms and throwing of rocks."[22] Later, the Founders acquired epaulets, performing a "triumphal march: See the conquering tort law comes."[23] Like Sherman's Yankees, this unlikely ragtag of a few judges and professors cut a wide swath through the commercial heartland of America. In removing products liability from contract, they vexed an author with a touching attachment to a Halcyon age when people were strong, self-reliant individuals and markets worked on the basis of personal choice.

Just one example of Huber's penchant for exaggeration as it applies to doctrine is his announcement that "the once broad defense of 'contributory negligence' was abandoned." His principal evidence consisted of two cases, including one rather extraordinary decision, not cited to an official report, involving a speeder who died when a tire exploded.[24] He made no reference to the multitude of decisions in which contributory negligence and its variants continued to win cases for defendants.[25]

One of Huber's more serious accusations lay in his assertion that under the developing products law, jurors began "redesigning" various kinds of products.[26] It is certainly fair to ask, even to speculate, about the effects on

---

20. *Id.* at 41.

21. *Id.* at 8.

22. *Id.* at 29.

23. *Id.* at 33.

24. *See id.* at 40. Huber's summary of this case, which cites only a periodical article, may refer to LeBouef v. Goodyear Tire & Rubber Co., 623 F.2d 985 (5th Cir. 1980), *aff'g* 451 F. Supp. 253 (W.D. La. 1978). Huber neglects, among other things, to refer to the Fifth Circuit's comment that the 425 horsepower engine of the vehicle at issue, and its capability for being driven at least 100 miles an hour, enhanced its "allure" for young drivers.

25. A liberal sprinkling of these cases appears in 2 M. Shapo, The Law of Products Liability (1990), chapters 20-21 *passim* (hereafter, Shapo, Products Liability).

26. *See* Huber at 39.

manufacturer conduct of jury decisions in design defect cases. But juries do not make design choices. Thus, it seems rather misleading to use this terminology in a book aimed in part at non-lawyer readers, when every lawyer knows that the most a jury does, subject to several layers of judicial control, is to say what it thinks may have been wrong with a product.

This is not to denigrate the argument that liability rules may influence product design. Nor is it to deny that the effect of some liability rules may be to diminish the spectrum of product models available to consumers, and particularly to low income consumers.[27] Yet, even if one were philosophically disposed against strict liability, Huber's line of argument amounted to a complaint against the entire system of the negligence law he seemed to favor. Any time that any court decides that an act or omission is negligent, it constrains some manufacturer and consumer choice in some fashion.

Huber's obsession with a conspiracy to remake tort law carried into his discussion of warnings doctrine, which he contended was a response to the fact that although "[t]he new rules of strict liability were ... firmly in place" by the 1970's, "theory was not working out as originally planned." As the warnings dimension of the conspiracy took hold, "the courts concluded that an inadequate warning, like defective design, need not be defeated by the victim's own foolishness or culpability."[28] To support this assertion, Huber summarily referred to a tiny pastiche of cases, at least half of them extracted from secondary sources.[29] He ignored the rather considerable jurisprudence in which courts overlap such concepts as contributory fault, the obviousness defense and warnings law with the exact result of holding consumers to their own culpable conduct.[30]

Huber's fondness for the polemic image inspired his metaphor of the "Institutional Nanny," which he applied to the risk that excessive imposition of liability would reduce the incentive for potential victims to take care for themselves. In the service of this austere figure of speech, he declared, with no visible evidence, that "[i]n nine cases out of ten, the best and cheapest protection from accidents lay very close to the victim herself."[31]

In a concluding *tutti* to this diatribe, Huber insisted that in "modern tort law," "consent counts for nothing,"[32] thus ignoring reams of recent cases elucidating assumption of risk type defenses.[33]

---

27. Huber hints at this argument early, *id.* at 42, and later, *id.* at 162 and *id.* at 229.
28. *Id.* at 52-54.
29. *See id.* at 55.
30. *See supra*, this work, chapter 10, *passim*. See also 1 Shapo, Products Liability ¶ 19.11; 2 *id.* ¶¶ 20.02, 20.05, 20.06, 21.08.
31. *See* Huber at 175-176.
32. *Id.* at 188.
33. *See, e.g.,* 2 Shapo, Products Liability ¶ 20.03 (1990).

Huber's solution, in two words, fixed on contract and consent. "The answer," he said, was "to reanchor the law of warning to its contractual roots."[34] The principle was that of "informed choice, deliberately made outside the courtroom and before the accident," and it "should count for everything."[35] The advantage of "[a] return to contract, built on open warning and informed consent," was that "it would permit once again infinite calibration to the varying needs of individual consumers."[36] If it was unclear how infinite a calibration would be possible with mass produced goods, the declaration of faith was a powerful one: "Contract and contract alone allows us to anticipate problems and to cover contingencies sensibly in advance, whether our objective is insurance or safety."[37] It seemed beside the point that the law had striven to adapt itself, including its contractual components, to modern realities. There was this concession, however: Huber would contend for a "[c]ontract reinvented, with a more human face."[38]

Fixated to the end with his preoccupation with "the Founders," Huber concluded with a mock sympathetic view of this spectral band of guerrillas as "traditional utopians."[39] Anyone who understood this area of the law and also enjoyed a good argument would find the book stimulating, but it had a particular and vexing irony. In a work devoted to arguing that tort law is an instance of the bad driving out the good,[40] the style of argument itself, so flashy and self assured, tends to supplant serious discussion of what all agree is a very serious subject.

Priest's History

On the more scholarly side, one of the most notable contributions came from George Priest, in an article entitled "The Invention of Enterprise Liability: A Critical History of the Intellectual Foundations of Modern Tort Law."[41] This historical essay, itself an important chapter in the academic

---

34. Huber at 212.
35. *Id.*
36. *Id.* at 216.
37. *Id.* at 226.
38. *Id.*
39. *Id.* at 231.
40. Huber speaks of a heaven in which "there would be no law," and a hell in which "there will be nothing but law," *id.* at 232.
41. George Priest, The Invention of Enterprise Liability: A Critical History of the Intellectual Foundations of Modern Tort Law, 14 J. Legal Studies 461 (1985).

literature, identified "enterprise liability" as the central concept in "modern tort law." Priest interpreted modern tort developments as "reflect[ing] a single coherent conception of the best method to control the sources of product-related injuries," and he defined the "enterprise liability" theory as one that "provides in its simplest form that business enterprises ought to be responsible for losses resulting from products they introduce in commerce."[42]

Yet the "simplest form" of the liability to which Priest referred was elementary indeed; few proponents of any expanded tort liability could be taxed fairly with so reductionist an approach. Indeed, the courts that have fashioned the law of strict liability have not engaged in such simplistic analysis. The evolving products liability law has always incorporated numerous limitations — on the duty issue, increasingly on the theory of liability, and surely by way of defenses based on the consumer's conduct. Symbolically, in the first judicial formulation of a "strict liability" theory for a majority opinion, Judge Traynor was careful to require that the use of the product be an intended use.[43]

Even taken on its own terms, Priest's analysis fluctuated in the use of language where one might have wished precision. For example, he employed rather interchangeably the terms "risk distribution," "loss distribution" and "risk spreading," which at various points he used to describe the central rationales of a theoretical model he ascribed to such writers as Fleming James. At one point early in the article, Priest said that "James promoted one principle—risk distribution—above all others."[44] On the next page, he associated with James the notion that "[l]oss distribution reduced the risk and uncertainty that would otherwise inhibit desirable activities by substituting a small calculable cost for the risk of a loss ruinous to a single individual."[45] A few pages beyond that, in a more general discussion, he referred in one sentence to "[t]he concepts of internalization and risk distribution" and in later sentences in the same paragraph, apparently synonymously, to "[i]nternalization and risk spreading" and "internalization and risk spreading concepts."[46] Perhaps this simply represented a striving

---

42. *Id.* at 463.

43. *See* Greenman v. Yuba Power Prods., Inc., 59 Cal.2d 57, 64, 377 P.2d 897, 901, 27 Cal. Rptr. 697, 701 (1963).

44. *Id.* at 470.

45. *Id.* at 471.

46. *Id.* at 483-84. Compare Priest's statement, *id.* at 481, that he was "certain that James perceived that the careful internalization of costs to activities that give rise to them can often conflict with distributing risks most broadly, in particular where neither of the parties to the dispute is an insurer or a large enterprise."

for elegant variation, but more precise terminology might have embodied a more rigorous critique.

In other scholarly works, Priest repeatedly contended that true solicitude for consumer welfare required expanded recognition of individual consumer taste for risk. For example, in a 1981 essay, he reasoned that because consumers can make certain "allocative or insurance investments ... more cheaply than the manufacturer," consumers themselves can be said to "demand" disclaimers and exclusions.[47] In a later article, Priest elaborated his concern about the insurance market consequences of the heterogeneity of consumers who would be beneficiaries of liability coverages. Because "[v]ery little information about individual risk ... is available to third-party insurers," he argued, insurers would not be able effectively to segregate risk pools.[48]

However, even as Priest wrote, multitudes of judicial decisions were taking into account precisely the levels of use and punishment to which diverse consumers subject products. The consumer who uses a product for something other than its intended purposes is always vulnerable to the defense of misuse, and consumers who use products foolishly must reckon with the doctrine of assumption of risk, not to mention the defense of contributory negligence.

Viscusi's Economics

Matching and raising the bids of Huber and Priest as champions of the consumer welfare, the economist Kip Viscusi weighed in with a 1991 book titled *Reforming Products Liability*.[49] Where Priest's "enterprise liability" analysis had taken products liability scholarship to represent the key idea of "modern tort law," Viscusi appeared to conflate the products liability problem with a broader set of tort and insurance issues. For example, he elided from statistics indicating a quintupling of "general liability insurance premiums" to a reference to a "fivefold increase in the total cost of products liability insurance."[50] Then he linked "the explosion in products liability costs" with "the expansion in tort liability,"[51] and particularly

---

47. George Priest, A Theory of the Consumer Product Warranty, 90 Yale L.J. 1297, 1313 (1981).
48. George Priest, The Current Insurance Crisis and Modern Tort Law, 96 Yale L.J. 1521, 1557-58 (1987).
49. W. Kip Viscusi, Reforming Products Liability (1991) [hereafter, Viscusi].
50. *See* Viscusi at 26.
51. *Id.* at 28.

with the "development of design defect doctrine and the application of defect tests to hazard warnings."[52]

Viscusi presented an overview of problems in the insurance market, including high loss ratios[53] and denials of coverage because insurers could not predict and pool risks.[54] He also inferred "a crisis in insurance availability" from decreases in insurance exposure levels for products liability.[55] After summarizing several specific incidents of stock market losses for product manufacturers,[56] Viscusi elided again to the language of "crisis."[57] However, his principal illustration of areas afflicted by a "crisis in availability" of liability insurance — semi-anecdotal in this later rendition — related not to products but to "day care centers or municipal playgrounds that were denied liability coverage."[58]

Unfortunately, Viscusi's chapter on the litigation process gave little feel for how attorneys approach lawsuits and for how litigation proceeds, nor for the complex conceptual reality of products liability doctrine. He adduced statistics from one of his prior studies indicating that claimants who plead strict liability increase their "chance of success by 20 percent,"[59] but his concept of strict liability seemed rather uncertain. Thus, one of his definitions of strict liability asserted that "the plaintiff need only show a causal relationship between a product defect and his injuries"[60] — a definition that is challenged on the same page by the statement that "[s]ome states do . . . permit comparative negligence defenses even in strict liability cases."[61] Further undercutting his broader definition are the observations that "strict liability is not tantamount to absolute liability,"[62] and that under strict liability "most jurisdictions allow some weakened version of the usual defenses (for example, contributory negligence)."[63]

No matter what the method of analysis, this conceptual vagueness about the doctrine seems to leave the statistical finding unmoored with respect to the meaning of "strict liability." Moreover, Viscusi did not indicate how he

---

52. *Id.*
53. *See id.* at 34.
54. *Id.* at 35.
55. *Id.* at 36.
56. *See id.* at 37-39.
57. *Id.* at 41.
58. *Id.*
59. *See id.* at 51.
60. *Id.* at 45.
61. *See id.*
62. *Id.* at 75.
63. *Id.* at 45.

would account for the many lawsuits in which plaintiffs alternatively plead strict liability and other theories including negligence. Nor did he appear to consider the fact that many lawyers say that they tend to litigate products cases on a negligence platform, whatever the announced theory of liability.

As we would expect from a superior economist, Viscusi effectively depicted the game of chicken that routinely occupies attorneys in bargaining over settlement,[64] and he nicely captured the function of expected judgments in influencing settlement figures.[65] He did permit himself a quotation from Justice Neely on what Viscusi characterized as the satisfaction that judges feel in "raiding corporate defendants' deep pockets."[66]

An air of unreality hung over proposals that Viscusi advanced as solutions for the "mass tort" problem of disease caused by toxic products. He suggested that "deterrence for current and future risks is best provided through effective government regulation of risk exposure levels" and that "[p]romotion of broadly based social insurance compensation for all disease victims, irrespective of cause, would meet society's objective of providing insurance to individuals in need."[67] The goals of effective regulation and adequate social insurance have been major political ambitions of Americans concerned with social justice for many decades. The assertion of these hopes, however, hardly assures continued improvement in those areas. In his response to this segment of the problem, Viscusi presents a somewhat unlikely apparition: the economist as utopian.

We should further remark on a large gap in the analysis of both Viscusi and Priest. This is the failure of both authors to take account of the importance of how products are portrayed in the marketplace. As this book has shown, a major underlying theme of products liability law resides in its response to advertising appeals, and to their tendency to influence consumer preferences and choices.

A "Reporters' Study" for the American Law Institute

One of the more disappointing chapters in recent criticism of products liability in the last decade appears within a broad analysis of tort law in a

---

64. *See id.* at 54-55.

65. *See id.* at 58, 61.

66. *See id.* at 56, characterizing and quoting Neely, The Products Liability Mess 1 (1988).

67. *Id.* at 174.

"Reporters' Study" commissioned by the American Law Institute. Heightening the reader's sense of an opportunity lost was the historical background of the products liability component of the study. It was the A.L.I. that had placed section 402A of the Second Restatement of Torts in intellectual commerce. Now, reacting to criticism of the development of products liability law associated with widespread judicial acceptance of section 402A, the Institute sought a reexamination of the issue. It was unsuccessful.

In its chapter on "products defects and warnings," the study revealed many analytical defects. Using brush strokes as exaggerated as Huber's, the reporters asserted in a summary of the development of strict liability theory that the doctrine "meant that the maker of a 'defective' product had to compensate any person who was injured by it."[68] The reporters also wrote that the courts had "expanded the substantive basis of strict liability" to include design defects as well as manufacturing defects.[69] This statement relied on one decision, *Larsen v. General Motors Corp.*,[70] which did involve allegations of poor design but which invoked negligence and not strict liability.

Like several other critics, the authors of the study failed to recognize the reality of the creation of consumer product demand. Their broadside at the consumer expectations test for defect, referring to the "uninformed safety expectations" of "uninformed consumers,"[71] did not give even implicit credence to the conditioning of consumer safety expectations by advertising.

With respect to the consumer expectations test, the authors relied on one outlandish example: "[A] consumer drives a car into a lake and is injured when it sinks," and "testifies honestly that he had believed the car would float." The authors commented that "[t]he consumer's expectation is unreasonable because the safety feature that the consumer said he expected would fail any conceivable risk-utility test." They saw this fanciful vignette as providing a basis for their assertion that the consumer expectations notion "has no independent existence," but "rather, it collapses into other tests or legal rules."[72] Again, they neglected the central importance of the process by which expectations are created, especially by media. One should note that even if we focus, for example, on risk-utility analysis rather than "consumer expectations," the techniques of product promotion are central to consumer formulation of the calculus of risks and benefits. It was per-

---

68. 2 ALI Reporters' Study, Enterprise Liability for Personal Injury: Approaches to Legal and Institutional Change, at 35 (1991) [hereafter, "Reporters' Study"].

69. *Id.*

70. 391 F.2d 495 (8th Cir. 1968).

71. 2 Reporters' Study at 44.

72. *Id.* at 44-45.

haps telling that the authors presented no real examples of the problem to which this part of their analysis addressed itself.

In line with the faith of the broader study that one may effectively assign various legal tasks to "institutions,"[73] the authors of this products liability chapter emphasized a proposal to exculpate defendants who complied with "specific government regulations respecting the form and content of product warnings."[74] Although a later chapter discussed the "shortcomings" of regulation,[75] this proposal seemed to override the many objections to complete reliance by private law on any regulatory framework: the problem of the captive agency, the problem of outright bribery, and the risk of insufficient analysis by agencies of specific products. The authors asserted that agencies "usually have more expertise than do even well informed juries at assessing the communicative impact of particular language and warning formats,"[76] but they did not explain how this "expertise" necessarily would triumph over politics in agency approval of particular warnings. Indeed, they did not demonstrate why agencies, under political pressure, would consistently perform better on warnings issues than juries informed by experts and trained advocates.

In sum, the Reporters' study exhibited several defects. At its foundations, it lacked depth of historical focus. Among other faults, it oversimplified doctrine, it ignored the process by which sellers generate consumer demand, and it relied on excessive faith in the effectiveness of regulation.

Summary

A deficiency common to many critiques of products liability law — despite numerous apt observations about its weaknesses — is a failure to appreciate the difficulty of the issues with which products cases confront courts. In their oversimplification of judicial efforts to respond to social realities, many critics have neglected the factual richness of the subject as it is revealed in the thousands of decisions that have created the present corpus of law. They appear to have underestimated the achievement of American courts in developing this body of jurisprudence over the last third of a century.

---

73. *See, e.g.*, 1 Reporters' Study, at 34 ("we might employ a variety of devices, each tailored to the particular role that is parceled out to it"), and, more generally, *id.*, section B.
74. 2 Reporters' Study at 72.
75. *See id.* at 85-86.
76. *Id.* at 74.

Truly, these commentators have placed before us a variety of useful perspectives: from the bench, from history and from economics, as well as from legal theory. They have, in some measure, succeeded as critics, indicating various ways in which we could enhance our analysis of legal problems. But in pursuing the critic's role, they have often refused to acknowledge the distance between the ideal of reform and the trudging road to systemic improvement. Perhaps they have ignored the truth that sometimes a real second best is better than a model theoretical universe. This failure of perception parallels a myopia about the successes of the courts — despite many flaws in performance — in responding to the problems of justice to which we all address ourselves.

12

In Pursuit of Justice

This book began with a personal recollection of an episode of Senate testimony. I have done that several times, and it never ceases to give me a thrill. As I said to Senator Heflin on one such occasion, I think it would have made my parents very proud that their son should be "discussing the law with members of the Senate Judiciary Committee."[1]

For old Washington hands, of course, Senate committee hearings are just another part of an ordinary day. Given the stylized way that Senate staffs set up the panels that testify—they try to keep them balanced with respect to points of view—it is pretty routine stuff. Yet with one casual exaggeration, an unknown actor in the vignette that opened the book captured a great deal of the reason that the subject has endured in the Congressional hopper: To the question, "Why are all these people here?" he replied, "Half the people in this town make their livings from products liability."

Indeed, lobbying over proposed products liability legislation, not to mention representation of clients in products litigation, has been a profitable enterprise for many people over the years. There persists, however, the most basic version of the baffled question by the naive interlocutor: Why?

In the last three decades, this branch of the law has generated a powerful set of symbols that, taken together, tell us a lot about our social views. In this chapter I seek to summarize the wide public controversy over this seemingly technical part of the law, indicating why it has become such a focus of political discussion and where I believe the balance of justice lies.

The Legal and Political Battlefield

Some of the arguments about the legal rules on products liability deal with doctrines that are specific to the field. These include the theories of

---

1. The Products Liability Reform Act, Hearing before the Senate Committee on the Judiciary, 101st Cong., 2d Sess., Serial No. J-101-89, at 31 (1990).

liability, the concept of defect and the law governing warnings issues. Some general doctrines of tort law have taken on a particular coloration in products liability; among these are the rules dealing with defenses based on consumer conduct. Other controversial doctrines apply more broadly throughout tort law. These include various damages rules—those relating to pain and suffering and punitive damages, and also to the apportionment of liability, for example, the rules on "joint and several liability." Besides seeking to change these rules, some legislative proposals have tried to modify the process of dispute resolution, for example by introducing various incentives for settlement.

From my observation over several years of attending and testifying at hearings, and my reading of many volumes of testimony, I interpret what happened through the 1980s this way: the proponents of federal products liability legislation began with a most comprehensive ambition. They would try to swallow the entire law of the subject in a broad legislative framework, fixing every possible perceived problem—and even codifying some parts of the law that "weren't broke," as the aphorism has it.[2]

By the early 1990s, the configuration of the legislative proposals had changed. The proponents of federal legislation increasingly began to act like many lobbyists dealing with complicated subjects: they stopped seeking to enact an ideal comprehensive law and started trying to splice together a series of provisions that would, taken together, sell.[3]

Why had these bills tended increasingly to a smorgasbord approach?[4] One other personal recollection may shed some light on that subject. During a Senate committee hearing in the mid-eighties, there was a break during which the Senators had to go to a roll-call. The testimony to the panel had been focusing on a proposal that would have considerably expanded the market for products liability insurance, by simple virtue of broadening the exposure of manufacturing firms on a non-fault basis.

I was standing next to a prominent lawyer who oversees a major corporation's litigation in these matters. "I don't think I like this part of it," he murmured. That simple declaration highlighted the political problems that

---

2. One example of such a bill, presented in the early 1980s, was S. 2631, reprinted in Product Liability Reform: Hearings before the Consumer Subcommittee of the Senate Commerce Committee, 97th Cong., 2d Sess., Serial No. 97-109, at 161-190 (1982).

3. An example of this would be S. 1400, a 1990 bill reprinted in The Products Liability Reform Act, *supra* note 1, at 466-491. This proposal includes a few provisions dealing with substantive liability, a section on expedited settlements and alternative dispute resolution procedures, and individual sections on punitive damages and offset of workers' compensation benefits.

4. Professor Viscusi speaks of the "Chinese menu approach." See W. Kip Viscusi, Reforming Products Liability 211 (1991).

faced proponents of federal legislation. A change that seemed entirely rational, not to mention profitable, to one big actor on stage—the insurance industry—was anathema to another—the manufacturing community.

The Practical Justice of Products Liability

As the decade of the nineties opened, the political spotlight on products liability became even more intense than in the eighties. Vice President Dan Quayle, as chair of the President's Council on Competitiveness, announced in 1991 a new initiative on "civil justice reform." The Council's Report included several general proposals for change that would bear on products litigation, including a recommendation to "[r]equire expert testimony to be based on 'widely accepted' theories" and a recommendation to change the procedures and standards governing punitive damages.[5] Very early in the report, the Council focused on the "adverse effects of unconstrained litigation" in products cases in particular.[6] The continuing intensity of political interest in the subject, and the tensions even among groups that believed themselves to share a common interest in "reform," prompts us to ask, where does the balance of practical justice lie in products liability?

Quantitative Axis

One aspect of the subject that on first look seems most tangible is its quantitative dimension. One would think that after the fact, some statistics would be readily available to us: the percentages of injurious occurrences per product model, the costs of building safety features into particular products, and the transaction costs and damages payments associated with litigation.

The seeming certainty of this dimension of the problem appears more vaporous on close analysis. It is true that, now and then, judicial decisions mention the costs of making specific products safer, but that happens in a surprisingly small number of cases. Since courts usually are fairly careful about cataloguing even marginally relevant facts in the cases before them, this suggests considerable imprecision in our generally available knowledge on this critical question.

Concerning another quantitative feature of the subject, we should note that data on accident rates are not a staple of manufacturers' promotions.

---

5. President's Council on Competitiveness, Agenda for Civil Justice Reform in America, reprinted in Prod. Safety & Liab. Rptr. (BNA) (Aug. 16, 1991).

6. *Id.* at 3.

Indeed, when they exist, they frequently must be wrung from product sellers in lawsuits, through the expensive procedural process of discovery. If one believes in a marketplace for risk, one must assume a more lively market in information about risk than the one that exists for many, probably most, products.

Moreover, we must observe that the statistics that do exist on trends in products litigation indicate that two major mass tort types of litigation have recently dominated the scene. One of these is the cases dealing with the Dalkon Shield, which Peter Huber, no aficionado of the present law of products liability, calls a "bad" product.[7] The other is the massive galaxy of asbestos cases, which decision after decision has stressed involve manufacturer conduct that was at least culpable and perhaps very seriously culpable.[8]

Thus, some of what might seem the most salient data on products hazards are surprisingly absent in the decisions, much information most pertinent to informed consumers does not find its way into the market, and the statistics on litigation itself tend to undercut the notion that there is a general crisis in the law.[9]

The Market and the Law

We should note here the frequent discussion of the virtues of "the market" as a vehicle for regulating product risks.[10] Certainly, in a free economy, the market is the foundation stone of control. Using price, quality and varieties of goods, it sorts out consumer preferences, including risk preferences. But we must remember that "the market" is not independent of the law. Indeed, it is inconceivable that in modern society, markets could work without a fairly complex set of legal rules. The law of fraud alone places significant constraints on conduct. Moreover, although baseline assumptions about the workings of markets posit able and well-informed consumers, much of the law of products liability deals with situations in which

---

7. *See, e.g.*, Peter Huber, Liability: The Legal Revolution and Its Consequences 108 (1988); *see also id.* at 162 ("[t]he Dalkon Shield without question deserved to go").

8. *See, e.g.*, Johnson v. Celotex Corp., 899 F.2d 1281, 1288 (2d Cir. 1990) (affirming punitive award under "wanton or reckless" standards).

9. *Cf.* James Henderson, Jr., & Theodore Eisenberg, The Quiet Revolution in Products Liability: An Empirical Study of Legal Change, 37 U.C.L.A. L. Rev. 479 (1990), reporting that in recent years "both appellate and trial judges are reaching decisions favoring products defendants in unprecedented numbers," *id.* at 539.

10. *See, e.g.*, 1 Enterprise Liability for Personal Injury ch. 7 (A.L.I. Reporters' Study 1991) (hereafter, "Enterprise Liability").

consumers are not well-informed. And some rather broad judicial pronouncements, reaching well back into this century at a time of proudly un-
regulated markets, exhibit empathy for consumers of limited ability.

The Process of Product Portrayal

I have explained my view that a singularly important aspect of products
liability analysis lies in the process of product portrayal. In highlighting
this element of the problem, I contrast my perspective with that of economic theorists who focus on factors such as price, available information
and search costs, although I do not downplay those factors. To some extent,
I also distinguish my ideas from legal scholars who emphasize "consumer
expectations."

I observe that it is ironic that economists should rightly place such emphasis on consumer information, but fail to focus on the process by which
sophisticated promotional techniques create demand and fuel expectations. Noting also that the notion of "consumer expectations" is a reasonable shorthand for many of the factors to which courts do—and should—
respond in products liability cases, I emphasize that it would improve
analysis to focus initially on the way that sellers establish those expectations.

Sellers create product portrayals in many ways. Not only do they use direct advertising; they take advantage of product appearance and they cap-
italize on widespread social agreement that builds up over time about the
function of particular products. It is for those reasons that courts should
specifically refer their judgments of products liability cases to the integrated image of the product that emerges against its promotional background. In that connection, courts should take into account the nature of
particular products as vehicles for the creation of persuasive advertising
images.[11]

I realize that this approach does not convey the seeming certainty and
precision of more quantitative forms of analysis. But I believe that readers
who live in present day America will recognize that it captures more of the
nuances of an age filled with sophisticated electronic and print advertisements than does an exclusive focus on numerical comparisons of alternative
risks, or of the costs of injuries and accident avoidance.

Warnings, design, and a metaphysics of products. It is only by focusing
on the process of product promotion that we can understand why courts

---

11. *See generally* Shapo, A Representational Theory of Consumer Protection: Doctrine,
Function and Legal Liability for Product Disappointment, 60 Va. L. Rev. 1109 (1974) (thesis summarized at 1370).

have tailored the law as they have. This is especially so in the law concerning product warnings and design defects, which has been so much the subject of recent criticism.[12]

The point is relatively clear concerning warnings. Modern product promotion has created a set of mental images, including images of reliability and safety, that sometimes require the offsetting effect of joltingly specific information on product hazards.

In the case of design defects, the law has come to recognize, often implicitly, that sellers naturally take advantage of a modern metaphysics of products when they design their goods. Liability may arise from product appearance in context, or common agreement about product function, combined with a particular degree of hazard. In many of these cases, warnings may be beside the point. The key is the hazard, in the context of consumer understanding fostered by the portrayal. Indeed, as some decisions have insisted, even obviousness may be beside the point, for the law should "discourage misdesign rather than encouraging it in its most obvious form."[13]

Moral Dimensions

Product images. One might chalk up my focus on product promotion entirely on the axis of economic theory. For in theory, a fully informed consumer is entirely capable of choosing rationally, at a price, whatever combination of risks and benefits inheres in a particular product. But a deeper consideration of the wellsprings of products liability leads us to emphasize the moral dimensions of the law.

It was well enough, in the days when the court of the Exchequer Chamber decided the case of *Chandelor v. Lopus* in 1603, to say that if a seller "does not warrant" that "his wares are good," "it is no cause of action."[14] Much decisional law in our own century, however, recognizes that in our present era of mass media, sellers who take advantage of subtle imagery should be held to the intended consequences of their creation of demand even when they have not precisely generated express warranties.[15]

The realities of power. Yet we must go beyond product promotion to examine other aspects of the problem. One of these is the realities of the

---

12. *See, e.g.,* 2 Enterprise Liability, *supra* note 10, ch. 2; Huber, *supra* note 8, chs. 3, 4; Viscusi, *supra* note 4, chs. 4, 7.

13. Uloth v. City Tank Corp., 376 Mass. 874, 881, 384 N.E.2d 1188, 1192-93 (1978).

14. Cro. Jac. 4 (Ex. Chamber 1603).

15. *See* Shapo, *supra* note 11, *e.g.,* at 1204-1258.

power relationships between sellers and consumers. I am not suggesting that this balance always favors sellers. I have read and consulted about enough litigation that borders on the frivolous that I understand why many manufacturers believe that it is consumer plaintiffs who occupy the dominant power position. Some claimants choose to abuse products; others seek to extort money with claims essentially unsupported by evidence.

But it is product sellers who more typically hold the highest cards. It is they who initiate the process of design, and make choices among alternatives of more or less safety. Sometimes, it is they who help to create situations in which consumers who are practically bound by circumstances, including the circumstances of employment, must expose themselves to grievous risks of harm. Certainly, it is sellers who create promotional campaigns. And it is they who, entirely within the law, can employ legal trench warfare to delay meritorious litigation. Thus, sellers frequently are in the best position to exercise control over both product risks and products litigation and, taken together, these elements of power sometimes permit imposition.

The law responds to each of these profiles of power. It has tailored its rules on design defects—some would say it has expanded those rules unreasonably—to deal with the power of manufacturers to choose less safe alternatives. It has moved to a fuller recognition of what it takes for consumers truly to "assume the risk." Beyond its use of liability theories directly based on representations, it has generated applications of negligence and strict liability doctrine that take into account the realities of modern advertising. And it has combined liability and proof rules to deal with the ignorance that burdens consumers entering the litigation process.

How one chooses. Some related comments are in order about choice and the significance of how both sellers and consumers choose. In this discussion, I assume that both manufacturers and consumers possess approximately the same degree of rationality in approaching their respective roles.

As to manufacturers, they may—indeed must—engage in a serious deliberative process both as to product design and quality. They not only formulate the blueprint, but they select the strength of materials and the manner in which they will be processed. They also weigh competing considerations in making final decisions about the overall profile of a product.

On the other side of the transaction stands the consumer, who in some cases exercises the key prerogative. He may plant the seeds of his own disappointment by selecting a product that is cheaper than an alternative, and which falls below the task to which it will be put. This sort of choice may evoke different kinds of judicial responses. In some cases, the courts will say that the product was not defective for the use for which the consumer employed it. In others, they may declare that a purchaser assumed the risk of a use for which the product was not really suited. Moreover, in cases involving only economic loss, courts may also refuse recovery under tort theories, especially strict liability, on the grounds that it is up to the consumer to pick a product that will measure up to the job, and that any loss of bargain is the consumer's.[16]

On other occasions, however, the court will recognize that the consumer has not deliberated. Thus, it may refuse to bar recovery on the ground that she was only inadvertent. Or it may engage in an extended empathy, with overtones of social policy, in deciding that it will not hold a consumer to what is primarily an unfree bargain—for example, when she continues to work on a machine because the price of refusal is dismissal.

In these diverse ways, courts develop and enforce a morality of choice, based on the different kinds of choices, and deliberations, involved in seller and consumer roles.

Social justice. In one of the seminal cases of modern products liability, the New Jersey Supreme Court referred, by quotation from precedent, to the "demands of social justice" as a basis for decision.[17] This concept presents a craftsman's problem for lawyers, who are trained to think that courts should severely constrain themselves against any tendency to reach out for grand conceptions of justice. In this well accepted view of the judicial role, courts should limit themselves to the justice of individual cases, itself a difficult enough thing to track down. Yet there are some markings of trails on which courts may steer as they seek "justice" at the boundary of particular cases and zones of broader social concern.

Spreading. One of the most controversial rationales in products liability law is loss spreading. There are, to be sure, overlaps and confusions in the terminology of this subject. As we have noted, the reader of decisions and commentaries encounters apparently synonymous usages like "loss distribution," "risk distribution" and "risk-bearing ability." Yet the basic idea, as we described it in chapter six,[18] is simple enough. By slightly increasing the price of each unit of a good, a seller can build up a fund from consumers who benefit from the product that will defray the costs of the few who are injured by it.

---

16. *See, e.g.,* Seely v. White Motor Co., 63 Cal.3d 9, 18-19, 403 P.2d 145, 151-52, 45 Cal. Rptr. 17, 23-24 (1965).

17. Henningsen v. Bloomfield Motors, Inc., 32 N.J. 358, 384, 161 A.2d 69, 83 (1960) (quoting Mazetti v. Armour & Co., 75 Wash. 622, 135 P. 633, 635 (1913) (original quotation from Ketterer v. Armour & Co., 200 F. 322, 323 (S.D. N.Y. 1912)). *See* discussion, *supra,* chapter 2, text accompanying notes 9-10.

18. *See supra,* chapter 6, pp. 103-104.

The later chapters of this book further illuminate our initial discussion of the controversy about whether spreading is a proper basis for products liability. It certainly is a proper question whether courts should take unto themselves the seemingly legislative role inherent in a spreading solution. But in reality, we do not often have to decide about the propriety of judicially enforced spreading. The form of spreading that is the object of critics' ire goes along with very pure forms of strict liability. Yet in most strict liability cases, the courts are seizing upon, or intuitively reacting to, considerations less freighted with a quasi-legislative form of wealth redistribution. They are responding to a strong whiff of culpability; to a suspicion that the seller may know, or should have known, more than it is telling; to the seller's creation of product images.

We might be very concerned if it could be shown that courts were in effect tacking an automatic insurance premium onto the price of every risky product. It is not clear that that would be beyond the bounds of the judicial role, but it would be a subject for extended discussion. Yet in their reflexive chant of the litany that manufacturers are not the "insurers" of their products,[19] even courts in the forefront of the development of liability theories make clear their horror of the very idea.

There is a common sense morality to the idea of allocating risks, and losses, broadly among consumers of products that pose risks of injury. Yet, addressing a favorite straw person of critics of products liability law, we should note the broad consensus that the fact of a "deep pocket" is insufficient grounds to shift a loss. Without asserting that there is no subconscious Robin Hood-ism in the souls of judges, I disagree with Justice Neely's argument that products liability decisions are basically agents of wealth redistribution.[20] Courts appear to be fairly scrupulous about not imposing liability just because a defendant is wealthy.

Knowledge. One factor that does appear to influence courts, time after time, is knowledge on the part of sellers. Knowledge of an established statistical trend of injuries associated with a product, or even awareness of a few severe accidents with which the product has been connected, can be the stuff of tort awards. This factor is often crucial on those relatively unusual occasions when courts award punitive damages. In an illustrative case, the Minnesota Supreme Court affirmed a punitive award against a maker of pajamas that ignited when a four-year-old child reached across a stove. The court drew on a memorandum written thirteen years before the accident, in which a top company official declared that the firm was sitting on a "pow-

---

19. *See, e.g.,* Azzarello v. Black Bros. Co., 480 Pa. 547, 553, 391 A.2d 1020, 1024 (1978).
   20. *See supra,* chapter 11, text accompanying notes 3-4.

der keg" concerning the flammability of the flannelette used in the garment.[21]

Moralizing deterrence. The element of producer information on hazards may often fit comfortably into a standard economic explanation of liability rules. But in the law, deterrence is not only a technical economic concept. It has moral properties. Courts hold it proper to announce rules aimed at making sellers behave more safely than they do, even when it might be technically inefficient for them to do so.[22] This is a point at which many lawyers and most economists part company. Perhaps they must, from the point of view of professional roles. In this area of legal conflict, most economists have one craft-oriented focus, and that is on efficiency. But lawyers have a broader aim, and that is to secure justice. That is why courts often take the position that on disputed issues, they will tilt their judgments toward saving life and limb.

In saying this, we recognize the insight that in some cases, to require more safety concerning the product feature that injured an individual claimant may have adverse safety consequences in other aspects of the product's function. An Illinois appellate decision makes this point in a case involving fatal injuries to a worker, who was struck in the chest by a "small bullet-like piece of metal" while he was using a sledgehammer to repair a track shoe on a tractor. In upholding a summary judgment for the defendant, the court noted that the plaintiff's own expert had admitted that suggestions he made for design changes "would actually increase the propensity for brittle failure" of the track shoe.[23] Analogously, we also recognize that specialized uses of a product may make certain safety features impossible to incorporate. That is the lesson, for example, of an Arkansas case in which a forklift lacked an overhead protective guard because the purchaser wanted to use the machine to enter trailers with low ceilings.[24]

Our primary point, however, is that there are many cases in which courts may appropriately employ a deterrence rationale that focuses on net savings of lives rather than net theoretical gains in consumer welfare. Crucial to this point is a factor central to judicial decision making, if not economic analysis: the moral authority of the law.

---

21. Gryc v. Dayton-Hudson Corp., 297 N.W.2d 727, 740-41 (Minn.), cert. denied, 449 U.S. 921 (1980). More generally on knowledge as a factor in punitive damages, *see* 2 Shapo, The Law of Products Liability, ¶¶ 29.04[3],[4], [9].

22. *See* A.B.A., Special Comm. on the Tort Liability System, Towards a Jurisprudence of Injury: The Continuing Creation of a System of Substantive Justice in American Tort Law 4-3 - 4-12 (M. Shapo Rptr. 1984).

23. Mason v. Caterpillar Tractor Co., 139 Ill. App. 3d 511, 517-18, 487 N.E.2d 1043, 1047 (1986).

24. *See* White v. Clark Equip. Co., 553 S.W.2d 280 (1977).

Individualization. When we speak of the moral aspects of injury law, we must also underline the individualizing tendencies of our litigation system. Despite the well-publicized warts of that process, the individualizing property of litigation is both theoretically and practically important. It provides a moral focus for dispute resolution. It preserves the dignitary interests of human litigants. And it ensures defendants—most of whom are business enterprises—as well as plaintiffs a specific day in court.

In our modern day, we have access to realms of specialized knowledge that can be very helpful in tracking injury patterns, in technologically enhancing safety, and, indeed, in more precisely identifying the safety trade-offs in many decisions about products. Yet in employing this information, we ought not to forget a basic lesson: justice between persons, as conceived in the long treks from Canaan to Egypt and back to the land of Israel, is individual business. In saying this, we do not ignore the broader goal of general distributive justice. And we keep in mind Professor Alfred Conard's eloquent argument that even in the realm of personal injury we should concern ourselves with "macrojustice."[25] But we do well to remember the virtues of a focus on individual cases, and the value of principles that emerge from the clash of fact and policy in the crucible of litigation.

I note that some of these principles unavoidably involve subjectivization. This is so, for example, when courts make particularized judgments under a doctrine like assumption of risk, which requires that in order to bar claimants, defendants must show a knowing and unreasonable confrontation with a risk. Holmes, the great proponent of objective theories, might have been displeased with the way this defense has come to the fore in products cases. But given the kinds of risks that frequently are involved in consumer encounters with products, the balance of justice seems to lie with a degree of subjectivity.

I have spoken with enough company executives and defense lawyers about products liability to understand their vexation about what they view as a legal lottery. I understand that from the trenches of individual cases, it is often difficult to perceive an overall rationality in the system. But from my reading of the cases over a quarter century, I discern a broad and generally rational pattern in the law. I see the judicial system performing its classic role: sifting out the obvious losers, narrowing the issues on the close cases, and deriving a reasonable set of principles tailored to particular subject matter from highly specific fact situations.

Perhaps most remarkably, and significantly by contrast with bureaucracies—including regulatory and other social bureaucracies—courts do all

---

25. *See* Conard, Macrojustice: A Systematic Approach to Conflict Resolution, 5 Ga. L. Rev. 415 (1971).

of this in the open, subject to challenge at every step and on the record all the way. Many will say that the price—in discovery costs, delay, lawyers' fees and litigants' anguish—is too high. My reply is that there are ways—through procedural reforms and tighter judicial control[26]—to deal with these problems. But I also respond that the individualizing virtues of the system help to redeem its costs.

Notice. A great deal of life, and law, centers on expectations. We would not be human without wishing to know where we stand in particular relationships. And in formulating our expectations, we desire fair notice of what is coming next. Sometimes, of course, "life is unfair"; it surprises us. But the desire is relatively fixed, for sellers and consumers alike.

The idea of notice, indeed, is at the root of many complaints from business persons about the way that products liability law affects them. They assert that the law is so capricious that they do not know how to plan: producers cannot figure out how to design their products to avoid liability, and insurers cannot fashion actuarially sound pricing schemes because they cannot adequately calculate their risks.

In some particular situations, these complaints have bite. But I have shown that overall, the developing law communicates a fairly strong set of guidelines for seller conduct and levels of product safety. Moreover, we must consider that manufacturers trying to calculate potential liabilities are often trying to decide how far to venture into grey areas. We now have enough law to tell them where the zone gets grey: where they are taking chances, and where their risks as business persons turn chancier than the risks all of us take in daily life.

There is another aspect to the subject of fair notice, however, and it reminds us of why so much of products law has developed as it has. This is the subject of notice to consumers. Frequently, the law of products liability responds to situations in which the consumer in effect claims unfair surprise. This helps to explain why the idea of consumer expectations has become a central feature of products liability law. No matter how much critics may inveigh against that concept—I myself find it vague in some applications—we deny our humanity when we deny that our expectations, in significant measure, define our lives. We cannot ignore the fact that a lot of our law, and not only products liability law, has evolved because of disputes about the fairness of certain expectations.

Products liability law thus embodies a robust set of arguments between two kinds of notice interests, and corresponding interests in certainty. We simply reiterate here that issues of notice often arise from the way products are portrayed.

---

26. *See generally* Towards a Jurisprudence of Injury, *supra* note 22, chapter 13.

The Proper Forum for Lawmaking—and Proper Lawmaking

At base, much of the controversy over products liability concerns the question of whether courts are the best forum for lawmaking on this subject, and whether they have overstepped their bounds in the law they have made. As an outgrowth of that controversy, fervent political argument has raged around the question of whether Congress should pass federal products liability legislation. The effort to enact such a law has consumed millions of dollars and generated thousands of pages of testimony. My initial focus in this conclusion is on that issue. I shall also comment generally on the relation between courts and legislatures, including state legislatures, with reference to the proper and necessary provinces of decision making on this subject.

I believe that the proponents of federal legislation have insufficiently credited the efforts of state and federal judges to get to the root of the problems of risk, conduct, and injury that bring products claimants to court. In those efforts, the courts have responded to real controversies, sifting them through a refined process of dispute resolution.

It is paradoxical that, in an America grown suspicious of federal involvement in many lines of activity, many representatives of the business community should seek to nationalize a body of law that has developed through the application of local jurisprudence in individual disputes. Federal legislation on this subject would stultify a creative process of local lawmaking, and at the same time pose baffling problems of interpretation and reconciliation to state courts.

Moreover, federal products liability legislation would surely complicate the work of the federal judicial system. It would involve federal judges in interminable wrangles over the meaning of a prolix new set of words and phrases. Indeed, federal as well as state courts would find themselves caught between the inevitable ambiguities of a new statute and the rich body of case law that the legislation was designed to supersede. This seems an especially unfortunate result when judges and scholars have complained for years about the workload of the Supreme Court—which presumably would have to be the arbiter of many disputes about the meaning of such a statute—as well as about the burdens of the federal courts generally.[27]

---

27. Much of this criticism would apply to proposals to achieve an analogous result through decisions of the Supreme Court. *See, e.g.*, the suggestions of Neely, The Products Liability Mess (1988), discussed *supra*, chapter 11, text accompanying notes 9-11.

I speak here primarily of the arguments about construction of such a statute that would rage for decades. I mention only in passing the disputes that would be sure to arise about the constitutionality of the legislation. And it would not take a seer to predict that amendments to the statute would begin in the first Congressional session after its passage, and would further complicate its interpretation.

I have noted that many of the perceived problems in products liability law are related to the expensive and delay-inspiring procedures that have become a hallmark of modern litigation. In objecting to proposals for federal legislation, I amplify my prior suggestions concerning these problems: instead of performing amputations on a hard-won body of substantive rules, it would be better to concentrate on streamlining the process and achieving tighter judicial control of the costs of litigation. Generic reforms of this sort would not only end many complaints about products liability law. They would improve considerably the general process of civil justice, with which the law of products liability is frequently, and misleadingly, equated.

More generally, I would observe that whatever sort of products liability legislation might be passed, the courts necessarily will continue to play a major role. This will be so even with the products liability statutes enacted over the last few years by state legislatures. It would have to be so, in an area of law so tied to advancing technology and so rooted in the facts of particular cases. Probably only courts can respond with appropriate sensitivity and dispatch to developing clusters of risk. And in all cases worthy of litigation, only courts can probe the factual intricacies of particular disputes.

Courts, indeed, provide a vital bridge between the political process and the need for law that boils up from individual cases. For all the complaints about the lottery aspects of products liability litigation, the American courts have engaged in a linear and modulated process of reasoned development. Indeed, the judicial process is indispensable for specific fact finding, reasonable in its use of social facts, and by its nature much more rigorously focused than the legislative process. I conclude this from my study of thousands of judicial decisions, and my attendance at and reading of many Congressional hearings on the subject. Congress, and the federal establishment, often generate interesting data. But when it comes to developing rules that respond to the data, the courts have produced what is probably the best working balance of justice.

It is true that courts do not exist to define culture. However, in their responses to some of the most intense disputes in our society, judicial decisions often reflect culture accurately. Courts deciding products liability cases have achieved a relatively exact representation of our beliefs about important aspects of our relationship to our material possessions: about how much of our personal safety we are willing to trade for the benefits conferred by risky consumer goods; about the meaning of choice, the locus of power and the valuation of personal dignity as they become prominent in the course of making and using those goods; and about competing moralities of selling and buying in a marketplace awash in images, both garish and subtle.

Index